Eating Disorders

Eating Disorders

Pamela K. Keel

University of Iowa

Upper Saddle River, New Jersey 07458

Library of Congress Cataloging-in-Publication Data

Keel, Pamela K.
  Eating disorders / Pamela K. Keel.
    p. cm.
  Includes bibliographical references and index.
  ISBN 0-13-183919-5
  1. Eating disorders. I. Title.

RC552.E18K44 2005
616.85′26—dc22

                  2004021632

Senior Acquisitions Editor: Jeff Marshall
Editorial Director: Leah Jewell
Assistant Editor: Dawn Stapleton
Editorial Assistant: Patricia Callahan
Marketing Assistant: Julie Kestenbaum
Asst. Managing Editor (Production): Maureen Richardson
Production Liasion: Marianne Peters-Riordan
Manufacturing Buyer: Benjamin Smith
Art Director: Jayne Conte

Cover Design: Kiwi Design
Cover Illustration/Photo: Matthias Kulka/ Corbis
Photo Researcher: Kathy Ringrose
Image Permission Coordinator: Cathy Mazzucca
Composition/Full-Service Project Management: Penny Walker, *The GTS Companies*/York, PA Campus
Printer/Binder: RRD-Harrisonburg
Cover Printer: Lehigh Press

Credits and acknowledgments borrowed from other sources and reproduced, with permission, in this textbook appear on appropriate page within text.

Pearson Education LTD.
Pearson Education, Singapore, Pte. Ltd
Pearson Education, Canada, Ltd
Pearson Education—Japan
Pearson Education Australia PTY, Limited

Pearson Education North Asia Ltd
Pearson Educación de Mexico, S.A. de C.V.
Pearson Education Malaysia, Pte. Ltd
Pearson Education, Upper Saddle River, New Jersey

PEARSON
Prentice
Hall

10 9 8 7 6 5 4 3 2 1
ISBN 0-13-183919-5

Contents

Preface

The question I have most often encountered is "What got you interested in eating disorders?" This is a challenging (although fair) question because there is no right answer. First, there is no one issue that got me interested in the topic. Instead, several factors converged to make it compelling to me, and it would take at least a chapter to answer the question adequately. Second, there are highly divergent views concerning who can speak authoritatively on the topic. Some people feel that only individuals who have personally suffered from eating disorders can truly understand their nature. Others feel that these individuals are unable to objectively differentiate aspects of their own experience from those of most individuals who have these disorders. I do not agree with either view. I believe that people who have not suffered from eating disorders are capable of understanding and appreciating their complexity. In addition, I believe that individuals who have suffered from these disorders have not, by definition, lost their ability to employ a scientific approach in examining these conditions. So, instead of attempting to answer the question of why I became interested in eating disorders, I will attempt to explain why I think you should be interested in them. After all, I have already chosen to specialize in this area, whereas you may be trying to discover what you feel passionate enough about to make a lifelong pursuit.

Eating disorders provide the perfect opportunity to examine the intersections of culture, mind, and body. To truly appreciate the causes and consequences of these disorders, one must be willing to consider topics that span the humanities (history, art, and literature), the social sciences (psychology, anthropology, women's studies, and economics), and the natural sciences (anatomy, physiology, pharmacology, and genetics). As a consequence, there is truly something for everyone in the study of eating disorders. Few topics of inquiry allow individuals from so many different disciplines to make significant contributions.

Eating disorders are all around us. Almost anyone who picks up this book knows someone who has suffered from an eating disorder. Unlike other topics in academia, eating disorders are often part of our personal lives. Even individuals who are fortunate enough to have never personally had an eating disorder, or to have watched a loved one suffer from it, probably know someone who has.

Eating disorders are very topical. Many famous individuals have acknowledged the impact of these disorders on their lives. Thus, even people who do not personally know someone with an eating disorder have a sense of familiarity with the problem. This topicality has two aspects. First, people probably know more about eating disorders than about many other subjects that might be covered by a textbook. Second, they probably have far more misinformation about eating disorders than they do about other textbook topics. Thus, eating disorders can be both familiar and challenging (rather than familiar and boring or challenging and intimidating).

Eating disorders is a young field. Sections of this book were difficult to write because there is a still much that we simply do not know about these disorders. However, this limitation represents an opportunity. Because there is so much left to learn, there are many ways that people can make a significant contribution to the knowledge base of these disorders. In this new field, young people have completed many fascinating and illuminating studies. This book includes many studies conducted by college undergraduates because of the important conclusions that can be drawn from them.

CASE STUDIES

Like most textbooks on psychopathology, this one uses case studies to help bring eating disorders to life. Moreover, eating disorders never exist in a vacuum. They occur in the context of an individual's life. In order to balance the competing demands of breadth and depth, three case studies are followed throughout the book so that the topics of different chapters are integrated into the lives of these individuals. Instead of presenting 25 different cases briefly, each chapter provides further insight into the three case studies. For this reason, it is best if the chapters are covered in the order in which they occur. Even for individuals who are intimately familiar with the definitions of eating disorders, it would be worthwhile to read Chapter 1 first because this is where I introduce the cases that will guide you throughout the text. Similarly, even if the final chapter is not part of the assigned reading due to the time constraints that are always present in any course, it is still worth reading to learn more about how things turn out for the individuals introduced in Chapter 1.

FEATURES FOR STUDENTS

Terms that may be new to students are defined within chapters and are included in a glossary at the end of the book. Glossary terms are presented in boldface type the first time they appear in text and are listed at the end of the first chapter in which they appear. Italic type is used for other key terms to draw students' attention to important topics within chapters. Tables and figures are also included as study aids. Figures reinforce the information described in the text. In contrast, tables often provide additional information. Thus, figures are illustrative, and tables provide concise reviews of information not presented elsewhere. Each chapter includes a brief conclusion. These conclusions are not intended to serve as an abstract for the full chapter. Instead, they provide an empirically supported conclusion regarding the topic covered in the chapter when such conclusions are possible.

This book includes a chapter devoted to research methodology (Chapter 4), with examples from studies of eating disorders. This chapter is designed for students who have not completed prior coursework on research methods so that they can critically evaluate the strengths and weaknesses of conclusions that may be drawn from the empirical literature. The chapter also may serve as a refresher for students in advanced psychology courses who have already completed coursework on research methods.

Acknowledgments

This book exists because of the efforts of many individuals. First, I want to acknowledge my husband, Josh, because much of the time I spent working on the book on weekends was time that I did not spend at home with him and our son. I also want to thank the 15 students in my eating disorders seminar who dutifully read and provided feedback on the text when it was in first draft (and often dreadful) form: Emily Adkins, Phil Behrens, Laura Durso, Caitlin Ferriter, Mindy Jellin, Cameron Moccari, Lyndsay Murray, Vanessa Oullette, Lufi Paris, Jennifer Reich, Lauren Sheerr, Christine Sieberg, Erin Valenti, Ann Yee, and Alyson Zalta. Shari Jager-Hymen, Alissa Haedt, and Crystal Edler all deserve appreciation beyond what I can express in writing for their assistance in pulling this work together.

The feedback (both positive and negative) from the reviewers of chapters was extremely helpful in making this book more useful for a broader audience.

I am deeply indebted to the efforts of many members of the Prentice Hall staff, including Jayme Heffler, who solicited the book proposal; Stephanie Johnson (Sponsoring Editor–Psychology) when I started the book; and Jeff Marshall (Senior Acquisitions Editor), who never gave me a moment's doubt that the book would come to fruition. I am also indebted to Jill Liebowitz for her assistance.

Finally, I want to thank you for your interest in this topic.

Pamela K. Keel

Eating Disorders

CHAPTER 1

Introduction:
What Are Eating Disorders?

The goal of *Eating Disorders* is to provide a research-based overview of what currently is known about eating disorders, including anorexia nervosa, bulimia nervosa, and eating disorders not otherwise specified. The text will span topics such as historical and cross-cultural trends in the prevalence of eating pathology, biopsychosocial bases of eating disorders, and treatment of eating disorders. This investigation will be conducted through integration of recent theoretical, review, and empirical journal articles. The text will present the current understandings of the causes, correlates, and outcomes of eating pathology, as well as the complexity and controversy surrounding these topics.

Prior to embarking on this investigation, it is important to define what eating disorders are. Eating disorders are a form of mental disorder currently recognized within the fields of psychology, social work, nutrition, and medicine. As for mood disorders or anxiety disorders, diagnostic criteria have been established for eating disorders and have been presented within widely used textbooks, such as the *Diagnostic and Statistical Manual of Mental Disorders* (*DSM,* published by the American Psychiatric Association) and the *International Classification of Diseases* (*ICD,* published by the World Health Organization). Two eating disorders, anorexia nervosa and bulimia nervosa, have received the majority of attention within research and clinical spheres. In addition, there are eating disorders not otherwise specified, such as binge eating disorder, that have received less study but are gaining greater attention within the field. This chapter will describe these syndromes and provide a case history that exemplifies a patient suffering from these disorders.

Caraline, 28 years old, told a reporter, "I'm not telling you how much I weigh because I'm ashamed I don't weigh less." She later died of complications due to anorexia nervosa. ([Oltmanns & Emery (2001). *Abnormal Psychology, 3rd ed.* Upper Saddle River, NJ: Prentice Hall, 353.])

ANOREXIA NERVOSA

Anorexia nervosa (AN) can be characterized as a self-starvation syndrome. The major sign of the syndrome is emaciation caused by food refusal. In addition, there is an intense fear of becoming fat or gaining weight as well as other body image disturbances, including misperception of being overweight despite being emaciated, undue influence of weight or shape on self-evaluation, or denial of the seriousness of low weight. Finally, in women who are past the age of **menarche,** there is **amenorrhea,** defined as the loss of menstrual periods for 3 consecutive months. Although there is no specific duration criterion for a

TABLE 1–1   Definitions of Anorexia Nervosa

DSM-IV-TR Diagnostic Criteria for Anorexia Nervosa

A. Refusal to maintain body weight at or above a minimally normal weight for age and height (e.g., weight loss leading to maintenance of body weight less than 85% of that expected; or failure to make expected weight gain during period of growth, leading to body weight less than 85% of that expected).

B. Intense fear of gaining weight or becoming fat, even though underweight.

C. Disturbance in the way in which one's body weight or shape is experienced, undue influence of body weight or shape on self-evaluation, or denial of the seriousness of the current low body weight.

D. In postmenarcheal females, amenorrhea, i.e., the absence of at least three consecutive menstrual cycles. (A woman is considered to have amenorrhea if her periods occur only following hormone, e.g., estrogen, administration.)

ICD-10 Diagnostic Guidelines for Anorexia Nervosa

(a) Body weight is maintained at least 15% below that expected (either lost or never achieved), or Quetelet's body-mass index (weight (kg)/height (m)^2) is 17.5 or less. Prepubertal patients may show failure to make the expected weight gain during the period of growth.

(b) The weight loss is self-induced by avoidance of "fattening foods" and one or more of the following: self-induced vomiting, self-induced purging; excessive exercise; use of appetite suppressants and/or diuretics.

(c) There is body-image distortion in the form of a specific psychopathology whereby a dread of fatness persists as an intrusive, overvalued idea and the patient imposes a low weight threshold on himself or herself.

(d) A widespread endocrine disorder involving hypothalamic-pituitary-gonadal axis is manifest in women as amenorrhea and in men as a loss of sexual interest and potency. (An apparent exception is the persistence of vaginal bleeds in anorexic women who are receiving replacement hormonal therapy, most commonly taken as a contraceptive pill.) There may also be elevated levels of growth hormone, raised levels of cortisol, changes in the peripheral metabolism of the thyroid hormone, and abnormalities of insulin secretion.

(e) If onset is prepubertal, the sequence of pubertal events is delayed or even arrested (growth ceases; in girls the breasts do not develop and there is a primary amenorrhea; in boys the genitals remain juvenile). With recovery, puberty is often completed normally, but the menarche is late.

Source: DSM-IV-TR criteria reprinted with permission from the *Diagnostic and Statistical Manual of Mental Disorders*, Copyright 2000. American Psychiatric Association, p. 589; *ICD-10* criteria from World Health Organization, 1992, p. 177.

diagnosis of AN, the required duration of amenorrhea places the length of malnutrition at a 3-month minimum. Table 1–1 presents the diagnostic criteria for AN in the *DSM-IV-TR* and in the *ICD-10*.

There are two currently recognized subtypes of AN, the restricting type (ANR) and the binge-eating/purging type (ANBP). Although a person with ANBP may meet all diagnostic criteria for bulimia nervosa (BN), defined below, the presence of AN precludes a diagnosis of BN. Data on treatment response and long-term outcome support the hierarchy of diagnosing ANBP rather than giving dual diagnoses of AN and BN because women with ANBP are more similar to women with ANR than they are to women with BN (see Chapters 9 and 11). Differences between the ANR and ANBP groups have also been reported. Compared to ANR, ANBP is associated with older age, greater impulsiveness, more substance use disorders, and more suicidal behavior. In general, these differences support the distinct behavioral presentations of the two subtypes. The ANR subtype is more perfectionistic and constrained in their eating and other behaviors, and the ANBP subtype is more impulsive and out of control with their eating and other behaviors (see Chapter 7). However, longitudinal data (Eddy et al., 2002; Herzog et al., 1999; Strober, Freeman, & Morrell, 1997) suggest that a high proportion of women with ANR go on to develop binge-eating episodes later in the course of their illness. Thus, the two subtypes may reflect different stages of the same illness for many individuals with AN.

AN predominantly affects women. Studies suggest that the ratio of AN in women versus men is approximately 10:1. The overall percentage of women who have had AN at some point in their lifetimes (**lifetime prevalence**) is 0.5%. A recent review paper indicates that the number of women suffering from AN increased over the 20th century (Keel & Klump, 2003). AN usually develops during middle to late adolescence (ages 14 through 18 years) in girls.

Case Study

Emily described herself as being "forced into treatment" by her school. She was a sophomore at a prestigious university. Emily made it clear that she thoroughly resented the university's interference in her private life since she had top grades in all of her classes and was clearly fine. She saw no reason to be in therapy or any sort of treatment. Emily was 5 feet 10 inches tall and weighed 109 pounds. This placed her weight at approximately 76% of that expected for her height and age. Her college roommates were extremely worried about her because she had to be taken to the emergency room after fainting in the dining hall. When asked about the incident, Emily said that she had lost track of the time, hadn't eaten all day, and became lightheaded after her afternoon run. However, she asserted that this was very unusual for her and that she always had a high-energy snack before exercising. In fact, she said that she always carried food with her because she had a tendency to be hypoglycemic and that, in contrast to what people thought, she was eating all the time. When asked to describe what she would eat during a given day, Emily said that she had cereal for breakfast, snacked throughout the day, had a salad for lunch, snacked throughout the afternoon, and then ate a full dinner. Upon further questioning, she stated that she ate one packet of instant oatmeal made with spring water for breakfast in her room. Her snacks consisted of celery sticks, carrot sticks, or sugar-free gum. For lunch, she ate a "huge" plate of salad greens without dressing from the dining hall's salad bar. Dinner was the only meal that varied from one day to the next. She might eat skinless chicken breast with half of a baked potato and a green vegetable. Occasionally, she ate half of a cup of pasta with tomato sauce and vegetables added from the salad bar. On days when the dining hall served nothing she liked, she ate two slices of bread with cottage cheese spread over each slice and tomatoes on top—she likened this to pizza—with a large salad. She stated that she didn't eat red meat because she didn't like the idea of eating cute, furry animals. In fact, she didn't care for meat as a food group but made sure that her diet always included protein because she knew it was important for muscle development. Emily considered muscle development to be important because she felt that she was constantly struggling with a "lopsided" body. She felt that her shoulders and arms were too thin and sticklike, while her hips, thighs, and buttocks were rotund. She described herself as having a "classic pear shape." To improve her muscle definition, Emily exercised rigorously. She ran every afternoon between classes and dinner. On weekends, she added weight training to her routine. She had read that metabolism increased both during and after exercise and felt that this pattern increased the probability that the dinner she ate would be used to fuel her body rather than being stored as fat. She was terrified of becoming fat. When asked about her menstrual cycle, Emily stated that it had "always been irregular." She started menstruating later than most girls, around 14 years of age, and had a period only every 3 months. When she was 16, her doctor prescribed birth control pills to increase the regularity of her menstrual cycle. This had caused her to gain weight, and this was when she first began to diet and lose weight. Her mother attributed the weight change to Emily's loss of her "baby fat," and her friends expressed admiration of her self-control. Emily once was approached in the shopping mall, asked if she had ever considered becoming a model, and given the card of a modeling agency. Although flattered, she did not pursue this opportunity because she planned to go to a good college, then go to law school, and eventually become a judge. She felt that a career in modeling would be a waste of her intellect and that it required people to focus on superficial things like appearance.

According to the *DSM-IV* (APA, 1994), Emily meets diagnostic criteria for ANR. Although it is unclear that she missed three consecutive menstrual cycles (Criterion D), the use of birth control pills makes this last criterion inapplicable for Emily (similar to cases of AN in men).

BULIMIA NERVOSA

Bulimia nervosa (BN) is characterized by recurrent binge-eating episodes coupled with inappropriate compensatory behavior and the undue influence of weight or shape on self-evaluation. Binge eating is defined both as consuming a large amount of food within a limited period of time and experiencing a loss of control over eating during the episode. Inappropriate compensatory behaviors include self-induced vomiting, laxative abuse, diuretic abuse, fasting, and excessive exercising. The first three forms are considered purging because they all involve the forceful evacuation of matter from the body. Fasting and excessive exercise are considered nonpurging forms of compensatory behavior because caloric intake during binge episodes is balanced by not allowing calories into the body (fasting) or exercising strenuously so that the body burns calories at a higher rate (excessive exercise). In the United States, self-induced vomiting appears to be the most common form of inappropriate compensatory behavior among women with BN. Unlike AN, BN carries explicit frequency and duration criteria in the *DSM-IV*. Binge-eating episodes and inappropriate compensatory behavior must occur, on average, twice per week over a 3-month period. Table 1–2 presents *DSM-IV-TR* and *ICD-10* diagnostic criteria for BN.

As with AN, there are currently two subtypes of BN: the purging subtype (BNP) and the nonpurging subtype (BNnP). As indicated by the names, BNP involves the regular use of purging methods, to compensate for binge eating episodes, while BNnP involves the use of nonpurging methods (i.e., excessive exercise or fasting). Limited data support this distinction. Some studies (e.g., Hay, Fairburn, & Doll, 1996) suggest that BNP is associated with higher levels of psychopathology and a worse 1-year outcome than BNnP, but other studies (e.g., Tobin, Griffing, & Griffing, 1997) suggest no significant differences between BNP and BNnP. The majority of research on BN is based upon women with BNP; thus, less is known about individuals who use excessive exercise or fasting as their primary forms of compensatory behavior.

Like AN, BN predominantly affects women. The overall percentage of women who have had BN at some point in their lifetimes (lifetime prevalence) is approximately 1–3%. The lifetime prevalence in men is approximately 0.1–0.3%. Also as with AN, the number of women suffering from BN increased in the second half of the 20th century (Keel & Klump, 2003). BN usually develops during late adolescence to early adulthood. Thus, individuals with BN tend to be older than individuals with AN, and approximately 30% of women with BN have a lifetime history of AN.

TABLE 1–2 Definitions of Bulimia Nervosa

DSM-IV-TR Diagnostic Criteria for Bulimia Nervosa

A. Recurrent episodes of binge eating. An episode of binge eating is characterized by both of the following:

(1) eating, in a discrete period of time (e.g., within any 2-hour period), an amount of food that is definitely larger than most people would eat during a similar period of time and under similar circumstances.

(2) a sense of lack of control over eating during the episode (e.g., a feeling that one cannot stop eating or control what or how much one is eating).

B. Recurrent inappropriate compensatory behavior in order to prevent weight gain, such as self-induced vomiting; misuse of laxatives, diuretics, enemas, or other medications; fasting; or excessive exercise.

C. The binge eating and inappropriate compensatory behaviors both occur, on average, at least twice a week for 3 months.

D. Self-evaluation is unduly influenced by body shape and weight.

E. The disturbance does not occur exclusively during episodes of Anorexia Nervosa.

ICD-10 Diagnostic Guidelines for Bulimia Nervosa

(a) There is a persistent preoccupation with eating, and an irresistible craving for food; the patient succumbs to episodes of overeating in which large amounts of food are consumed in short periods of time.

(b) The patient attempts to counteract the "fattening" effects of food by one or more of the following: self-induced vomiting; purgative abuse, alternating periods of starvation; use of drugs such as appetite suppressants, thyroid preparations or diuretics. When bulimia occurs in diabetic patients they may choose to neglect their insulin treatment.

(c) The psychopathology consists of a morbid dread of fatness and the patient sets herself or himself a sharply defined weight threshold, well below the premorbid weight that constitutes the optimum or healthy weight in the opinion of the physician. There is often, but not always, a history of an earlier episode of anorexia nervosa, the interval between the two disorders ranging from a few months to several years. This earlier episode may have been fully expressed, or may have assumed a minor cryptic form with a moderate loss of weight and/or a transient phase of amenorrhea.

Source: DSM-IV-TR criteria reprinted with permission from the *Diagnostic and Statistical Manual of Mental Disorders,* Copyright 2000. American Psychiatric Association, p. 594; *ICD-10* criteria from World Health Organization, pp. 178–179.

Case Study

Jean was a 27-year-old secretary who lived with her boyfriend of 2 years. She was 5 feet 4 inches tall and weighed 138 pounds. She came in for treatment because of a return of eating problems that she thought had ended in college. In college, she had experienced binge-eating episodes and had engaged in self-induced vomiting. She spent a great deal of time trying to hide these behaviors from her roommates and from her family when she went home during breaks. However, her roommates confronted her after a particularly bad episode in which she had gone to the bathroom to self-induce vomiting four times within a 2-hour period. She had received treatment that allowed her to stop binge eating and purging on a regular basis. She continued to have occasional slips—times when she felt she had eaten too much and purged to avoid weight gain. However, these had occurred rarely, and there were times when she prevented herself from vomiting when she felt she had eaten too much. About a year and a half ago, she noticed that she was gaining weight and could no longer fit into the same size jeans she had worn since high school. Jean said that she couldn't bring herself to buy larger jeans because she couldn't feel good about herself unless she fit into that specific size. She decided to diet and go to the gym more regularly. At first, her new fitness routine worked, and she lost approximately 7 pounds. At 125 pounds, Jean felt great about herself, and found that she was more likely to want to go out with friends and to flirt with and get attention from men. However, when she and her boyfriend started living together, she had a hard time resisting the tempting foods he kept in the kitchen. When she lived alone, she never had cookies, ice cream, or potato chips in the house because these had been common triggers for binge-eating episodes. Now these foods were always around. At first, she simply resisted eating them because they were not part of her diet. However, one night while her boyfriend was out with his friends, Jean ate an entire bag of potato chips, and finished off a package of cookies and three fourths of a gallon of ice cream. Disgusted with herself and in pain from the amount of food she had consumed, she made herself throw up. Afterward, she went to the store to replace what she had eaten. She ended up throwing out some of the new ice cream and cookies in order to hide all evidence of her binge. Jean vowed that she would not eat any more of these "dangerous foods" and told herself that this was just a slip. However, the next week, when she was alone in the apartment, the same cycle happened again. She would binge and purge only when she was alone, because when she was alone she could not resist. Bingeing and purging were now happening several times per week. She regained the weight she had lost and found that it was creeping up above her prediet weight. She then redoubled her efforts at dieting to counteract the effects of her binge episodes in addition to using self-induced vomiting. She even began vomiting when she ate normal amounts of food because she believed that it was necessary to eat as little as possible in order to get rid of the unwanted weight. She felt disgusted with herself. As her weight increased, she felt worthless and revolting.

According to *DSM-IV* (1994), Jean meets diagnostic criteria for BNP. This appears to be a recurrence of the disorder from which she suffered in college and apparently recovered. It is unclear whether she ever fully recovered from her earlier eating disorder because it seems that she continued to base her self-evaluation on her weight and shape even after her binge eating and purging had remitted.

EATING DISORDER NOT OTHERWISE SPECIFIED

Eating disorder not otherwise specified (EDNOS) represents the largest category of eating disorders because it includes all clinically significant disorders of eating that do not meet the specific diagnostic criteria for AN or BN. Clinical significance is defined by present distress, impairment, or increased risk associated with the pattern of symptoms. Thus, individuals who experience distress as a result of their disordered eating, but fail to meet all the diagnostic criteria for either AN or BN, can be diagnosed with EDNOS. Table 1–3 provides several examples of EDNOS. In many cases, the disorders can be characterized as

TABLE 1–3   Eating Disorders Not Otherwise Specified in the DSM-IV-TR

1. For females, all of the criteria for Anorexia Nervosa are met except that the individual has regular menses.
2. All of the criteria for Anorexia Nervosa are met except that, despite significant weight loss, the individual's current weight is in the normal range.
3. All of the criteria for Bulimia Nervosa are met except that the binge eating and inappropriate compensatory mechanisms occur at a frequency of less than twice a week or for a duration of less than 3 months.
4. The regular use of inappropriate compensatory behavior by an individual of normal body weight after eating small amounts of food (e.g., self-induced vomiting after the consumption of two cookies).
5. Repeatedly chewing and spitting out, but not swallowing, large amounts of food.
6. Binge-eating disorder: recurrent episodes of binge eating in the absence of the regular use of inappropriate compensatory behaviors characteristic of Bulimia Nervosa.

Source: Reprinted with permission from the *Diagnostic and Statistical Manual of Mental Disorders,* Copyright 2000. American Psychiatric Association, p. 594.

subthreshold because they fail to meet full diagnostic criteria. There is evidence that cases of EDNOS are less severe than cases of AN or BN (Garfinkel, Lin, et al., 1995). However, this is not true of all examples of EDNOS. Data suggest that there are no differences in level of clinical severity between women who meet all criteria for AN versus women who meet all criteria for AN, except that the latter continue to menstruate on a regular basis (Cachelin & Maher, 1998; Watson & Andersen, 2003). Although they may be at decreased risk for osteoporosis, the risk of other complications does not seem to differ from that of women with AN or BN. Research also suggests a similar level of clinical severity in women with BNP compared to women who would meet criteria for BNP except that they do not have large binge episodes (Keel, Mayer, & Harnden-Fischer, 2001; Keel, Haedt, & Edler, in press). However, EDNOS is rarely studied, and individuals with EDNOS are often excluded from studies of treatment efficacy. Thus, little is known about this heterogeneous category of eating disorders.

The most frequently studied EDNOS is binge eating disorder (BED). BED is characterized by recurrent binge-eating episodes in the absence of inappropriate compensatory behavior. Binge episodes in BED are defined as they are for BN and are also characterized by eating more rapidly than normal, eating until feeling uncomfortably full, eating large amounts of food when not hungry, eating alone because of feeling embarrassed by the amount eaten, and feeling disgusted, depressed, or very guilty after overeating. For a diagnosis of BED, three of these characteristic features are required; however, from the case study of Jean, it is clear that many of these factors also characterize binge episodes in BN. In addition, individuals must endorse marked distress regarding their binge eating. As with BN, specific frequency and duration criteria are provided for BED. The binge-eating episodes must occur, on average, 2 days per week over a period of 6 months. As with BN, there is a diagnostic hierarchy in which a person who simultaneously meets diagnostic criteria for AN and BED is given a diagnosis of ANBP only. Because a diagnosis of BED requires the absence of inappropriate compensatory behavior, it is also not possible to be diagnosed with both BN and BED. Suggested research diagnostic criteria for BED appear in Table 1–4.

TABLE 1–4   DSM-IV-TR Diagnostic Criteria for Binge Eating Disorder

A. Recurrent episodes of binge eating. An episode of binge eating is characterized by both of the following:

(1) eating, in a discrete period of time (e.g., within any 2-hour period), an amount of food that is definitely larger than most people would eat during a similar period of time and under similar circumstances.

(2) a sense of lack of control over eating during the episode (e.g., a feeling that one cannot stop eating or control what or how much one is eating).

B. The binge-eating episodes are associated with three (or more) of the following:

(1) eating much more rapidly than normal

(2) eating until feeling uncomfortably full

(3) eating large amounts of food when not feeling physically hungry

(4) eating alone because of being embarrassed by how much one is eating

(5) feeling disgusted with oneself, depressed, or very guilty after overeating

C. Marked distress regarding binge eating is present

D. The binge eating occurs, on average, at least 2 days a week for 6 months.

E. The binge eating is not associated with the regular use of inappropriate compensatory behaviors (e.g., purging, fasting, excessive exercise) and does not occur exclusively during the course of Anorexia Nervosa or Bulimia Nervosa.

Source: Reprinted with permission from the *Diagnostic and Statistical Manual of Mental Disorders,* Copyright 2000. American Psychiatric Association, p. 787.

Like AN and BN, BED is more common in women than in men. In weight-control programs where the prevalence of BED is greatest, women are 1.5 times more likely to have the disorder than men (APA, 2000). In community samples, the ratio of women to men with BED is closer to 60:40 (Spitzer et al., 1992). Approximately 0.7–4.0% of people report meeting criteria for BED in community samples (APA, 2000). Age of onset of BED may be bimodal, with many individuals reporting problems with overeating since childhood and others reporting significant problems beginning in late adolescence or early adulthood after a period of significant dieting (Spurrell, Wilfley, Tanofsky, & Brownell, 1997). Individuals with BED tend to be significantly overweight or obese.

Case Study

Jamie's problem was simply stated as follows: "I eat too much. For some people, it's alcohol, for some it's cocaine; for me it's food." Jamie said that this had always been true; even as a small child, a whole box of Twinkies was a single serving. For a junior high school bake sale, Jamie's mother had baked a cherry pie. The pie, Jamie's favorite dessert, was gone before the start of school that day. When asked for the dessert, Jamie lied to conceal the gluttony. There had been many times like this throughout childhood, episodes of eating all of something rather than just one serving. However, because Jamie was tall and athletic, the big appetite was often a source of pride rather than embarrassment. In fact, everyone on the athletic teams ate large amounts of food, so Jamie didn't feel unusual most of the time. The realization that there was an eating problem did not emerge until the end of college, when Jamie started interviewing for jobs. It was the first time Jamie needed to buy a suit but couldn't fit into any of the sizes offered in the normal department store. Jamie was embarrassed by having to go to a special store that stocked larger sizes. Currently, Jamie weighed 360 pounds despite several diets and several different weight loss programs. Jamie was frequently able to lose some weight on these programs; the greatest weight loss was 50 pounds, down from 280 to 230 pounds. However, as at all other times, the weight came back—and more. Jamie denied eating when not hungry but acknowledged eating to the point of being uncomfortably full. Jamie felt that this was because, when hungry, eating occurred at one rate: "as much and as quickly as possible." This was true for all favorite foods. Jamie said it was like being a "food addict"; there was no way to stop until all of the food was gone. For example, Jamie would consume three supersize value meals from the local fast food restaurant in the car on the way home from work. Eating alone in the car was "the best" because "I can just zone out." However, terrible guilt followed these episodes because Jamie knew that eating so much junk food contributed to the weight problem—and could lead to heart problems. However, Jamie didn't like salads, vegetables, or fruit because they were bland and boring. Jamie said, "I wish I felt about fast food the way that I feel about salads because then I would be thin as a rail." Jamie wanted to know if there was any medication that would cause weight loss or make it easier not to eat. Based on all of the TV advertisements, Jamie felt like a good candidate for medication because there was definitely an eating problem occurring every day—often throughout the day.

Jamie meets the *DSM-IV* research diagnostic criteria for BED. Although the distress over eating was a consequence of being overweight, the extent to which Jamie viewed the eating problems as contributing to the weight problems led Jamie to experience marked distress over the eating as well.

EATING DISORDERS AS A CONTINUUM OF PROBLEMS

Describing the definitions of AN, BN, and BED and their prevalence represents a categorical approach to eating disorders. That is, an individual either does or does not have one of these eating disorders. In contrast, many experts prefer to think of eating disorders as existing on a continuum. One end of the continuum represents diagnosable eating disorders, and the other end represents healthy eating attitudes and behaviors. This perspective seems to match what is known about the presence of disordered eating attitudes and behaviors in the general population and within the course of individuals' lives.

Many people experience disordered eating at some point in their lives. Some of these people may be experimenting with disordered eating behaviors and never develop any significant problems. Nevertheless, many of them probably have genuine problems with their eating and body image that do not fall within the narrowly defined disorders characterized in the *DSM* or *ICD*. For example, body image disturbance may be present in many women who do not meet criteria for AN or BN. This may be coupled with severely restricted dieting and excessive exercise and may contribute to diminished self-esteem. Although such a pattern may not warrant an eating disorder diagnosis, it is likely worthy of both clinical attention and research. Understanding the factors that lead to these problems may help reveal the causes of AN, BN, and EDNOS.

It is most likely the case that people with eating disorders (defined categorically) experienced disordered eating before developing a full-threshold syndrome, because it seems unlikely that an adolescent girl would shift suddenly from completely healthy eating habits to BN. Thus, viewing eating disorders as a continuum helps us understand the progression of these problems within an individual's life.

Others have argued that eating disorders represent distinct categories that do not lie on a continuum of disordered eating behaviors and attitudes. This view is supported by studies demonstrating qualitative differences between AN and BN. While these individuals acknowledge the limitations of arbitrarily set frequency or duration criteria for distinguishing eating disorders from normal eating, they still believe that eating disorders are best conceptualized as distinct categories.

Whether or not eating disorders lie on a continuum, many decisions require a categorical approach. For example, the decision of whether or not to provide treatment is a categorical decision. The decision of whether or not to include a person in a research study is a categorical decision. Further, a categorical approach occasionally allows us to detect differences that lead to improved understanding or treatment of an eating disorder. For example, BN responds to treatment with selective serotonin reuptake inhibitors (see Chapter 9), but AN does not. If no distinction had been made between AN and BN in treatment studies, this finding may have eluded eating disorder researchers.

CONCLUSION

In conclusion, there are two currently recognized forms of eating disorders, AN and BN. In addition, there is a larger set of EDNOS, the most widely recognized form of which is BED. AN is best summarized as a self-starvation syndrome. BN is most often a binge-purge syndrome. Both AN and BN involve significant body image disturbance. BED involves recurrent binge-eating episodes in the absence of inappropriate compensatory behavior. It does not require body image disturbance but is frequently associated with significant overweight/obesity. Other examples of EDNOS include purging in the absence of binge-eating episodes, as well as syndromes that resemble AN or BN but fall short of meeting the full diagnostic criteria. In addition to the 2.2–7.5% of individuals who meet criteria for AN, BN, or BED, there are many more who experience disordered eating behaviors or harbor disordered eating attitudes but never develop a diagnosable disorder. These individuals may be conceptualized as falling along a continuum with those who suffer from AN, BN, or EDNOS.

Roughly two thirds of this book is devoted to understanding the **etiology** of eating disorders: understanding what causes these conditions to occur. The last third of the book is concerned with treatment and prevention of eating disorders and the outcome for individuals with these conditions. Although eating disorders represent mental disorders on par with mood or anxiety disorders, they have been particularly associated with modern Western culture. Chapter 2 addresses the question of whether eating disorders represent culture-bound syndromes by examining evidence of eating disorders outside of their current sociohistorical context. Just as Chapter 2 examines **epidemiological** patterns across history and culture, Chapter 3 examines epidemiological patterns across different ethnic groups and between the genders. Epidemiological investigations allow identification of when, where, and in whom the risk of eating disorders is increased. As such, they are crucial for unraveling the causes of eating disorders.

Chapter 4 introduces approaches to understanding the causes of eating disorders. This chapter presents the logic of research methods used in studies reviewed in subsequent chapters. Some risk factors are discussed in this chapter; more complete reviews of social, psychological, and biological risk factors are presented in Chapters 5 through 8.

Social risk factors for eating disorders include both societal ideals and family environment. Chapter 5 discusses the societal idealization of thinness and denigration of fatness, gender roles, and the impact of societal messages on women's body image and the pursuit of thinness. The associations among body image, dieting, and eating disorders are reviewed in this chapter. Chapter 6 addresses a second sphere of social influence—the role of families. This chapter begins to introduce a biopsychosocial model, as the influence of families can be interpreted at social, psychological, and biological levels. It focuses specifically on the rearing environment provided by families in which eating disorders emerge, as well as the rearing environment provided by women who have suffered from eating disorders.

Chapter 7 reviews psychological factors that contribute to the risk of eating disorders. Because social learning and psychoanalytic/psychodynamic models are explored in the context of family factors in Chapter 6, Chapter 7 examines personality, cognition, and behavior. The extent to which these factors represent causes or consequences of disordered eating is also discussed.

Chapter 8 introduces biological factors that contribute to the risk of eating disorders. In addition, this chapter reviews biological correlates and consequences of eating pathology. The chapter marks the transition from examining the etiology of eating disorders to discussing treatment and outcome.

Chapter 9 covers eating disorder treatment. As in Chapter 6, the role of different theoretical models in shaping treatment approaches is discussed. The efficacy of interventions is reviewed as well.

Chapter 10 discusses theories of prevention and evidence concerning the impact of prevention on disordered eating knowledge, attitudes, and behaviors. This chapter provides examples of prevention programs aimed at three different levels of intervention: a general school population, girls recruited from schools, and college-age women reporting high levels of body dissatisfaction. Results from studies of the reviewed prevention programs are included.

Chapter 11 reviews the outcomes associated with eating disorders. Statistics on mortality, recovery, relapse, and crossover are presented for AN, BN, and BED. Predictors of outcomes are discussed in this chapter. Particular attention is given to the impact of treatment on long-term outcome.

Chapter 12 concludes the book by summarizing information within the context of the case histories presented in Chapter 1. In addition, this chapter introduces current debates surrounding different topics reviewed in the book. The chapter ends with a discussion of future directions within the field of eating disorders.

The book is designed to provide a thorough research-based review of what is currently known about eating disorders. Several topics are covered from different perspectives to represent the different theoretical orientations in the field. Similarly, certain findings are reviewed in terms of how they may reflect social, psychological, and biological factors in the etiology of eating disorders. Rather than pointing to one underlying cause for all eating disorders, this book strives to reveal how multiple factors conspire to produce these debilitating and sometimes deadly disorders.

KEY TERMS

Amenorrhea	Lifetime prevalence
Epidemiology	Menarche
Etiology	

CHAPTER 2

Are Eating Disorders Culture-Bound Syndromes?

Eating disorders are more prevalent in industrialized and often Western cultures and are far more common among women than men. Furthermore, the prevalence of eating disorders seems to have increased among younger women during the second half of the 20th century. These patterns suggest that current Western ideals of beauty motivate the behaviors associated with the development and maintenance of these disorders. Indeed, popular accounts of eating disorders, such as those presented in *People* magazine or *Glamour* magazine, draw prominent connections between eating disorders and the idealization of thinness in Western culture. This particular explanation of eating disorders will be explored in Chapter 5. This chapter explores the extent to which eating disorders, specifically AN and BN, represent culture-bound syndromes.

Prince (1985) defined a culture-bound syndrome as, "a collection of signs and symptoms (excluding notions of cause) which is restricted to a limited number of cultures primarily by reason of certain of their psychosocial features" (p. 201). With this definition, he proposed that AN might represent a culture-bound syndrome. However, he cautioned that "the decision hinges on the empirical question of whether or not the syndrome occurs in non-Western cultures or segments of them which are not markedly influenced by Western cultures" (p. 201). Thus, this chapter examines evidence of AN and BN outside of modern Western culture. AN and BN are reviewed separately, and information is divided into three sections for each: historical accounts of the disorder prior to its recognition, changing rates of the disorder following its recognition, and presence of the disorder in non-Western cultures. If a disorder exists only in the modern era, if disorder rates increase with the emergence of modern ideals, and if the disorder does not exist in the absence of Western influence, then it could be considered culture-bound.

ANOREXIA NERVOSA

Attempts to examine evidence of AN across time or across cultures have been marked by debates concerning the definition of the illness. While there is universal agreement that AN represents a disorder marked by starvation, some experts (Beumont, 1988; Habermas, 1989) have argued that fear of fat (weight phobia) (Criterion B; see Table 1–1) is a necessary motivating force behind food refusal. However, other experts (Banks, 1992, 1994; Katzman & Lee, 1997; Lee, 1995) have argued that weight phobia is not a core feature of AN. These experts argue that when individuals become ill with any disease, their culture shapes their experience and understanding of the disease. Similarly, there have been debates over whether or not amenorrhea (Criterion D) should be retained as a diagnostic criterion or viewed as a consequence of malnutrition (Cachelin & Maher, 1998). Because definitions of AN change with each edition of the *DSM,* differ between the *DSM* and *ICD,* and continue to be contested, this chapter considers evidence from studies using various definitions of AN and notes how these definitions differ from that presented in the *DSM-IV-TR* (APA, 2000) (presented in Chapter 1).

Historical Accounts of Self-Starvation in Adolescent Girls

Early Christianity offers a possible case of AN from the late 4th century in *Blessila,* in which a 20-year-old woman died from self-starvation (Bemporad, 1996). Cases of self-starvation attributed to demonic possession and cured by exorcism also were documented during the 5th and 8th centuries (Bemporad, 1996). Some time between the 8th and 9th centuries, St. Wilgefortis allegedly engaged in self-starvation resulting in emaciation and lanugo (growth of fine, downy hair all over the body) (Bemporad, 1996; Lacey, 1982a). However, these early cases are controversial. For example, Bynum (1987) characterized the description of St. Wilgefortis as having AN as a "bizarre communication to a British medical journal" (p. 194). Moreover, details for the oldest historical cases are extremely limited. Thus, starvation could have been caused by physical or psychological conditions unrelated to AN.

For examples of AN from the 12th to the 17th century, probably the most has been written about fasting medieval religious **ascetics.** Bell (1985) reported that approximately 90 saints living on the Italian peninsula from A.D. 1200 onward suffered from "holy anorexia." Holy anorexia, like AN, involved food refusal resulting in emaciation but was believed to be an act of God. The cases of St. Catherine of Siena and St. Veronica are summarized from Bell (1985).

Case Study

The story of St. Catherine begins with a "robust, happy, obedient child" (p. 52) who goes on to seek spiritual perfection by conquering all of her bodily drives (hunger, fatigue, and sexual desire). She began fasting at around 16 years of age. At various stages of her life, her diet was restricted to raw vegetables, bread, and water; raw vegetables and water; and then water and the sacrament. She engaged in vigorous physical activities, including long, fast-paced walks. She constantly chewed on bitter herbs and spit out the juice and saliva. St. Catherine was also known to self-induce vomiting. The following comment on her life is attributed to one of St. Catherine's contemporaries, Raymond of Capua: "she was constrained every day to vomit what she had eaten. To do this she regularly and with great pain inserted stalks of fennel and other plants into her stomach, otherwise being unable to vomit" (p. 28). According to Bell, when she was "warned that

St. Catherine of Siena refused to eat despite repeated pleas and commands from Church superiors.

by such eating habits she was bringing about her own death, Catherine shot back that eating would kill her anyway so she might as well die of starvation, and do as she wished in the meantime" (p. 24). St. Catherine died from starvation in 1380 at approximately 32 years of age.

St. Catherine had many of the characteristics of patients with AN. She engaged in food refusal, excessive exercising, and self-induced vomiting. In addition, her constant chewing of bitter herbs may be analogous to the use of sugar-free gum in modern patients with AN to satisfy the urge to eat without actually eating. Both Catherine's age of onset and eventual death from starvation are also characteristic of patients with AN.

Case Study

St. Veronica (Veronica Giuliani) began a pattern of self-starvation at age 18. Like St. Catherine, she ate little (i.e., bread, water, "five orange seeds") or nothing, slept little, and was very active. When forced to eat, St. Veronica also vomited (although without obviously inducing the episodes). She was observed by her sisters to have periods in which she gorged on food. According to an account of Abbess Ceoli, "the sisters sometimes found Sister Veronica in the kitchen, the refectory, or the dispensary, where she ate everything there was" (p. 75). These instances were particularly likely to occur at times when she was less likely to be discovered. St. Veronica was also accused of having intercourse with her confessor. Clearly, St. Veronica was in conflict with her fellow sisters; "most of the time she reasoned that she was in a race against all the other novices to show who loved God the most. She was losing, and so despite all the sleepless nights spent crying over she knew not what, Veronica carried more water and chopped more wood than anyone else" (p. 71). St. Veronica's life was filled with contests of will between her and her superiors. Early in her career, she openly defied orders. In response to a confessor's commanding her to provide a genuine confession versus confessing to trivial errors, she replied, "Father, what do you want that we should do, since we are always silent and cloistered, or to say it more clearly, imprisoned?" (p. 71). Unlike St. Catherine, St. Veronica ultimately achieved recovery sometime between her 30s and 50s and lived until the age of 67 (dying in 1727).

———————— •◆• ————————

Although St. Veronica's case differs significantly from that of St. Catherine, she does resemble some patients with AN. She engaged in self-starvation, excessive exercise, and binge-eating episodes. In addition, she demonstrated a competitive drive to be better than her fellow novices and engaged in battles of will.

For the 17th and 18th centuries, Bliss and Branch (1960) found nine dissertations on anorexia written between 1685 and 1770. Morton (1694) described "nervous atrophy" or "a Nervous Consumption" characterized by loss of appetite, extreme emaciation, amenorrhea, overactivity, and indifference to the condition. The case of Mr. Duke's daughter from Morton (1694) is now summarized.

Case Study ———————————————— •◆• ————————————————————

Mr. Duke's 18-year-old daughter experienced amenorrhea and significant weight loss, "like a Skeleton only clad with skin" (p. 9), that could not be attributed to tuberculosis or chlorosis (a form of anemia). The patient engaged in "continual poring upon Books, to expose her self both Day and Night to the injuries of the Air" (p. 8). After initial compliance with treatment, she "quickly tired with Medicines, she beg'd that the whole Affair might be committed again to Nature, whereupon consuming every day more and more, she was after three Months taken with a Fainting Fit and dyed" (p. 9).

———————— •◆• ————————

The cause of Miss Duke's death is unclear; however, **refeeding syndrome** seems to be one plausible explanation (see Walsh, Wheat, & Freund, 2000, for a review of treatment complications in AN). At around this time, "Miraculous Maids" (predominantly girls between the ages of 14 and 20) emerged throughout the European countryside; they were considered "miraculous" for their self-imposed fasts (Bemporad, 1996).

Fasting girls throughout the 18th and 19th centuries gained great attention in popular and scholarly media throughout America and Europe (Bemporad, 1996; Brumberg, 1989; Vandereycken & van Deth, 1994). Typically, these cases involved adolescent girls who abruptly refused to eat. They created a mixture of medical concern and religious awe. Some fasting girls were acclaimed as miracles for their ability to eat nothing yet remain completely healthy (including maintaining a healthy weight). Conversely, other fasting girls became extremely emaciated, in some cases dying. Among them were Lina Finch [1886], Kate Smulsey [1885], and Lenora Eaton [1881], who all reportedly died of starvation before the age of 22 as a result of their food refusal (Brumberg, 1989).

Sarah Jacobs [1869], the "Welsh Fasting Girl," represents a particularly tragic case of self-starvation leading to death (Bemporad, 1996; Brumberg, 1989; Vandereycken & van Deth, 1994).

Case Study

Sarah Jacobs began to fast in 1867 at the age of 12. Her parents publicized her behavior with the support of a local clergyman who confirmed the authenticity of the claims. She became a tourist attraction for the curious and a source of inspiration for religious pilgrims. As with other fasting girls of her time, Sarah's fame attracted concern and skepticism from the medical profession. To resolve the ongoing debate over her case, nurses from Guy's Hospital were dispatched to watch the girl. As a condition of the watch, her parents insisted that she not be offered unsolicited food. Over the course of the week, Sarah grew feeble and lost the ability to regulate her body temperature. The nurses and supervising doctors attempted to end the watch and recommended refeeding, but her parents refused to end or modify the conditions of the test, and Sarah never requested food. After 10 days, she died of starvation.

According to Brumberg (1989), Anglo-American girls during the Victorian era were well acquainted with the religious fasting of medieval saints, and St. Catherine of Siena's biography was included in inspirational books for girls. Indeed, the actions of Sarah Jacobs' parents seem to reflect a deep faith in a divine source of their daughter's food refusal. However, the growing field of psychiatry viewed these girls as suffering from "nervous" conditions. Thus, fasting girls of the 18th and 19th centuries embraced the continuity between the religious medieval fasting of saints and their own behaviors. Meanwhile, psychiatrists endorsed the continuity between the extreme fasts leading to death among adolescent girls in the United States, England, France, and Germany and the newly identified syndrome of AN.

Introduction of Anorexia Nervosa as a Syndrome in the Late 19th Century

The term *anorexia nervosa* was first introduced in the medical literature by William Gull (1874) to describe four adolescent girls with deliberate weight loss, three of whom went on to achieve full weight recovery. At around that time, independent descriptions of a similar syndrome appeared under the labels *l'anorexie hysterique* in France (Lasegue, 1873) and *anoressia* in Italy (Brugnoli, 1875, as described in Habermas, 1992; Ruggiero, Prandin, & Mantero, 2001). Similarly, just before the turn of the 20th century, American physicians were beginning to differentiate anorexia as a syndrome distinct from the larger category of hysteria (Vandereycken & Lowenkopf, 1990), and German physicians were differentiating AN from the larger category of **neurasthenic disorders** (Vandereycken, Habermas, van Deth, & Meermann, 1991). A paper read at a meeting of the South Australian branch of the British Medical Association in 1882 documented two cases of anorexia in young women in Australia (Vandereycken & Beumont, 1990), and Kissyel reported a case of severe hysterical anorexia in an 11-year-old girl in Russia in 1894 (as reported in DiNicola, 1990b).

Despite the sudden psychiatric attention given to fasting girls around the world, Gull's characterization of the disorder gained the most prominence. The case of Miss K. R., a 14-year old girl, is now described by Gull (1888, pp. 516–517).

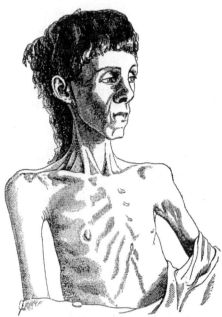

Photographed April 21st, 1887.

Miss K. R. at age 14 years, height 5 feet 4 inches, weight 63 pounds, diagnosed with anorexia nervosa. (Photographed April 21, 1887.)

Source: Reprinted with permission from Elsevier (*The Lancet,* 1888, Vol. 1, pp. 516–517).

Case Study

The patient, who was a plump, healthy girl until the beginning of last year (1887), began early in February, without apparent cause, to evince repugnance to food; and soon afterwards declined to take any whatever, except half a cup of tea or coffee. On March 13th, she traveled from the north of England, and visited me on April 20th. She was then extremely emaciated, and persisted in walking through the streets to my house, though an object of remark to the passers-by. [. . .] Patient expressed herself as quite well. A nurse was obtained from Guy's, and light food ordered every few hours. In six weeks Dr. Leachman reported her condition to be fairly good; and on July 27th the mother wrote: "K. is nearly well. I have no trouble now about her eating. Nurse has been away three weeks."

Gull's (1874, 1888) descriptions of AN provide the first accounts of the disorder as it is recognized and defined today. They also are strikingly similar to the accounts of fasting girls, nervous consumption, and holy anorexia of earlier periods.

Both Gull (1868, 1874, 1888) and Lasegue (1873) acknowledged the presence of several cases of anorexia before giving the syndrome a specific name. Lasegue (1873) commented, "I wish to treat of a symptomatic complexus *too often observed* to be a mere exceptional occurrence" (p. 265, emphasis added). Similarly, Gull (1888) stated that his case was "an illustration of most of these cases" (p. 517) and in an earlier paper referred to "young women emaciated to the last degree through hysteric apepsia" (1868, p. 175). Thus, the language used in these papers, as well as the widespread attention and confirmation

Photographed June 14th, 1887.

Miss K. R. following successful treatment for anorexia nervosa. (Photographed June 14, 1887.)
Source: Reprinted with permission from Elsevier (*The Lancet,* 1888, Vol. 1, pp. 516–517).

these works received from other physicians, indicate that the condition was a familiar entity, although previously known by other names or viewed within a larger category of mental disorders.

The features of Gull's (1888) AN included significant weight loss, slow pulse rate, skin changes, and loss of menstruation, with "perversions of the 'ego' being the cause and determining the course of the malady" (p. 517). Gull (1874) specifically noted that "The want of appetite is, I believe, due to a morbid mental state. I have not observed in these cases any gastric disorder to which the want of appetite could be referred" (p. 25). In a similar vein, Gull (1874) advised physicians to treat the illness with feeding despite the likely protests of the patient. Lasegue (1873) viewed *l'anorexie hysterique* as a form of hysteria in which psychological distress was converted into food refusal motivated by "disgust" or "uneasiness after food, vague sensations of fullness, suffering, and gastralgia *postprandium*" that, "although hypothetical, is dreaded in advance" (p. 265). Lasegue's (1873) description, based on eight cases, resembled present-day AN in that his patients were primarily girls between the ages of 15 and 20 years.

Both Gull's (1874) and Lasegue's (1873) formulations of the syndrome focused on the food refusal itself; emaciation (Criterion A) and amenorrhea (Criterion D) were viewed as consequences of the syndrome. This resembles the current view of hair loss and constipation as sequelae of AN rather than core features of the syndrome. Another distinction in the descriptions of the illness by both Gull (1888) and Lasegue (1873) from present-day AN was the absence of mention of weight or shape concern.

Examination of historical cases reveals the following patterns. A syndrome of self-starvation existed before the modern era. Like AN, this syndrome predominantly affected adolescent girls and young adult women. Like AN, cases could end in either full recovery or death. Unlike AN in the modern era, starvation was not motivated by a fear of becoming fat. Reasons for self-starvation included pursuit of moral superiority, attention seeking, and fear about the danger food posed to the body. Of interest, these all represent features that can be present in modern-day AN.

The absence of weight/shape concerns in most (though not all) historical cases may reflect the importance of modern cultural ideals in producing body image disturbance. However, the similarities between historical and modern cases appear to outweigh this one difference. This raises the question of whether body image disturbance is really necessary to produce AN.

Historical Trends in the Incidence of Anorexia Nervosa During the 20th Century

Incidence represents the number of new cases of an illness per 100,000 people per year. Thus, if there were 360 new cases of a disorder during a year in a population of 2.5 million, then the incidence would be 14.4 per 100,000 population per year. Table 2–1 provides incidence rates for AN per 100,000 persons per year in ascending order of year. Similar to difficulties encountered when looking at historical cases of AN, the definition of AN has changed over recent decades. Such differences in diagnostic criteria have contributed to incidence rates that differ more across studies than across time (see Table 2–1).

Across studies, nine articles reported a significant secular increase in AN incidence, ten reported no significant increase, and one reported a significant decrease (see Table 2–1). A recent **meta-analysis** of results across studies (Keel & Klump, 2003) supported a statistically significant but modest increase in AN incidence across cohorts over time (see Figure 2–1).

If the core feature of AN is taken to be this intentional yet nonvolitional self-starvation, then evidence of AN appears to trace back to early medieval times. Although the incidence of AN appears to have increased during the 20th century, cases of AN that closely resemble modern cases are not restricted to a period characterized by an idealization of thinness. Furthermore, across historical contexts, this disorder demonstrates a particular tendency to affect adolescent girls.

Anorexia Nervosa in Non-Western Cultures

Numerous case reports have revealed the presence of self-starvation syndromes around the world (Keel & Klump, 2003). Although significant weight loss and emaciation are reported in all cases, the presence of weight concerns as a motivating factor for food refusal does not appear to be universal. Cases of AN have been described in South Africa, Nigeria, Zimbabwe, Egypt, the United Arab Emirates, Iran, China, Japan, Korea, Russia, India, Pakistan, and Malaysia (Keel & Klump, 2003) (see Figure 2–2). In many cases, there is evidence of exposure to Western culture. For example, Buchan and Gregory (1984)

TABLE 2–1   Incidence of Anorexia Nervosa

Mid-point	Range	Location	Criteria	Reported Incidence	Study
1945	1931–1960	Sweden	—	0.24	Theander (1970)
1962	1935–1979; 1935–1984; 1985–1989	Rochester, Minnesota	DSM-III/ III-R	7.3 8.2 8.3	Lucas et al. (1988)[b] Lucas et al. (1991)[a] Lucas et al. (1999)[a]
1968	1960–1969; 1960–1976	New York	—	0.37 0.47	Kendell et al. (1973)[a] Jones et al. (1980)[a]
1968	1965–1971	London	—	0.66	Kendell et al. (1973)[a]
1974	1966–1969; 1965–1982	Scotland	Russell (1970)	1.6 4.06	Kendell et al. (1973)[a] Szmukler et al. (1986)[b]
1976	1956–1975; 1983–1985; 1993–1995	Zurich, Switzerland	—	0.38–1.12 1.43 1.17	Willi & Grossman (1983)[a] Willi et al. (1990)[b] Milos et al. (2004)[b]
1977	1972–1981	England	—	—	Williams & King (1987)[b]
1978	1965–1991	Northeast Scotland	ICD-8	—	Eagles et al. (1995)[a]
1980	1970–1989	Bornholm County, Denmark	ICD-10	1.6–6.8	Pagsberg & Wang (1994)[a]
1981	1977–1985	Ireland	ICD-8/9	4.18	Shinkwin & Standen (2001)[c]
1982	1970–1989 1973–1987 1970–1993	Denmark	ICD-8	 0.42–1.17 1.04 —	Møller-Madsen & Nystrup (1992)[a] Nielsen (1990)[b] Munk-Jørgenson et al. (1995)[a]
1982	1977–1986	Fyn County, Denmark	DSM-III-R	11.0	Joergensen (1992)[b]
1982	1977–1986	Wellington, New Zealand	DSM-III	5.0	Hall & Hay (1991)[b]
1987	1985–1989	Netherlands	DSM-III-R	8.1	Hoek et al. (1995)[b]
1989	1978–1992	Yamagata Prefecture, Japan	DSM-III-R	—	Nadaoka et al. (1996)
1991	1988–1993	England and Wales	DSM-IV	4.2	Turnbull et al. (1996)[b]

[a]Reported significant increase in incidence.
[b]Reported no significant change.
[c]Reported significant decrease.

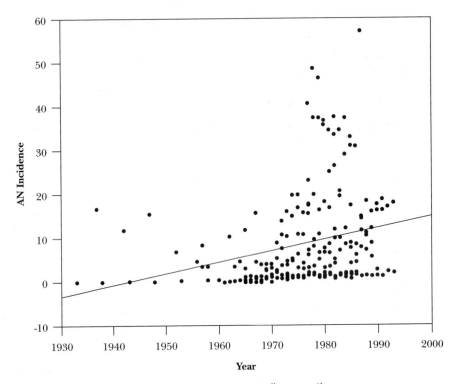

FIGURE 2–1 Incidence of anorexia nervosa across studies over time.

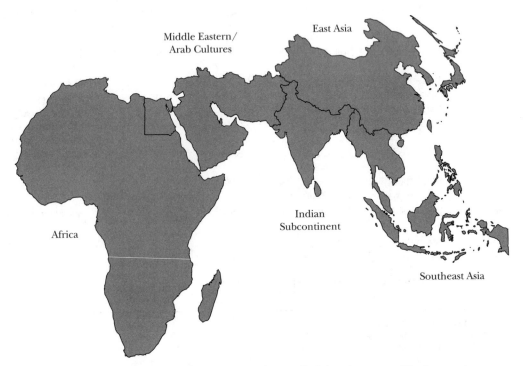

FIGURE 2–2 Anorexia nervosa has been reported in all of the above non-Western regions.

described AN in a Black Zimbabwean woman who had lived in England for many years as a child and recalled being ridiculed about her weight. However, there are examples of AN emerging in individuals with no apparent exposure to Western ideals. Abou-Saleh, Younis, and Karim (1998) described AN in a woman who was a nomad from the Empty Quarter of the United Arab Emirates. This patient apparently had no previous contact with Western ideals of beauty and, like the historical cases reviewed above, refused to eat for reasons unrelated to her weight.

Similar to historical cases, many non-Western cases do not report weight phobia. Lee, Ho, and Hsu (1993) suggested that Westernization and industrialization bring about certain aspects of AN without being necessary to produce the syndrome. Thus, they predicted that Western influence in China would result in an increased incidence of AN there, as well as an increased presentation of AN with weight phobia. Consistent with this hypothesis, Lee and Lee (2000) found that weight concerns were greatest in Hong Kong and least prominent in Hunan, suggesting an association between Westernization and body image disturbance. Further, Lee (2000) and Lai (2000) have both described an increasing prevalence of AN characterized by body dissatisfaction in the East. Still, prior to the increasing influence of Western culture, evidence of a self-starvation syndrome predominantly affecting young women existed in China.

Excluding the criterion of weight phobia for a diagnosis, AN has been found with equal frequency in Western and non-Western cultures. For example, Lee et al. (1987) found no difference in the lifetime prevalence of AN in a nationwide epidemiological study in Korea compared to the Epidemiological Catchment Area study for lifetime prevalence of AN in New Haven or St. Louis. A recent study (Nobakht & Dezhkam, 2000) reported the lifetime prevalence of AN to be 0.9% in Iranian schoolgirls, a value higher than the lifetime prevalence reported in the *DSM-IV-TR* (APA, 2000), and the incidence of AN in Hong Kong reported by Lee, Chiu, and Chen (1989) (just under 0.4 per 100,000 person-years) is similar to the incidence rates reported in Western nations (e.g., Kendell, Hall, Hailey, & Babigian, 1973; Moller-Madsen & Nystrup, 1992; Theander, 1970; Willi & Grossmann, 1983). According to reports from Buhrich (1981) and Goh, Ong, and Subramaniam (1993), AN comprised between 0.05% and 0.16% of psychiatric cases seen in Malaysia, and Okasha (1977) reported that 0.19% of psychiatric cases in Egypt presented with AN. These figures are comparable to those reported by Götestam, Eriksen, Heggestad, and Nielsen (1998) for Norway from 1990 to 1994. Thus, AN does not appear to be limited to Western cultures.

Evaluating the cross-historical and cross-cultural evidence together suggests the following conclusions. A syndrome characterized by deliberate self-starvation, sometimes resulting in recovery, sometimes resulting in death, and primarily affecting adolescent girls and young adult women does not appear to be culture-bound by the definition of Prince (1985). Although this syndrome is not characterized by weight phobia, the similarities to AN far outnumber this difference.

BULIMIA NERVOSA

Several authors have reviewed historical cases of binge syndromes prior to the formal recognition of BN (Habermas, 1989; Parry-Jones, 1991; Parry-Jones & Parry-Jones, 1991; Stein & Laakso, 1988; Ziolko, 1996). Although these cases involved the coupling of binge eating with self-induced vomiting, it is unknown whether these behaviors were accompanied by preoccupations with weight or shape. Like arguments concerning the necessity of weight phobia for defining AN, assertions that concerns over weight and shape are core features of BN have been made (Russell, 1979). However, it seems unreasonable to review cases of AN without weight phobia but disallow such instances for BN. Further, body image disturbance was not a required feature of bulimia when it was first introduced in the *DSM-III* in 1980 (APA, 1980).

Historical Accounts of a Binge-Purge Syndrome

Crichton (1996) speculated on whether the Roman emperors Claudius (A.D. 41–54) and Vitellius (A.D. 69) represented cases of BN in the early part of the first millennium A.D. Ziolko (1996) rejected these cases on the basis that excessive food intake appeared to be based on intentional gluttony, with self-induced vomiting used to allow continued consumption. However, descriptions of Vitellius suggest that the emperor's excessive food intake may not have been under his control; "he was a man of not only such extreme and impulsive, but also disgusting, gluttony that he could not even curb it during a sacrifice or on a journey" (Suetonius quoted in Crichton, 1996, p. 204). This suggests loss of control, currently required to define binge-eating episodes within BN (Criterion A2). Crichton (1996) noted that vomiting distinguished Claudius and Vitellius from their historical peers; nevertheless, Seneca is known to have commented, "*vomunt ut edant, edunt ut vomant*" ("they vomit so that they may eat and eat so that they may vomit"). This suggests that binge eating and purging may have represented a common behavioral pattern among the elite in the Roman Empire and, in the case of Vitellius, a not entirely volitional pattern of eating.

Roman vomitoriums have been presented as further evidence that binge-purge behaviors were common in the Roman Empire. However, the definition of Roman vomitoriums as places to purge after feasts is erroneous and first arose in 1923 (*Oxford English Dictionary*). The original and correct definition describes these architectural features as "a passage or opening in an ancient amphitheatre or theatre" from which audience members would exit. Classics professor Alice Radin speculates that the incorrect definition emerged as a "misunderstood pseudo-Latin colloquialism that arose in what folklorists call 'unofficial culture,' probably British schoolboy humor" (http://www.apaclassics.org/AnnualMeeting/03mtg/abstracts/radin.html). She goes on to describe the proliferation of this misunderstanding as fact in both popular and academic media. Thus, the true frequency of binge-purge syndromes in the Roman Empire remains unknown.

In the 8th century A.D., Avicenna prescribed self-induced vomiting to undo the ill effects of overeating; however, he warned:

> to procure emesis (vomiting) to an undue degree is injurious for the stomach. It is also prejudicial to the thorax and to the teeth. The custom of some people of eating to excess and then procuring emesis . . . is one of the things which ends in chronic disorders.
> *(Gruner, 1930, p. 498)*

This suggests awareness of the morbidity associated with chronic self-induced vomiting and that a disorder characterized by overeating and self-induced vomiting was known in Arabic medicine. No further information is provided concerning the victims of this disorder or whether the disorder was maintained at normal weight.

From the 12th to the 17th centuries many of the fasting saints were reported to engage in binge eating (e.g., St. Veronica) and self-induced vomiting (e.g., St. Catherine; Bell, 1985; Rampling, 1985). These cases appear to fall within the diagnosis of ANBP (*DSM-IV-TR*). It is unclear whether there were cases of binge eating and purging among normal-weight women of this time. If these cases were common in convents, there is little reason to think that they would go unnoticed given the religious significance of women's eating during medieval times (Bynum, 1987).

In 1678, a 50-year-old man experienced uncontrollable eating followed by vomiting for 20 days each year. Following the 20-day binge-purge cycle, the man fasted for 20 days and then resumed normal eating for the remainder of the year (Parry-Jones & Parry-Jones, 1991; Ziolko, 1996). Robert Whytt [1714–1766] provided a description of *fames canina,* originally observed by Richard Lower in the 17th century (Silverman, 1987). According to Whytt [1764], Dr. Lower observed "an uncommon hunger" among hypochondriac and hysteric patients that produced "a great craving for food" (Silverman, 1987, p. 145). "In other cases, however, the morbid matter affecting the nerves of the stomach in hypochondriac and hysteric patients, sometimes occasions a want of appetite and a *nausea*" (Silverman, 1987, p. 145). Although *fames canina* is supposedly a disorder characterized by large food intake followed by vomiting (Stein & Laakso, 1988), Whytt's [1764] review of Lower's [1631–1691] observations does not make a clear connection between the presence of "uncommon hunger" and "want of appetite and a nausea" in the same patients (Silverman, 1987). Parry-Jones and Parry-Jones (1991) reviewed 12 potential cases of BN from the 17th to the 19th centuries. Five of these cases are described below. Among the remaining seven cases, none were associated with inappropriate compensatory behavior, and parasitic worms were found in four cases. According to Ziolko (1996), Forestus [1602] described a nun afflicted with canine appetite (*fames canina* or **kynorexia**) who was miraculously cured after several unsuccessful medicinal treatments by physicians. Like *fames canina, kynorexia* was defined by insatiable appetite, eating that is out of control, and then compulsive vomiting as a result of excessive food intake (Stein & Laakso, 1988; Ziolko, 1996). However, weight is not reported for this case, and the nun may have represented a forerunner to St. Veronica.

For the 18th century, Parry-Jones (1992) detailed the case of Samuel Johnson [1784] as meeting *DSM-III-R* criteria for BN.

Case Study

Dr. Samuel Johnson was known for his gluttonous behavior. In an autobiography, he reported that his eating patterns began in childhood and elicited comments from relatives when he was 9 years old. At one particularly notorious meal, Dr. Johnson consumed large portions of venison, fowl, pork, goose, and dessert in one sitting. To control his weight, he engaged in fasting and used senna as a purging agent. He was very concerned about his excessive weight and his health in general. According to accounts of the time, Dr. Johnson appeared to lose awareness of his surroundings while eating and would tear though food with his bare hands, sweating profusely, until no food remained.

Like modern-day BN patients, Dr. Johnson suffered from binge-eating episodes and engaged in inappropriate compensatory behavior to control his weight. Unlike modern-day BN patients, he was an obese middle-aged man whose disorder began with binge eating alone in childhood. This clinical picture is more characteristic of BED.

Pope, Hudson, and Mialet (1985) concluded that the major psychiatric texts of the 19th century, including those of Esquirol [1838], Briquet [1859], and Lasegue [1871], included no apparent cases of *DSM-III* bulimia. Conversely, Habermas' (1989) review of Briquet [1859] revealed a case of apparent BN in a woman who "ate well" but vomited everything she had eaten and maintained a normal weight (p. 267). Van Deth and Vandereycken (1995) reviewed cases of hysterical vomiting and noted that some of them occurred in individuals of normal weight who also engaged in binge eating and fasting behaviors. Notably, most of these cases occurred in female adolescents. However, the authors equated these cases more with a modern-day **conversion disorder, psychogenic vomiting,** or AN rather than BN (Van Deth & Vandereycken, 1995). Rosenvinge and Vandereycken (1994) reviewed a case of "hysteria" described by Selmer [1892] in which a 12-year-old girl refused to eat but maintained normal weight. This apparent contradiction was explained one night when the girl's mother observed her "'eating butter, herrings, potatoes and all the food she was able to find in the house'" (Selmer quoted in Rosenvinge & Vandereycken, 1994, p. 280). Thus, this girl appeared to fast during the day and binge eat at night (Rosenvinge & Vandereycken, 1994). One 1870 report described a 14-year-old girl who would fast for 18 days and then enter a period during which she ate voraciously (Parry-Jones & Parry-Jones, 1991). Other cases of purported bulimia in the 19th century include one 30-year-old man [1897] who consumed large quantities of food day and night and two men whose voracious consumption included living animals and human flesh, but none engaged in purging or other forms of inappropriate compensatory behavior (Parry-Jones & Parry-Jones, 1991).

For the first half of the 20th century, Pope et al. (1985) reviewed four cases presented by Pierre Janet in 1903. However, the combination of binge eating with purging is presented in only one case. It involved a 17-year-old boy, "Ron," who experienced episodes of "'voracious' appetite," "never felt satiety," and engaged in self-induced vomiting after periods of heavy food consumption (Pope et al., 1985, p. 741). Habermas (1991) presented Ludwig Binswanger's description of Irma, published in 1909, as "the first known report on a case of bulimia nervosa at normal body weight" (p. 361). The 22-year-old patient engaged in recurrent binge eating and fasting and experienced fear of becoming overweight. The case histories of Ellen West [Binswanger, 1944] and Laura [Lindner, 1940] have been interpreted as examples of BN in the first half of the 20th century (Stein & Laakso, 1988). However, several experts in the field of eating disorders have reviewed Ellen West as representing AN, and it is unclear that binge eating and purging ever occurred at normal weight in her case (DiNicola, 1990a). Cases described by Wulff [1932], Bergmann [1932], and Feuchtinger [1942] in the German psychiatric literature have been characterized by binge eating and purging as well (Habermas, 1989, 1992a; Stunkard, 1990).

According to Habermas (1989), Wulff's [1932] cases included four women and one man, all of whom experienced periods of compulsive eating at normal weight. In three cases, onset occurred during puberty. In two cases, vomiting was present in addition to dieting. Finally, in three cases, body image disturbance was recorded. However, a different picture emerges from Stunkard's (1990) translation of Wulff's [1932] work. First, Wulff [1932] described marked obesity in two of the four cases (Cases A and C). Further, in three of the four cases (Cases A, B, and C), binge eating and fasting or purging occurred in distinct phases. Only Case D experienced a binge-purge cycle within one period; these periods alternated with short periods of abstinence and fasting.

According to some reviews, BN existed in a limited number of patients before its formal recognition. According to other reviews, cases of binge eating more closely resembled ANBP or BED. Unlike deliberate self-starvation, the earliest historical accounts of binge-purge syndromes do not seem to preponderate in adolescent girls. In fact, prior to the 19th century, the cases involved mostly adult men. Although there is clear evidence of a binge-purge syndrome existing outside of its present historic confines, this evidence is quite sparse compared to that for a self-starvation syndrome.

Introduction of Bulimia Nervosa as a Syndrome in the Late 20th Century

BN was first identified as a distinct disorder approximately a century after the recognition of AN. In 1979, Russell used the term *bulimia nervosa* to name a binge-purge disorder in a series of 30 patients seen over a period of 6.5 years. Earlier reports of a binge-purge syndrome in women were published in German (Ziolko, 1994) and Spanish (Dorr-Zegers, 1972) journals, but these reports did not suggest widespread awareness of this syndrome before 1960. Based on BN's recent appearance and dramatically increasing incidence (Soundy, Lucas, Suman, & Melton, 1995), Russell (1997) concluded, "Bulimia nervosa is a new disorder." (p. 23)

Historical Trends in the Incidence of Bulimia Nervosa During the 20th Century

Table 2–2 presents studies tracking the incidence of BN from 1970 to 1993. All studies suggest a significant increase in the rate of this disorder over time (Keel & Klump, 2003) (see Figure 2–3). Soundy et al. (1995) reported that the incidence of BN increased nearly sevenfold from 1980 to 1983 and then remained relatively stable at around 30 per 100,000 females from 1984 to 1990 (representing a four-fold increase). Soundy et al. (1995) noted that the particularly high rate in 1983 was inflated by a BN treatment study that year for which participants were being actively recruited from the community. Pagsberg and Wang (1994) reported that the incidence of BN quadrupled from 1970–1985 to 1985–1989. Hoek et al. (1995) reported a significant increase in BN incidence from 1985 to 1989 despite having found no significant time trend for AN. Similarly, Hall and Hay (1991) found a significant increase in referral rates for BN but not AN from 1977 to 1986. There are no incidence data for BN prior to 1970, supporting Russell's (1997) assertion that BN is a new disorder. However, it is possible that observed trends resulted from the

TABLE 2–2   Incidence of Bulimia Nervosa

Midpoint	Range	Location	Criteria	Reported Incidence	Study
1980	1970–1989	Bornholm County, Denmark	ICD-10	0.7–3.0	Pagsberg & Wang (1994)
1982	1977–1986	Fyn County, Denmark	DSM-III	5.5	Joergensen (1992)
1982	1977–1986	Wellington, New Zealand	DSM-III	6.0–44.0	Hall & Hay (1991)
1985	1980–1990	Rochester, Minnesota	DSM-IIIR	13.5	Soundy et al. (1995)
1987	1985–1989	Netherlands	DSM-IIIR	11.5	Hoek et al. (1995)
1989	1978–1992	Yamagata Prefecture, Japan	DSM-IIIR	—	Nadaoka et al. (1996)
1991	1988–1993	England and Wales	DSM-IV	12.2	Turnbull et al. (1996)

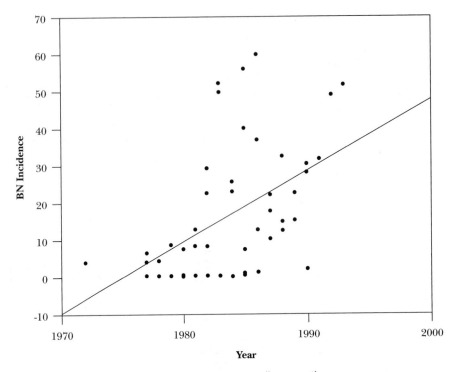

FIGURE 2–3   Incidence of bulimia nervosa across studies over time.

formal recognition of a disorder that had existed as a hidden form of psychopathology in earlier periods.

The limited evidence regarding BN is related to its recent recognition as a distinct syndrome. Attempts to characterize its incidence and prevalence do not precede the second half of the 20th century. Incidence data suggest an increase in rates of BN over this period of increasing idealization of thinness.

Bulimia Nervosa in Non-Western Cultures

Characterizing the presence of BN outside of a Western context has proven challenging. For example, in several reviews of eating disorders cross-culturally (Davis & Yager, 1992; Dolan & Ford, 1991; Miller & Pumariega, 2001; Pate, Pumariega, Hester, & Garner, 1992; Tsai, 2000), references to AN far outnumbered references to BN. This difference is also reflected in the range of countries reporting BN among their citizens; in a recent review (Keel & Klump, 2003), reports of AN were found in five of five non-Western regions of the world, whereas BN was reported in only three of five non-Western regions (see Figure 2–4). Unlike patients with AN in non-Western cultures, those with BN uniformly express weight concerns. Notably, no studies reported the presence of BN in an individual with no exposure to Western ideals (Keel & Klump, 2003). If BN emerges in non-Western countries only as a result of Western influences, then this may explain why there does not appear to be a "non-weight concerned" form of BN.

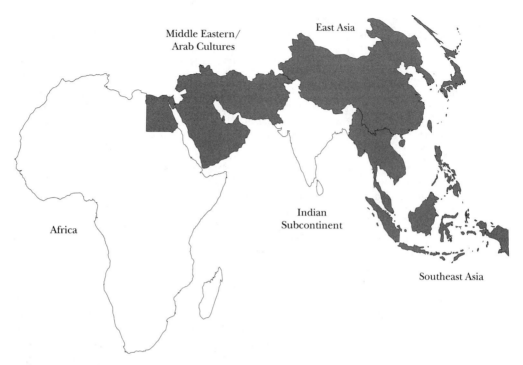

FIGURE 2–4 Bulimia nervosa has been reported in the Middle East, East Asia, and Southeast Asia.

With the exceptions of Japan and a recent study in Iran, prevalence estimates of full BN in non-Western nations were below the range reported for Western nations in the *DSM-IV-TR* (APA, 2000). The degree of Western influence may account for a good deal of variance in BN prevalence estimates. For example, following World War II, Japan emulated some of the ideals of the United States. Indeed, the *Cassell Dictionary of Modern Politics* (East & Joseph, 1994) indicates that Japan is sometimes included in the definition of the West. So, it is not surprising that BN prevalence is most similar between the United States and this non-Western nation. Epidemiological data suggest a lower prevalence for BN than for AN in non-Western countries, a pattern that is the opposite of that observed in Western nations. The point prevalence of AN has been found to be four to five times greater than that of full-syndromal BN in Japan (Nakamura et al., 2000), and it has been noted that AN is more prevalent than BN in Hong Kong (Chun et al., 1992; Lee, Hsu, & Wing, 1992). Thus, even when BN is found in non-Western nations, it is not found in the absence of Western influence, and it seems to be less common than AN.

CONCLUSION

Divergent patterns emerged in the examination of cross-historical, epidemiological, and cross-cultural evidence of AN and BN as culture-bound syndromes. Unlike previous conclusions that eating disorders either *are* or *are not* culture-bound (Habermas, 1989; Lee et al., 1993), these findings suggest that BN is culture-bound and that AN is not.

AN appears to have existed outside of its current sociohistorical context. Conversely, BN appears to be relatively confined to its current sociohistorical context. The conclusion for BN is necessarily weaker than the conclusion for AN because there are fewer articles concerning BN than AN. Although this may represent the relatively longer recognition of AN as a syndrome (and thus greater time to accumulate papers on AN), the majority of the articles reviewed were published since the introduction of BN to the *DSM-III* in 1980. Further, this publication pattern is the inverse of that observed for the treatment literature in AN versus BN. So, it remains unclear whether the recent recognition of BN is the cause or the result of limited data concerning its existence.

The limited data for BN cannot be construed unequivocally as indicating the absence of the disorder because BN may have existed but eluded detection. This seems plausible because there is no overt sign of BN such as the emaciation that characterizes AN. Indeed, Whitehouse, Cooper, Vize, Hill, and Vogel (1992) found that 50% of the cases of BN determined in the community were unknown to their general practitioners, despite referrals made for complications of bulimic pathology in half of these hidden cases. No such hidden cases of AN were found in this study, suggesting that the low weight of AN likely makes it easier to detect outside of the confines of a recognized syndrome.

There are reasons why concerns about detection of BN may be overstated. Further, these reasons contribute to the understanding of why BN may represent a culture-bound syndrome, whereas AN does not. First, although self-starvation can occur in any context, binge eating requires large quantities of readily edible food. Thus, cases may be validly limited to places and periods with abundant food, such as the palaces of the Roman Empire or affluent households in Victorian England. Prior to mass production of food, use of preservatives, and refrigeration, most homes did not contain adequate amounts of food to supply recurrent binge episodes. A loaf of bread would be prepared for a meal and distributed within a household, with the largest portions going to men, who were larger and engaged in manual labor. This may explain why cases prior to the 19th century more commonly involved men, as men were given greater access to food. Leftover food was immediately incorporated into the next day's meal to prevent loss due to spoilage. In earlier historical contexts, food distribution was closely monitored. Thus, it seems that most women would have been unable to binge eat or binge eat without detection. Even if the purported binge eater were the person in charge of food stores, food preparation, or food distribution within an affluent household, the rate at which food required replacement likely would be noticed for two reasons. First, individuals did not obtain food anonymously. A woman purchasing large quantities of food repeatedly for no obvious reason would be quite conspicuous. Second, food purchases required a greater proportion of household budgets than they do now (Bailey & Earle, 1999). Large quantities of food would require large sums of money that would be noticed in most households. Thus, while individuals can deliberately starve themselves regardless of access to food—in some cases refusing even the meager portions allotted to them—they cannot binge eat without free access to large quantities of food. If large amounts of food were obtainable, it is difficult to believe that recurrent binge episodes would go unnoticed. Certainly, the food intake of Dr. Samuel Johnson was not only noticed but recorded by several individuals during and following his lifetime (Parry-Jones, 1992). The modern ability to obtain large amounts of food inconspicuously may explain why BN is more common in urban than rural areas (Hoek et al., 1995).

Similar to the difficulties that would have been encountered in attempting to binge eat without detection, purging would be a difficult behavior to hide prior to the wide availability of modern plumbing. The ability to flush evidence of self-induced vomiting, or laxative or diuretic abuse, away from the privacy of one's indoor bathroom would greatly facilitate secretive purging. Outhouses and chamber pots would not. Thus, in earlier historical periods, symptoms of BN would have been more noticeable. Thus, the relative dearth of evidence of BN outside of its current cultural context may be due to its lack of existence.

The distinct epidemiological patterns suggest that modern Western culture may play a more central role in the etiology of BN compared to AN. However, evidence that the incidence of both disorders increased since their recognition suggests that the emerging thin ideal is relevant to both disorders. The thin ideal and other societal factors will be reviewed in Chapter 5. Chapter 3 continues the epidemiological investigation of eating disorders by examining whether particular segments of modern Western society are at increased risk.

KEY TERMS

Ascetics
Conversion disorder
Fames canina
Incidence
Kynorexia

Meta-analysis
Neurasthenic disorders
Psychogenic vomiting
Refeeding syndrome

CHAPTER 3

Eating Disorders in Ethnic Minorities and Men: Stereotype Versus Reality in Who Suffers from Eating Disorders

STEREOTYPE OF WHO SUFFERS FROM EATING DISORDERS

In Chapter 1, three case studies of individuals with eating disorders were presented. Emily suffered from AN, Jean suffered from BN, and Jamie suffered from BED. In reading the case studies, you may have formed a mental image of these people. Most likely, you imagined that they were all White women, although no specific information was given concerning their race and no specific information concerning gender was given for Jamie. This automatic process of assigning a race and gender to these individuals is related to what is generally believed concerning who suffers from eating disorders—upper-middle-class White girls. Beyond representing a general stereotype, this has been presented as fact by experts in the field of eating disorders (e.g., Bruch, 1966; Crisp, Palmer, & Kalucy, 1976; Garfinkel & Garner, 1982). Furthermore, this representation of eating disorder patients matches observations within treatment-seeking samples.

Evidence from Treatment-Seeking Samples

In the year 2000, less than 70% of the U.S. population was White of non-Hispanic origin, and approximately half were female. In comparison to these national statistics, the demographic characteristics of eating disorder patient samples demonstrated a preponderance of White women. Notably, many controlled treatment studies include only women (e.g., Bulik, Sullivan, Carter, MacIntosh, & Joyce, 1998; Mitchell et al., 1990; Stice & Agras, 1999;

Walsh et al., 1997). Even in a study recruiting both women and men, 96% of participants were women (Goldstein, Wilson, Thompson, Potvin, & Rampey, 1995). No treatment study restricts admission on the basis of racial or ethnic background. Despite this, over 90% of participants have been White in several independent studies of treatment-seeking individuals (Bulik, Sullivan, Carter, MacIntosh, & Joyce, 1998; Goldstein et al., 1995; Keel, Mitchell, Miller, Davis, & Crow, 1999; Strober, Freeman, & Morrell, 1997b; Sullivan, Bulik, & Kendler, 1998). Notably, much of this research has been conducted in areas in which approximately 90% of the local population is White (e.g., Minnesota, the United States, and Christchurch, New Zealand). However, even in a study recruiting participants from a more ethnically diverse area such as New York City, 83% of participants were White (Walsh et al., 1997). Ethnic breakdown of the remaining participants included 6% Black, 6% Hispanic, and 5% Asian.

These data indicate that patients with eating disorders are more likely to be female and White than might be expected from the general population. However, these data may best represent demographic data for *patients* with eating disorders. Because most individuals with eating disorders may never seek treatment (Fairburn, Welch, Norman, O'Connor, & Doll, 1996), treatment-seeking samples may be unrepresentative. Thus, school- and community-based samples may provide less biased estimates of gender and ethnic minority representation among individuals with eating disorders.

Evidence from Non-Treatment-Seeking Samples

An examination of studies evaluating the presence of eating disorders in school- or community-based samples suggests greater representation of men and ethnic minorities than has been observed in treatment-seeking samples. Pemberton, Vernon, and Lee (1996) assessed the prevalence of BN and bulimic behaviors among college students from two universities in Texas. The prevalence of BN was 1.3% for women and 0.2% for men, and the authors found no significant difference in the prevalence of BN or bulimic behaviors on the basis of racial/ethnic background. Among White undergraduates, 5.5% had bulimic behaviors. Among non-White students, 5.3% had bulimic behaviors. In a population-based study of the prevalence of BN, Bushnell and colleagues (1990) reported that the lifetime prevalence of the disorder was 1.9% in women and 1.0% in men. Further, the proportion of adult women diagnosed with BN who were of "European" descent did not differ significantly from the surrounding population. Reiss (1996) evaluated the presence of abnormal eating attitudes and behaviors and diagnosable eating disorders among two ethnic groups recruited from family planning clinics in the British Urban population. In this study, African-Carribean women reported *higher* levels of disordered eating attitudes and behaviors than White women. Clinical interviews confirmed BN in six women. Among these women, one was White, two were African-Carribean, one was African, one was Asian, and one was "other/mixed race." Thus, when individuals with eating disorders are drawn from the community, ethnic minorities are well represented, and gender differences appear to be less dramatic than in treatment studies. Thus, the stereotype that all eating disorders occur in White women seems false.

This chapter reviews research concerning the associations between eating disorders and ethnicity and gender. The essential issue of this chapter is the extent to which the risk of eating disorders differs across specific sociodemographic groups. Because ethnic minority groups cannot be assumed to be all alike, evidence of eating disorders is examined separately in four ethnic minority groups: African-American/Black, Hispanic, Asian, and Native American. Unfortunately, research is too limited to allow examination of differences among specific cultural backgrounds within these groups. Following the examination of eating disorders in ethnic minority groups, this chapter explores eating disorders in men. In addition to examining rates of eating disorders in underrepresented groups, this chapter reviews how features inherent in each group may influence the presentation of eating disorder symptoms.

EATING DISORDERS AND ETHNICITY

Eating Disorders in African-American or Black Samples

Cases of AN and BN have been recognized in Black individuals for a long time (Dolan & Ford, 1991; Gray, Ford, & Kelly, 1987; Johnson, Lewis, Love, Lewis, & Stuckey, 1984; Pate et al., 1992). Indeed, Lawlor, Burket, and Hodgin (1987) described a Black male adolescent hospitalized for an eating disorder over fifteen years ago. However, early cases were recognized with the caveat that they were "rare." It was generally believed that Black individuals were "protected" from developing eating disorders because the ideal of beauty was heavier and more voluptuous for Black women than it was for White women (Williamson, 1998).

In support of this belief, African-American women appear to be less likely to experience body dissatisfaction, disordered eating, and BN compared to White American women (Abrams, Allen, & Gray, 1993; Chandler et al., 1994; Edwards-Hewitt & Gray, 1993; Gray et al., 1987; Rhea, 1999; Rosen et al., 1991). Wilfley, Schreiber, Pike, & Striegel-Moore (1996) found comparable levels of disordered eating in Black and White women. However, after controlling for degree of overweight, White women were found to have more body dissatisfaction. That is, at a given weight, Black women were more satisfied with that weight than were White women. Across studies, African-American women appear to be more accepting of higher weights. For example, Black college students reported greater body satisfaction despite weighing more than White college students (Chandler et al., 1994).

Correlates of disordered eating in Black women have included actual weight problems, the degree to which they assimilated to mainstream culture, depression, anxiety, and low self-esteem (Abrams et al., 1993). Conversely, a strong African-American cultural identity appears to protect Black women from disordered eating attitudes and behaviors (Pumariega, Gustavson, Gustavson, & Motes, 1994). Given these patterns, one might predict that this protection would be limited to AN and BN for which the undue influence of body weight or shape on self-evaluation is symptomatic. Supporting this prediction, Mulholland and Mintz (2001) found that rates of AN and BN were both 0% in 413 African-American college women; however, 2% met criteria for an EDNOS. Similarly, Smith and colleagues (1998) found equivalent prevalence rates for BED among Black and White women. These studies suggest that Black women may not be protected from eating disorders per se but may be protected from those disorders in which body image disturbance is a defining feature.

A recent study of eating disorders in 985 White and 1,061 Black women supported ethnic differences in lifetime prevalence rates and suggested that the magnitude of ethnic differences depended on eating disorder diagnosis (Striegel-Moore et al., 2003). Specifically, AN affected 1.5% of White women but affected no Black women (0%). BN was also more common in White compared to Black women, affecting 2.3% of White women and 0.4% of Black women. Finally, BED showed the least dramatic difference, affecting 2.7% of White women and 1.4% of Black women.

In preadolescence, Black girls have reported higher drive for thinness than White girls (Striegel-Moore, Schreiber, Pike, Wilfley, & Rodin, 1995). Hermes and Keel (2003) found that White and Black girls reported similar awareness of the thin ideal, but Black girls reported greater internalization of this ideal. It is unclear whether the increasing ethnic diversity of fashion models may explain such findings in young girls. Presenting thin women of color as icons of beauty may increase the relevance of the thin ideal to Black girls. However, this beauty ideal is not only thin, it is also quite White, and fashion models often possess traditionally "White" features, regardless of their ethnic background. Such models may only serve to reinforce multiple points of departure between a non-White girl's appearance and the ideal. Presented with several potential foci for feeling inadequate, non-White girls may focus less on weight as they mature. Supporting this possibility, as preadolescent girls in Striegel-Moore et al.'s study passed through puberty, the drive for thinness increased significantly in White girls but remained relatively unchanged in Black girls (Striegel-Moore et al., 2000b).

Eating Disorders in Hispanic Samples

Evaluation of eating disorders in Hispanic women has suggested rates that equal those found in predominantly White samples (le Grange, Stone, & Brownell, 1998; Lester & Petrie, 1998; Pumariega, 1986; Rhea, 1999; Smith & Krejci, 1991), with 1.4% to 4.3% of Mexican-American women being diagnosable with BN. When differences have been found in comparisons between White and Hispanic females, they have suggested more severe binge eating (Fitzgibbon et al., 1998) and greater body dissatisfaction (Robinson et al., 1996) in Hispanic women. Several studies have reported that acculturation to U.S. values is associated with higher levels of eating pathology among Hispanic individuals (Chamorro & Flores-Ortiz, 2000; Gowen, Hayward, Killen, Robinson, & Taylor, 1999; Pumariega, 1986). In particular, widespread adoption of U.S. beauty ideals has been associated with greater eating pathology (Lester & Petrie, 1995). Gowen et al. (1999) reported that among more acculturated Hispanic girls, 13.6% could be diagnosed with an EDNOS compared to 0% of less acculturated Hispanic girls. Additional risk factors include increased family rigidity (Kuba & Harris, 2001), increased weight or body mass index (BMI) (Fitzgibbon et al., 1998; Lester & Petrie, 1995), and depression (Fitzgibbon et al., 1998).

Similar to the effects of increasing diversity among fashion models, increasing diversity among female pop artists, such as Christina Aguilera and Jennifer Lopez, may produce Hispanic versions of the thin ideal. Like Barbie dolls of the world, such role models provide a seamless bridge between ethnic identity and dominant Western ideals of beauty, fame, and wealth.

Eating Disorders in Asian Samples

Asian college women were found to report less dieting and binge eating (Mintz & Kashubeck, 1999) and were less likely to score above the cutoff for eating pathology on the Eating Attitudes Scale (Lucero, Hicks, Bramlette, Brassington, & Welter, 1992) compared to White college women. In contrast to these findings, Tsai and Gray (2000) reported that the prevalence of BN was higher than previously thought among Asian women. Barnett, Keel, and Conoscenti (2001) found that Asian college women did not differ from White college women in levels of body dissatisfaction. Although Asian women were thinner than White women, they also selected a thinner ideal, so that differences between the current and ideal body were similar between the two ethnic groups (Barnett et al., 2001) (see Figure 3–1). Robinson et al. (1996) reported that among the thinnest girls

Caucasian Females

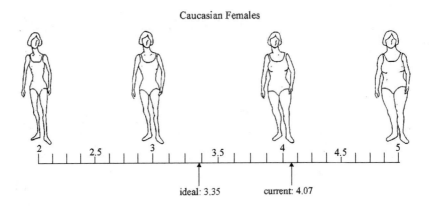

Asian Females

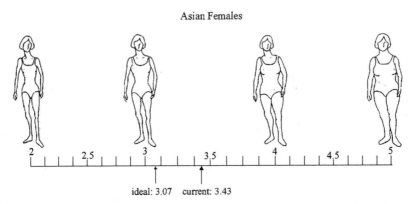

FIGURE 3–1   Mean figure ratings of Caucasian (top row) and Asian females (bottom row).

Source: Barnett, Keel & Conoscenti (2001). Body type preferences in Asian and caucasian college students. *Sex Roles,* 45, p. 871 with kind permission of Springer Science and Business Media.

in a school-based sample, Asian girls reported significantly greater body dissatisfaction than White girls. Notably, for White girls, shorter height was associated with higher body dissatisfaction, while for Asian girls, taller height was associated with higher body dissatisfaction. This suggests that Asian girls, like Jean, may be more concerned about being large, in general, rather than fat, in particular.

Case Study

Jean dreaded going home for vacation because she knew her mother would complain about two things—Jean's living with her boyfriend before marriage and Jean's weight. What was more, Jean's mother would tie the two complaints together into one theme. She would warn Jean that if she did not lose weight, she would never receive a wedding proposal. Jean's mother was a first-generation American from Korea. Although Jean's father was born in the United States, his grandparents had moved there from Korea. Jean's mother held traditional values that included the importance of Jean attracting a good husband, preferably a Korean husband. To reach this goal, Jean needed to remain thin and avoid revealing her age. Most of all, she needed to break up with her boyfriend. It was clear to Jean's mother that the boyfriend did not have honorable intentions.

In contrast to findings for Hispanic samples, several studies have failed to find a significant association between acculturation and body dissatisfaction or disordered eating among Asian women (Gowen et al., 1999; Haudeck, Rorty, & Henker, 1999; Yoshimura, 1995). These results, along with aspects of Jean's case, suggest that cultural factors that contribute to eating disorders may be native to some Asian cultures. Rieger, Touyz, Swain, and Beumont (2001) have argued that traditional values and practices in Asian cultures also idealize thinness. The virtues of fasting to the point of emaciation are included in the Daoist text *Sandong zhunang* (Rieger et al., 2001). Asian cultures may also emphasize the importance of gaining approval from family members and friends (Mukai, Kambara, & Sasaki, 1998; Mukai & McCloskey, 1996), who may encourage dieting even among underweight girls (Mukai, Crago, & Shisslak, 1994). Thus, rather than viewing all cultural contributions to eating pathology as originating in White Western culture, it is important to recognize that there may be non-Western cultural factors that increase the risk of disordered eating.

Eating Disorders in Native American Samples

There have been very few investigations of disordered eating among Native American individuals. However, those studies that have been conducted indicate alarmingly high rates of disordered eating behaviors (Rosen et al., 1988; Smith & Krejci, 1991; and Snow & Harris, 1989). Rosen et al. (1988) found that over half of Chippewa females employed one or more purging methods to lose weight. This is consistent with Smith and Krejci's (1991) finding of greater disordered eating among Native American compared to White high school students. Native American groups appear to be at increased risk for obesity, and increased BMI has been associated with the use of dangerous weight control methods among Chippewa women (Rosen et al., 1988). Similarly, Story and colleagues (1994) reported that Native American and Native Alaskan girls who felt overweight were more likely to use extreme measures to control their weight. In their sample, 27% of Native American girls endorsed a history of self-induced vomiting to lose weight.

Taken together, these studies suggest elevated rates of purging among Native American girls. Purging may be viewed as a less extreme behavior in Native American cultures because purging agents are traditionally used for purification. The use of special teas to induce vomiting during Native American healing practices may make this a more accessible behavior for girls who are concerned about their weight. Thus, not only are Native American girls not protected from disordered eating practices, they may be more likely to develop certain symptoms.

Summary of Eating Disorders in Ethnic Minorities

The apparent underrepresentation of ethnic minorities among women with eating disorders appears to be related more to biases in who seeks and receives treatment for eating disorders than to protection from eating pathology afforded by minority status. With the exception of African-American or Black women, most women of color appear to have the same risk of developing eating disorders as White women. Thus, the belief that White women are at particularly high risk of developing eating disorders appears to reflect a stereotype rather than reality. The role of acculturation or the adoption of dominant cultural values in increasing the risk of disordered eating among ethnic minorities is unclear. There is some support for the view that only those girls who attempt to conform to dominant cultural ideals fall prey to eating disorders (Chamorro & Flores-Ortiz, 2000; Gowen et al., 1999; Lester & Petrie, 1995; Pumariega, 1986). However, there may also be risk factors for eating disorders that are inherent in the cultural values of ethnic minority groups (Rieger et al., 2001).

EATING DISORDERS AND GENDER

Eating disorders are more common in women than men. This has been confirmed in population-based epidemiological studies, treatment studies, and school-based investigations of body dissatisfaction, disordered eating, and full-threshold eating disorders. That said, eating disorders occur more often in men than most people realize. Men comprise approximately 10% of those diagnosed with AN or BN. Yet, far less than 10% of the research conducted on eating disorders has evaluated these problems in men (Keel, Klump, Leon, & Fulkerson, 1998). Similarly, approximately 40% of BED occurs in men (Spitzer et al., 1992, 1993). Yet, both early (e.g., Arnow, Kenardy, & Agras, 1992; Berkowitz, Stunkard, & Stallings, 1993; de Zwaan, Nutzinger, & Schoenbeck, 1992) and more recent (Appolinario et al., 2002; Pendleton et al., 2001; Raymond, de Zwaan, Mitchell, Ackard, & Thuras, 2002; Williamson et al., 2002) investigations of BED have excluded male participants.

This pattern of excluding men from the study of eating disorders raises several questions. First, are findings for women true for men with eating disorders? Second, given that eating disorders are so uncommon in men, are there factors that uniquely increase the risk of eating disorders in men? Third, do men have problems with eating and body image that go unrecognized because the problems do not match the patterns exhibited by women? To address these questions, this section examines eating disorders in boys and men. As captured by Jamie's case, men with an eating disorder may feel marginalized with respect to their gender and marginalized with respect to others who suffer from eating disorders.

Case Study

Jamie was embarrassed about beginning treatment for an eating disorder because he had always been such a guy's guy. He had been an athlete throughout school, and he worked in a male-dominated business environment. When the possibility of group treatment was introduced,

Jamie immediately rejected it. He felt that he would stand out like a sore thumb as the only man in the group. The counselor told him that the group included both men and women but acknowledged that there were far more women. Jamie repeated that he was interested in the possibility of using medication to help him adhere to a weight loss program. He felt it would be hard to explain to his male friends where he was going every Monday night if he entered group treatment. In addition, attending the Monday night group meant missing Monday night football. As far as Jamie was concerned, if the group was really meant to include men, it would not meet on Monday nights during football season.

Despite Jamie's feeling of being different from other patients with eating disorders, most research suggests more similarities than differences between boys and girls with eating disorders (Keel et al., 1998; Leon, Fulkerson, Perry, Keel, & Klump, 1999). Chapter 4 reviews risk factor research, and a more complete review of susceptibility will be presented there and in Chapters 5–8. In general, results have not differed between the genders. However, there appear to be some correlates of eating pathology that are unique to men that are reviewed in more detail here. These include higher premorbid weight and higher proportions of premorbid obesity, participation in sports that emphasize maintenance of either low body weight (e.g., wrestling) or low percentage of body fat (e.g., body building), and homosexuality. In addition, men may present with a type of eating disorder that is not observed in women, an eating disorder characterized by unhealthy behaviors in the pursuit of muscularity.

FACTORS UNIQUE TO EATING DISORDERS IN MEN

Weight

Studies of adolescent boys and girls suggest that body dissatisfaction is associated with increased levels of disordered eating behaviors (Keel et al., 1998; Leon, Fulkerson, Perry, & Cudeck, 1993). Nevertheless, women are more likely than men to report that they are dissatisfied with their bodies because they are larger than their ideal weight (Barnett et al., 2001; Fallon & Rozin, 1985; Heatherton, Mahamedi, Striepe, Field, & Keel, 1997; Heatherton, Nichols, Mahamedi, & Keel, 1995). Gender differences in body dissatisfaction are found even among elementary school children (Keel, Fulkerson, & Leon, 1997a), with girls expressing concern that their thighs, hips, and stomach are too large.

Puberty may produce further gender differences in the risk for eating disorders. As girls enter puberty their percentage of body fat increases; this body fat is distributed in the development of breasts and increases in the size of hips and thighs. Thus, the process of puberty takes girls further from the feminine ideal portrayed in popular media (see Chapter 5). Conversely, as boys enter puberty, their percentage of lean muscle mass increases. Both boys and girls become taller, but sexual differences in height emerge during puberty, causing boys to be taller than girls. Further, boys experience an increase in the size of their shoulders relative to their hips. Thus, the process of puberty brings boys closer to the masculine ideal portrayed in popular media (discussed further below).

Although men and women are striving for different ideals, neither desire fat bodies. Indeed, a recent investigation indicated that elementary school children uniformly preferred thin children to fat children, regardless of the child's gender (Kraig & Keel, 2001). However, gender differences were found for preferences regarding average-weight children.

A thin girl was rated more positively than an average-weight or overweight girl. Conversely, a thin or average-weight boy was rated more positively than an overweight boy (Kraig & Keel, 2001). This pattern suggested that, for girls, the salient category is "thin," with social value being reserved for this quality. Thus, both average and overweight girls would be motivated to lose weight, and this conclusion matches patterns observed in school-based samples (Keel, 1997a; Leon et al., 1999; Rosen, Gross, & Vara, 1987). For boys, the salient category is "fat," with social devaluation reserved for this quality. Thus, only overweight boys would be motivated to lose weight, and this conclusion matches patterns observed in school-based samples (Keel et al., 1997a; Leon et al., 1999; Rosen et al., 1987). Given these results, it is not surprising that fewer adolescent boys diet to lose weight compared to adolescent girls (Neumark-Sztainer & Hannan, 2000), and this may account for a significant gender difference in the risk of developing an eating disorder (see Chapter 4). Further, it may explain why being overweight acts as a specific risk factor in men (Carlat & Camargo, 1991).

Sports

Compared to estimates of eating disorder prevalence in men in the general population (0.1% to 0.3% for AN or BN), higher rates of eating disorders have been reported in male athletes. Burckes-Miller and Black (1988) reported AN in 1.6% of male athletes and BN in 14.3%. Notably, this study employed less strict criteria in defining these disorders than are currently employed, explaining the particularly high rate of BN. However, these authors posited that athletic participation increased the risk of eating disorders. Supporting this assertion, subsequent studies reported elevated rates of disordered eating among male athletes (Enns, Drewnowski, & Grinker, 1987; Thiel, Gottfried, & Hess, 1993; Yates, Shisslak, Allender, Crago, & Leehey, 1992). Notably, these studies found increased rates of disordered eating for sports that require weight control for success. In a recent meta-analysis, Hausenblas and Carron (1999) suggested that weight can be important to athletic participation in at least three ways: (1) competitions occur within weight classes (e.g., wrestling), (2) reduced weight improves performance (e.g., long distance running), and (3) evaluation involves aesthetics (e.g., gymnastics). Results of their meta-analysis showed that participation in sports that emphasized weight restriction or aesthetics was associated with increased rates of disordered eating. Supporting the particular importance of sports for eating disorders in men, this effect was larger in men compared to women.

Given the results of Hausenblas and Carron's (1999) meta-analysis, one would not predict an increased risk of eating disorders among men competing in sports that emphasize strength through increased size (e.g., football). In fact, given that a relatively small proportion of male athletes participate in sports that emphasize weight control, it is not surprising that athletic participation, in general, is not associated with disordered eating in adolescent boys (Fulkerson, Keel, Leon, & Dorr, 1999) and may even be associated with increased self-esteem. Thus, the association between sports and eating disorders in men may be limited to certain kinds of sports. Further, it is difficult to determine whether disordered eating behaviors that are limited to the sports season should be equated with symptoms of an eating disorder (Enns et al., 1987).

Homosexuality

Several studies have reported an association between homosexuality and eating disorders in men (Beren, Hayden, Wilfley, & Grilo, 1996; French, Story, Remafedi, Resnick, & Blum,

1996; Heffernan, 1994; Williamson, 1999). A higher proportion of men with eating disorders are homosexual compared to proportions in the general population (Carlat, Camargo, & Herzog, 1997; Herzog, Norman, Gordon, & Pepose, 1984; Mangweth et al., 1997; Olivardia, Pope, Mangweth, & Hudson, 1995). Further, rates of eating disorders are higher among homosexual compared to heterosexual men (Russell & Keel, 2002; Yager, Kurtzman, Landsverk, & Wiesmeier, 1988). In contrast, there does not appear to be a consistent relationship between homosexuality and eating disorders in women (Moore & Keel, 2003). These patterns suggest that homosexuality may serve as a risk factor for eating disorders that is unique to men.

Russell and Keel (2002) examined whether increased rates of disordered eating attitudes and behaviors in homosexual men might reflect a general risk of increased emotional and behavioral problems or whether the association was specific to eating disorders. Potentially, a homosexual orientation is associated with increased psychosocial stressors that can be expressed as several different forms of psychological problems, including eating disorders. Results of Russell and Keel's investigation supported a specific association between sexual orientation and eating disorders. One explanation for this specific association is the greater emphasis in the gay male subculture on thinness for attractiveness (Epel, Spanakos, Kasl-Godley, & Brownell, 1996). Epel and colleagues examined personal advertisements and found that men seeking men placed the same emphasis on thin physiques as men seeking women. In contrast, heterosexual men were less likely to use characterizations of their own body weight to attract a mate. It has been argued that men seeking to attract men experience the same pressures to conform to appearance ideals as heterosexual women (Brand, Rothblum, & Solomon, 1992; Epel et al., 1996). Thus, like women, homosexual men are at increased risk for eating disorders.

One theme unites the three unique factors reviewed above. All three serve to increase the salience of body weight to men. Further, all three increase the pressure to attempt to control body weight. Thus, these factors simply make men more similar to women in terms of body image and weight concerns. The next section discusses problems with eating and body image that are rarely seen in women.

MUSCLE DYSMORPHIA—A DIFFERENT TYPE OF EATING DISORDER?

Thus far, this chapter has explored eating disorders in men as they have been defined in women. This assumes that eating disorders will be expressed in men as they are in women. Given this assumption, it is not surprising that risk factors show more similarities than differences between the genders and that the few differences that do emerge likely serve to make men more similar to women. However, there has been speculation that men may be at risk for a type of eating disorder not seen in women. This eating disorder has been described as **reverse anorexia** (Pope, Katz, & Hudson, 1993). Instead of viewing the body as much larger than it really is, men with **muscle dysmorphia** view it as puny despite their efforts and success at body building (Pope et al., 1993). This distorted perception contributes to more extreme efforts to increase lean muscle mass and overall body size. Extreme measures include excessive exercise, dietary manipulations that include extremely high protein intake, and the use of anabolic steroids. To the extent that this clinical pattern involves altered eating patterns, the use of extreme weight control behaviors, and body image disturbance, many have argued that it represents an eating disorder (Andersen, 1984; McCabe & Ricciardelli, 2001; Pope et al., 1993), albeit one rarely seen in women.

Similar to the cultural idealization of thinness for women, there is a cultural idealization of muscularity for men. Pope and colleagues (1999) examined changes in the

Luke Skywalker and Han Solo, 1978 (left); Luke Skywalker and Han Solo, 1998 (right).
From Pope, Olivardia, Gruber, & Borowiecki (1999). Evolving ideals of male body image as seen through action toys. *International Journal of Eating Disorders, 26,* 65–72, p. 70.

proportions of male action figures including GI Joe and the *Star Wars* characters Luke Skywalker and Han Solo. In recent decades, the shoulder-to-waist ratio has increased dramatically. Current action figures represent a distortion of bodily proportions on par with the distortions presented by Barbie dolls. According to Pope et al., the large, bulging, well-defined muscles of these action figures are obtainable only with professional weight training and the use of anabolic steroids.

As was noted earlier, in comparison to girls, boys who want to lose weight are more likely to be overweight, resulting in a difference in the percentage of girls and boys who want to lose weight (Cohn et al., 1987). However, the same study demonstrating this gender difference failed to find a gender difference in absolute levels of body dissatisfaction (Cohn et al., 1987), a finding that was mirrored in a study of college-age men and women (Fallon & Rozin, 1985). Although the desire to be smaller seems to be limited to overweight men, underweight men report the desire to be bigger. Indeed, in the Barnett et al. (2001) study, Asian men were smaller than White men but reported a similar ideal body size. This left no significant difference between current and ideal body size for White men but a significant discrepancy for Asian men who wanted to be larger (Barnett et al., 2001) (see Figure 3–2). Thus, the characterization of women as having more body dissatisfaction than men is more appropriately contextualized as dissatisfaction with being too large. Mirroring this difference, adolescent boys are significantly more likely to use anabolic steroids compared to adolescent girls (Bahrke, Yesalis & Brower, 1998; Drewnowski, Kurth, & Krahn, 1995; Neumark-Sztainer, Story, Falkner, Beuhring, & Resnick, 1999b). Rates of anabolic steroid use range from 4% to 12% among adolescent boys (Bahrke et al., 1998). Given the effects of anabolic steroids on liver, heart, and reproductive function, these rates are alarmingly high. More research is required to understand the relationship between muscle dysmorphia (Phillips, O'Sullivan, & Pope, 1997), which is

Caucasian Males

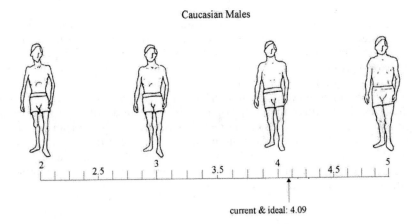

current & ideal: 4.09

Asian Males

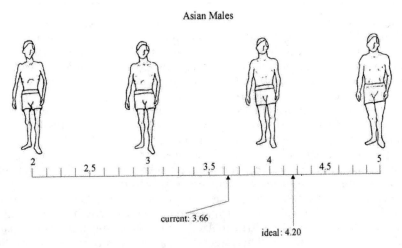

current: 3.66

ideal: 4.20

FIGURE 3–2 Mean figure ratings of Caucasian (top row) and Asian males (bottom row).

Source: Barnett, Keel & Conoscenti (2001). Body type preferences in Asian and caucasian college students. *Sex Roles,* 45, p. 872 with kind permission of Springer Science and Business Media.

viewed as a type of body dysmorphic disorder (Pope, Hudson, Katz, Gruber, Choi, Olivardia, & Phillips, 1997), and eating disorders (Pope et al., 1999; Pope, Phillips, & Olivardia, 2000).

Summary of Eating Disorders in Men

The stereotype that eating disorders are more common in women than men is an accurate reflection of reality. Nevertheless, the stereotype posits a significantly greater disparity than truly exists. Further, eating disorders are largely conceptualized on the basis of their occurrence in women. On this basis, eating disorders in men closely resemble eating disorders in women, and they have more similarities than differences. Factors that appear to be more relevant for men are those that increase the salience of weight control. However, the features that have come to be associated with eating disorders (e.g., weight phobia) may produce greater gender disparity in eating disorder prevalence than would exist if a more inclusive definition of eating pathology were used. Further work is needed on clinical patterns marked by an intense desire to attain a larger, more muscular physique, the undue influence of body weight or shape on self-evaluation, and the use of extreme and unhealthy eating and weight control behaviors.

CONCLUSION

The stereotype that eating disorders are most likely to occur in upper-middle-class White women is misleading. Although Black women appear to be somewhat protected from developing eating disorders, this protection does not extend to members of other ethnic minorities. Further, men make up a larger proportion of individuals with eating disorders than most people realize, and the diversity is even greater when eating disorders other than AN and BN are considered.

At the beginning of this chapter, a difference between the ethnic composition of treatment-seeking versus community-based samples was presented. This difference could reflect barriers to seeking treatment among members of ethnic minorities who have a stereotype-incongruent disorder. In a recent study of college undergraduates, Gordon, Perez, and Joiner (2002) found that race significantly influenced the likelihood of recognizing an eating disorder. Participants in this study were given a written summary of a 16-year-old girl's eating and other activities over a 5-day period. When "Mary" was depicted as White, 93% of participants recorded that she had an eating disorder. When she was depicted as either African American or Hispanic, only 79% of participants recognized an eating disorder. This effect did not depend upon the race of the participant. It is possible that, like college students, primary care physicians are less likely to appreciate the presence of an eating disorder when it occurs in a non-White woman. This may contribute to a difference in referral for treatment of the disorder.

Hermes and Keel (2003) conducted a study of primary care physicians, examining whether the gender and ethnicity of a college student influenced the recognition of eating disorder symptoms and the likelihood of referral for eating disorder treatment. Although the depiction of disordered eating patterns was held constant in the fictional student, physicians were significantly more likely to recognize and suggest treatment for an eating disorder when the student was female. Disturbingly, increased medical morbidity in men suffering from eating disorders may be attributable to delayed recognition of these disorders due to the patient's sex (Siegel, Hardoff, Golden, & Shenker, 1995). Thus, even when stereotypes appear to reflect a true difference, the overgeneralization of these stereotypes can create negative consequences for those who suffer from eating disorders but do not fit the stereotype.

Lawlor and colleagues (1987) characterized the presence of an eating disorder in a Black adolescent boy as "rare." In retrospect, perhaps what was rare was the appreciation that the disorder existed in a patient who differed so much from the expected norm. Future work would benefit from challenging stereotypes that prevent the recognition of individuals with eating disorders or eating disorders in individuals.

KEY TERMS

Muscle dysmorphia
Reverse anorexia

CHAPTER 4

Risk Factor Research: Methods for Determining the Causes of Eating Disorders

Before the causes of eating disorders are examined in Chapters 5–8, this chapter examines how research studies are designed to reveal causal factors. A common misperception is that statistics can be made to show anything. This is not true. Although people have believed that eating disorders were limited to White girls in the United States, epidemiological data do not support this perception (see Chapters 2 and 3). However, epidemiological data are fairly straightforward. The number of patients with AN in Rochester, Minnesota, in 1944 or the percentage of Asian girls with eating disorders represent descriptive statistics that do not require much interpretation. Although statistics cannot be made to show anything, their interpretation can lead to very different, and sometimes erroneous, conclusions.

This chapter reviews the logic behind different research methods used to examine risk factors in eating disorders and the limits to conclusions that can be drawn from different kinds of studies. Later chapters will refer back to this chapter. Thus, this chapter provides a working knowledge of the kinds of studies reviewed in the book.

HYPOTHESES

Just as there are common perceptions of who suffers from eating disorders, there are common understandings of the causes of these disorders. One common explanatory model attributes the increase in rates of eating disorders to increasing societal idealization of thinness. Another model attributes the development of an eating disorder to an individual's need for control or perfectionistic strivings. These models often reflect a combination of actual observations (of an individual or a group) and inferences about the meaning of these observations. Thus, they best represent hypotheses. Research studies are specifically designed to test hypotheses.

Several different research methodologies can be used to test these and other hypotheses concerning the causes of eating disorders. Because it would be unethical to actually cause an eating disorder in a person, these research designs operate by a combination of deduction and inference. Deduction comes in when a certain premise is stated (e.g., "Dieting causes binge eating"; Polivy & Herman, 1985), and then specific consequences of this statement are tested for their veracity (e.g., "If dieting causes binge eating, then individuals who diet should be more likely to report binge eating than individuals who do not diet"). This statement can be tested with a simple comparison of binge eating in dieters and nondieters. If the predicted difference is found, it is inferred that dieting may cause binge eating—although this is not actually demonstrated by this correlational study design. The finding does not prove the original premise because there are alternative explanations for the association between binge eating and dieting. For example, binge eating may cause weight gain that causes dieting. So, individuals who binge are more likely to diet than individuals who do not binge. However, for this alternative explanation to be true, dieting would need to follow binge eating, not vice versa. So, **longitudinal studies** are often used to infer causal relationships between a proposed risk factor and eating disorder onset. The logic is simply that for A to cause B, A must precede B in time.

LONGITUDINAL STUDIES

There are two basic types of longitudinal studies, retrospective follow-back investigations and prospective follow-up investigations. Each is associated with benefits and limitations. The basic design features of each type of study are described, as well as research findings that have emerged in the field of eating disorders using these approaches.

Retrospective Follow-Back Design

A retrospective follow-back investigation begins with individuals whose eating disorder status is known. A case-control design would include individuals with eating disorders demographically matched to individuals who have never suffered from an eating disorder. For example, a person with an eating disorder could be matched to an individual with no lifetime history of an eating disorder on factors such as sex, age, ethnic/racial background, and **socioeconomic status**. The purpose of matching across these factors would be to ensure that differences found between the eating disorder group and the control group could be attributed to the presence of the eating disorder (versus other factors that might differ between the groups). Matching participants on these variables assumes that these variables are not of interest. This could be because the matched factor is already known to be a risk factor (e.g., sex) and does not require further investigation. Alternatively, it may be because the factor is not believed to be related to eating disorder risk (e.g., socioeconomic status) but could operate as a **nuisance variable** if it happened to differ between comparison groups. A nuisance variable is anything that creates differences but that is irrelevant for understanding the problem under investigation.

TABLE 4–1   Variables Examined by Fairburn and Colleagues

Environmental Vulnerability Domain

Parental problems
    Low parental contact
    Separation from parents
    Parental arguments
    Parental criticism
    Parental high expectations
    Parental overinvolvement
    Parental underinvolvement
    Parental minimal affection
    Maternal low care and high overprotection
    Paternal low care and high overprotection
Disruptive events
    Parental death
    Change of parent figure
    Parental chronic illness
    Frequent house moves
    Severe personal health problems
Parental psychiatric disorder
    Parental depression
    Parental alcoholism
    Parental drug abuse
Teasing and bullying
    Teasing (not related to weight, shape, appearance, or eating)
    Bullying
Sexual and physical abuse
    Sexual abuse
    Repeated severe sexual abuse
    Physical abuse
    Repeated severe physical abuse
    Repeated severe physical or sexual abuse

Personal Vulnerability Domain

Childhood characteristics
    Negative self-evaluation
    Shyness (not included in AN study)
    Perfectionism
    Extreme compliance
    No close friends
    School absence through anxiety
Premorbid psychiatric disorder
    Major depression
    Drug abuse
    Alcohol abuse
Behavioral problems
    Marked conduct problems
    School absence (truancy)
    Deliberate self-harm
Parental psychiatric disorder (ever)[a]
    Depression
    Alcoholism
    Drug abuse

TABLE 4–1   *(continued)*

Dieting Vulnerability Domain

Dieting risk
    Family member dieting for any reason
    Family member dieting for shape or weight
    Family criticisms of body or eating
    Repeated comments by others about body or eating
    Teasing about body or eating
    Parental history of AN or BN
    Parental obesity
    Childhood obesity
Obesity risk
    Childhood obesity
    Parental obesity (ever)[a]
Parental eating disorder
    Parental history of AN or BN (ever)[a]

[a]"Ever" denotes before or after the onset of an eating disorder.

Source: Fairburn et al. (1997, 1998, 1999).

In a retrospective follow-back study using case controls, the onset of the eating disorder is used as a starting point. The study examines potential differences between groups on historical variables from before this starting point. Fairburn and colleagues (1997, 1998, 1999) have completed a series of studies using this approach to understand risk factors in the development of AN, BN, and BED. In each study they identified a group of individuals with the eating disorder under investigation, a group of individuals with other forms of psychopathology (general psychiatric controls), and individuals who were free of eating and general psychopathology (healthy controls). This approach allowed them to differentiate among factors that appeared to increase the risk for psychopathology in general (factors that were elevated in the eating disorder group relative to healthy controls but not general psychiatric controls) versus those that were specific for increasing eating disorder risk (factors that were elevated in the eating disorder group relative to both the general psychiatric and healthy control groups).

Table 4–1 lists the factors examined in this study. The investigators organized risk factors into three domains: environmental, personal, and dieting vulnerability. Environmental vulnerability factors represent characteristics in the individual's environment that may increase the risk of an eating disorder, such as parental criticism. Personal vulnerability factors represent characteristics within the individual that may increase the risk, such as perfectionism. Dieting vulnerability factors include features in the environment or in the individual that would have increased the likelihood of dieting, such as childhood obesity.

Table 4–2 presents results for specific risk factors from Fairburn et al.'s studies of AN (1999), BN (1997), and BED (1998). More risk factors were identified for BN than for AN or BED. For both BN and BED, difficult family environments and weight problems were risk factors (Fairburn et al., 1998). For both AN and BN, low self-esteem and perfectionism increased the risk. Interestingly, factors that would contribute to body image concerns and dieting were increased in BN but not AN (Fairburn et al., 1999), supporting hypotheses presented in Chapter 2 regarding the role weight concerns play in the development of each disorder.

TABLE 4–2 Specific Risk Factors for AN, BN, and BED (Differences from General Psychiatric Controls at $p \leq 01$)

Domain	Anorexia Nervosa	Bulimia Nervosa	Binge Eating Disorder
Environmental		Low parental contact High parental expectations Parental arguments Parental criticism Parental alcoholism	Low parental contact High parental expectations Severe personal health problems
Personal	Negative self-evaluation Perfectionism	Negative self-evaluation Perfectionism Parental alcoholism (ever)	
Dieting		Family member dieting for any reason Repeated comments by others about shape or weight Childhood obesity Parental obesity (ever)	Family criticisms of body or eating Childhood obesity

A benefit of the follow-back design is the ability to compare a large number of affected individuals to matched controls. Large samples increase statistical power to detect differences, and case controls eliminate the need to control statistically for potential nuisance variables. A drawback of the follow-back design is the potential influence of **retrospective recall bias.** For example, individuals who have an eating disorder may be more likely to recall criticism about their weight than individuals who do not have an eating disorder when no true difference occurred. One means of avoiding recall bias is to use objective historical records (e.g., medical or school records). However, these tend to be limited in terms of what variables can be obtained. For example, few medical records would include valid or reliable measures of perfectionism. For these reasons, prospective follow-up designs have been used in much risk factor research.

Prospective Follow-up Design

A prospective follow-up design begins with a large group of unaffected individuals and collects data both prior to and following the period of risk for onset of an eating disorder. Individuals who develop eating disorders over the course of follow-up are compared to individuals who do not develop eating disorders on factors measured before the eating disorder emerged. Several groups have conducted such investigations, and much of this work will be reviewed in later chapters. What follows is a review of findings from two major longitudinal studies of eating disorders.

Leon et al. (1999) conducted a longitudinal study of the development of disordered eating in over 1,400 adolescents. The study investigated girls and boys in the 7th through 10th grades. Each cohort was followed prospectively until they graduated or until the end

TABLE 4–3   Vulnerability Domains

Substance-related impulsivity
    Smoking cigarettes
    Drinking alcohol
    Constraint (personality measure of impulse control)
Development
    Puberty
    Grade in school
Negative affect/attitudes
    Body dissatisfaction (in girls, body dissatisfaction also loaded on development)
    Depression
    Negative emotionality (personality measure of the tendency to feel unhappy and anxious)
    Ineffectiveness
    Interoceptive awareness (difficulty recognizing and separating different feelings and
        internal sensations)

Source: Leon et al. (1999).

of the 4-year study. Students completed self-report assessments of *DSM-III-R* eating disorder symptoms, mood disturbances (e.g., depression), self-esteem, dieting, exercise, body image, personality (e.g., perfectionism), other risky behaviors (e.g., alcohol use), and pubertal status.

Table 4–3 shows how the investigators arranged the variables into vulnerability domains. Unlike Fairburn and colleagues' (1997, 1998, 1999) arrangement of factors by hypothesized associations, Leon et al. (1999) examined how the risk factors were associated with each other to define domains. Thus, smoking cigarettes, drinking alcohol, and a personality measure of impulsiveness (Constraint) were highly related to each other and formed a category of related factors: Substance-Related Impulsivity. Not surprisingly, puberty and grade in school were highly correlated and constituted the Development domain. Finally, body dissatisfaction, depression, a tendency to feel unhappy and anxious (Negative Emotionality), feeling ineffective, and difficulty recognizing different feelings (**Interoceptive Awareness**) were interrelated as a third factor: Negative Affect/Attitudes.

Over the course of follow-up, Negative Affect/Attitudes was a significant predictor of new onset of disordered eating attitudes and behaviors in both girls and boys (Leon et al., 1999). As a **diathesis,** negative affectivity is likely to be associated with negative attitudes toward the self, leading to low self-esteem and dissatisfaction with many aspects of the self, including physical appearance and weight. The authors posited that negative affectivity represented a nonspecific diathesis for the development of psychopathology and that cultural factors, such as an idealization of thinness for women, shapes the expression of this diathesis into an eating disorder (Leon et al., 1999).

In an independent 4-year prospective follow-up study, Killen et al. (1996) examined weight concerns, bulimia, drive for thinness, body dissatisfaction, interoceptive awareness, interpersonal distrust, ineffectiveness, maturity fears, perfectionism, personality, alcohol consumption, and height and weight as potential predictors of eating disorders in approximately 800 girls. Of these, only weight concerns predicted the new onset of EDNOS in high school girls. The overall incidence of EDNOS was 4%. Among girls with the highest weight concerns at baseline assessment, 10% developed an EDNOS. Among girls with the lowest weight concerns at baseline, 0% developed an EDNOS. Similar results for boys have been reported. Keel, Fulkerson, and Leon (1997a) demonstrated that poor body image predicted the onset of disordered eating in 102 elementary school boys at 1-year follow-up.

An advantage of prospective follow-up studies is the ability to test specific hypotheses concerning risk factors for eating pathology. In addition, concerns about retrospective recall bias are eliminated. A drawback is the need to begin assessments before eating disorders develop and to continue follow-up assessments throughout the entire period of risk. Most prospective risk factor studies are constrained by the need to retain a sample within a school setting. Thus, studies of adolescents typically end when students graduate from high school, and studies of college students begin well after eating problems have begun. Given that the transition from high school to college reflects a peak age of onset for both AN and BN, the limited number of studies bridging this period is a serious limitation in risk factor research.

Two studies (Tyrka, Waldron, Graber, & Brooks-Gunn, 2002; Vohs, Bardone, Joiner, Abrahamson, & Heatherton, 1999); have examined girls prospectively during this transition. Tyrka and colleagues (2002) examined 157 girls in the 7th to 10th grades and conducted 2- and 8-year follow-up evaluations. At the 8-year follow-up, interviews were conducted to determine the lifetime history of an eating disorder (either *bulimic syndrome* or *anorexic syndrome*). Notably, this introduces retrospective recall into the assessment of eating disorders. The authors found that initial perfectionism and low body weight predicted anorexic syndrome, and initial negative emotion predicted bulimic syndrome. This study replicated results from previous studies (e.g., Fairburn et al., 1997, 1999; Leon et al., 1999) and suggested that different risk factors contribute to AN versus BN. Vohs et al. (1999) examined a specific model for predicting increases in bulimic symptoms (not necessarily the development of BN) from the spring of the senior year of high school to the freshman year of college in 342 women. Their study supported a combination of perceived overweight, low self-esteem, and perfectionism as predicting increases in bulimic symptoms.

A consequence of follow-up ending when participants graduate from high school is that most of the individuals who will develop an eating disorder will do so after the period of observation ends. Indeed, a second drawback of prospective studies is that very large samples are needed because only a very small percentage of individuals will develop an eating disorder. Most prospective studies are not able to predict the onset of AN or BN because the rates of these disorders are extremely low. Leon et al. (1999) measured disordered eating attitudes and behaviors. Similarly, Killen et al. (1996) predicted partial syndrome eating disorders. Even those studies that do bridge the transition from adolescence to young adulthood use expanded (e.g., Tyrka et al., 2002) or continuous (e.g., Vohs et al., 1999) definitions of eating pathology due to their relatively smaller sample sizes. The validity of this approach rests on the extent to which eating disorders exist on a continuum with disordered eating (see Chapter 1) and the extent to which AN, BN, and BED share risk factors. This latter assumption does not appear to be supported by research (Fairburn et al., 1997, 1998, 1999; Tyrka et al., 2002).

An additional drawback of both retrospective and prospective longitudinal studies is that inferences concerning causation between variables remain inferences. For example, dieting may precede and be associated with an increased risk of binge eating without necessarily causing binge eating. A third underlying variable could cause both dieting and binge eating even though dieting emerges first. Perhaps appetite disturbances cause an individual to set external limits on food intake by dieting, and these same appetite disturbances cause binge-eating episodes. In order to demonstrate causation, experimental designs are necessary.

EXPERIMENTAL RESEARCH STUDIES

Experimental studies identify an independent variable that, when manipulated, causes a change in a dependent variable. Logically, experiments are a type of longitudinal study because manipulations of the independent variable always precede changes in the dependent variable in time. With appropriate experimental controls, these designs can be very powerful in demonstrating that one factor causes another. However, as noted above, it would be unethical to attempt to cause an eating disorder. Thus, most experimental studies start with a premise concerning a factor that causes eating disorders and then generate a hypothesis that would be true if the premise were correct. The study then tests this hypothesis as an indirect way of evaluating the original premise. In this case, the specific hypothesis usually involves some analogue of the factors thought to be important in causing eating disorders, and these investigations are called **analogue studies.** Most experimental analogue studies use college undergraduates as research participants. Thus, the value of these studies depends upon the extent to which causal patterns demonstrated in college students accurately represent causal patterns for eating disorders in the population at large.

Analogue Studies

Polivy and Herman (1985) and others (for review of early experimental research see Ruderman, 1986) have conducted a number of experimental analogue studies evaluating the premise that dieting causes binge eating. The classic design compares responses to experimental manipulations in individuals with high versus low scores on a measure of dietary restraint. For example, individuals will be asked to participate in a "taste test"; prior to this, they are randomly assigned to consume a milkshake or nothing (the experimental manipulation). When asked to consume nothing prior to the taste test, dieters consume less than nondieters, consistent with their being on a diet. When asked to consume a milkshake prior to the taste test, dieters consume a lot more than nondieters. This effect has been demonstrated and replicated by a number of labs (Heatherton & Baumeister, 1991; Ruderman, 1986). Thus, these studies show that a milkshake will cause a dieter to eat an unusually large amount of food (Criterion A1 for BN). However, increased food consumption in these studies is not necessarily a binge-eating episode, and dieters do not necessarily suffer from eating disorders.

Several experimental studies have examined and supported a causal relationship between media images and body dissatisfaction (Agliata & Tantleff-Dunn, 2004; Hargreaves & Tiggemann, 2002; Heinberg & Thompson, 1995; Stice & Shaw, 1994). Heinberg and Thompson (1995) randomly assigned women to view television commercials containing either appearance-related images or non-appearance-related images. Women in the appearance-related condition reported significantly greater body dissatisfaction after exposure compared to women in the non-appearance-related condition. Stice and Shaw (1994) randomly assigned women to view magazine pictures of very thin models, average models, or no models. Women assigned to view pictures of very thin models reported significantly greater body dissatisfaction than women assigned to the other two conditions. Notably, neither study demonstrated that media images portraying the thin ideal caused eating disorders. However, both studies provide evidence that such images contribute to discrepancies between women's current weight and the weight they believe is ideal.

Mills, Polivy, Herman, and Tiggemann (2002) compared dieters and nondieters on attitudinal and behavioral responses to exposure to thin ideal body images. Exposure to these images was the experimental manipulation. Only dieters who were exposed to the thin ideal demonstrated shifts in their current and ideal body size (both became smaller) and showed increased food intake. In addition to demonstrating a causal relationship between media images and actual eating behaviors, this study suggested that dieting may increase vulnerability to the effects of media exposure.

Clinical Experimental Studies

Clinical experimental studies evaluate mechanisms within individuals who are diagnosed with an eating disorder compared to individuals without eating disorders. As such, they do not test the new onset of eating disorders experimentally but instead seek to understand the mechanisms that may underlie the presence of eating disorders in one group versus another. A common example of this type of study involves the experimental manipulation of a biological factor and measured effect on other variables (including biological and behavioral indices). Smith, Fairburn, and Cowen (1999) examined the effect of consuming a beverage that would manipulate blood tryptophan levels in women clinically remitted from BN and controls (tryptophan is the biological precursor to serotonin; the hypothesized role of serotonin function in the etiology of eating disorders will be discussed in more detail in Chapter 8). Ten women remitted from BN and 12 healthy control women participated in two sessions. In one session, participants consumed a nutritionally balanced beverage; in the other session, they consumed a tryptophan-depleted beverage. Session type was counterbalanced across participants. Participants provided ratings of mood and eating disorder cognitions (e.g., "feeling fat," "urges to eat," and "weight concern") before and after consuming the beverage and recorded in a food diary any loss of control over eating in the 24 hours following the session. Consumption of a tryptophan-depleted beverage caused similar decreases in blood tryptophan levels in women with BN and controls. However, in women with BN, the drop in tryptophan concentration was associated with increased **dysphoria,** increased eating disorder cognitions, and increased loss of control over food intake (although no objectively large binge episodes occurred, according to the 24-hour food diaries). Similar differences have been reported for women currently ill with BN compared to controls (Weltzin, Fernstrom, Fernstrom, Neuberger, & Kaye, 1995). One possibility is that dieting causes decreases in tryptophan levels and the emergence of bulimic symptoms reflects a response to this biological change.

Case Study ●◆●

During Emily's intake evaluation, she was told about a research study that was being conducted at the university hospital. The study involved three assessments. The first assessment included questionnaires and interviews that would require 2 to 4 hours to complete. The second assessment included having blood drawn once before and twice after consuming a liquid meal. The third assessment included a scan for bone mineral density. For participating, she would be paid $150, and she would receive the results of the bone scan. This was a lab test that her doctor planned to have conducted, so Emily decided that she might as well get paid to have the procedure done and that she would be contributing to science in the meantime. In reading the consent form for the study, she learned that the research was designed to answer three basic questions: Was AN associated with increased levels of depression, a disturbed hormonal response to eating, and decreased bone density? Further, were levels of depression in AN related to the hormonal disturbances? Finally, were these hormonal disturbances related to bone mineral density? Participants in the study included individuals with no history of physical or mental disorders (including any eating disorder) and patients with AN. (Results of Emily's bone scan are discussed in Chapter 8.)

Clinical treatment trials represent another experimental study design with implications for understanding risk factors for eating disorders. Treatment condition is the independent variable, and eating disorder remission is the dependent variable. If certain factors contribute to remission of eating disorder symptoms, then inferences may be made about the roles of these factors in the etiology of eating disorders. For example, Fairburn and colleagues (1993) randomly assigned patients with BN to one of three treatment conditions: behavioral therapy, cognitive-behavioral therapy, and interpersonal therapy (discussed further in Chapter 9). At the end of treatment, patients assigned to cognitive-behavioral therapy had significantly greater decreases in binge eating and purging that were sustained at 12-month follow-up compared to patients in the other two treatment conditions. These results have been interpreted to support the role of cognitions and behaviors in the development of eating disorders (see Chapter 7).

A caveat to using clinical treatment studies to understand the causes of eating disorders is that curative factors do not need to be related to causative factors. The classic example is that aspirin may be effective in treating a headache even though the headache was not caused by an aspirin deficit.

Case Study

Because Jamie was very interested in the possibility of being treated with medication, he eagerly volunteered for a medication treatment study. A drug that had been successful in treating patients with Type II diabetes was going to be examined in patients with BED. He understood that he might be randomly assigned to receive either the active medication or the placebo, and that neither he nor the physician managing his medicine would know what Jamie was actually taking. Jamie did not mind this because he knew that he had a 50/50 chance of getting the active medication, and that at the conclusion of the study he would be offered the medication if it had been shown to be successful. He also knew that if the initial results of the study were dramatic, the active medication would be offered to all participants. The medication was associated with some minor side effects; these were known to diminish over time. In some instances, more serious reactions had developed. However, these severe reactions were very rare, and he would be monitored very closely throughout the study. Jamie felt he had nothing to lose. Unlike most other weight-loss programs, the treatment study was free, and it might work. (Results of Jamie's study participation are discussed in Chapter 9.)

Finally, prevention studies can take advantage of an experimental design in demonstrating that manipulation of a factor can prevent the onset of an eating disorder. Stice, Chase, Stormer, and Appel (2001) recruited 87 young adult women for participation in a study designed to improve body image. After eliminating participants who appeared to meet full criteria for BN or AN at baseline, participants were randomly assigned to one of two conditions: an intervention designed to help them reject the thin ideal or a healthy weight control condition. Results indicated that the intervention reduced internalization of the thin ideal, body dissatisfaction, dieting, negative affect, and bulimic symptoms compared to baseline. Nevertheless, the intervention and control condition produced similar decreases across most variables, including bulimic symptoms.

A concern in experimental studies is that the very controls used to ensure that causal conclusions are sound reduce the **ecological validity** of results. For example, in studies of the association between dieting and binge eating, participants are randomized into a condition in which they are forced to break their diet. In real life, individuals who diet face numerous opportunities to break their diets, and it is difficult to account for individual differences in response to these opportunities within experimental designs. Similarly, exposure to the thin ideal may cause body dissatisfaction, but only a very small proportion of individuals with body dissatisfaction go on to develop eating disorders. Thus, the phenomena that can be demonstrated to be caused within experimental studies support links within a causal chain but rarely connect these causal factors to the actual emergence of eating disorders.

NATURALISTIC INVESTIGATIONS

For certain causal factors, study designs that take advantage of naturally occurring or historical events are possible. These tend to be very powerful because they allow observation of causal relationships in the onset of eating disorders. For example, Polivy, Zeitlin, Herman, and Beal (1994) compared rates of binge eating in World War II combat veterans and prisoners of war in German concentration camps. If binge eating were simply a result of increased stress, then elevated rates would be expected in both groups. If it were a specific consequence of starvation, then elevated binge rates would be expected only among former prisoners of war. Results supported an association between starvation and subsequent binge eating.

Adoption and Twin Studies

Both twin and adoption studies present the opportunity to evaluate the effects of genes and the effects of environmental factors. Adoption studies examine rates of a disorder in adopted children and compare these with disorder rates in their biological and adoptive parents. If greater similarity is found between adoptive parents and children, then an effect of the rearing environment is inferred. If greater similarity is found between biological parents and children, then an effect of genes is inferred. If rates of a disorder are elevated only among children whose adopted and biological parents are both affected, then an interaction between genes and environment is inferred. Although adoption studies have provided very important insights into the etiology of various kinds of mental disorders, they have yet to be used in understanding the causes of eating disorders.

Twin studies use the natural occurrence of **monozygotic (MZ)** and **dizygotic (DZ) twins** to compare the contributions of genes and environment to the risk of developing a disorder. MZ twins share 100% of their genes, while DZ twins share, on average, 50% of their genes. However, when MZ and DZ twins are reared together, environmental factors such as parenting styles, socioeconomic status, neighborhood peers, and school peers are fully shared by both MZ and DZ twin pairs. The independent variable is twin status (MZ versus DZ, or 100% of genes shared versus ~50% of genes shared), and the dependent variable is similarity within twin pairs for the disorder **(twin concordance).** If twin concordance is similar between MZ and DZ twins, then the effect is attributed to a shared environment. If MZ twins show greater concordance for a disorder compared to

DZ twins, the effect is attributed to genes. Population-based twin studies of eating disorders have demonstrated significantly greater concordance rates for MZ compared to DZ twins, suggesting that genes play an important role in the etiology of eating disorders (see Chapter 8).

Cross-Cultural and Epidemiological Studies

Finally, examinations of the epidemiology of eating disorders both cross-historically and cross-culturally (reviewed in Chapter 2) provide interesting insights into etiology. Rates of eating disorders increased during the 20th century and tend to be more common in Western industrialized nations. These observations point to societal features of these nations. However, based on the information reviewed in Chapter 2, we have good reason to believe that AN and BN have unique etiological factors that help to explain their distinct patterns with regard to cross-cultural/cross-historical representation. These findings do not provide insight into specific risk factors; they do suggest that risk factors for BN are limited to specific cultural and historical contexts, whereas risk factors for AN are not. Thus, hypotheses concerning associations between media ideals of thinness and resulting dissatisfaction with weight or shape (reviewed in Chapter 5) may be more relevant for understanding the causes of BN than AN.

Although naturalistic observations often provide strong evidence of causal factors that are directly related to the emergence of eating disorders and can provide information for both BN and AN, they often do not point to specific factors. For example, concluding that genes contribute to the etiology of AN (Klump, Miller, Keel, Iacono, & McGue, 2001b) does not specify which genes increase the risk or what these genes do. Similarly, recognizing that something in modern Western culture increases the risk for BN does not narrow the list of potential culprits.

CONCLUSION

Several methodologies exist for examining risk factors in eating disorders. Due to ethical considerations and logistical constraints in time and financial resources, the majority of risk factor research examines correlates of disordered eating attitudes and behavior. Thus, rather than directly examining causal associations, studies operate on a series of logical relationships in which a relationship (correlation) between two variables must exist if a causal relationship exists. Those studies that examine causal relationships do not typically evaluate eating disorders. Despite these limitations, certain risk factors emerge across studies.

Stice (2002) conducted a meta-analysis of risk and maintenance factors in eating pathology. He only included prospective studies or experimental studies and differentiated between risk factors and *causal* risk factors (these terms map onto results from prospective versus experimental studies, respectively). Stice concluded that body dissatisfaction, negative affect, perfectionism, impulsivity, and substance use were risk factors for eating pathology. Causal risk factors included perceived pressure to be thin and thin-ideal internalization. Notably, the distinction between risk and causal risk factors was largely a result of the types of studies that have been conducted rather than demonstrated differences in these variables' impact on disordered eating attitudes and behaviors. Further, the review was restricted to understanding "eating pathology," not eating disorders. Due to prevalence differences between AN and BN, composite measures of disordered eating attitudes and behaviors most reflect predictors of bulimic symptoms (Stice, 2002).

Chapters 5 and 6 will review evidence for the role of social factors in the etiology of eating disorders. Psychological factors such as cognition, behavior, and personality will be revisited in Chapter 7. Rounding out the examination of etiology, biological factors will be reviewed in detail in Chapter 8. Although biological, psychological, and social factors are reviewed in separate chapters, they should not be viewed as operating independently or as representing competing models because there is no single factor that causes all eating disorders. Genes cannot fully cause eating disorders because concordance rates are not 1.0 in MZ twins. Similarly, sociocultural factors cannot fully cause eating disorders because most women in societies that idealize thinness do not suffer from eating disorders. Rather, several factors, operating at different levels, influence vulnerability to developing an eating disorder.

KEY TERMS

Analogue studies	Longitudinal studies
Diathesis	Monozygotic (MZ) twins
Dizygotic (DZ) twins	Naturalistic investigation
Dysphoria	Nuisance variable
Ecological validity	Retrospective recall bias
Experimental study	Socioeconomic status
Interoceptive awareness	Twin concordance

CHAPTER 5

Body Image, Dieting, and Eating Disorders: Is the Media to Blame?

Cultural context shapes beliefs and values, and beliefs and values influence behaviors. Cultural values can be communicated by families, religions, schools, and, in modern Western culture, by the media. A recent study examined the influence of Western television on the beliefs, values, and behaviors of adolescent girls in Fiji (Becker, Burwell, Gilman, Herzog, & Hamburg, 2002). Baseline assessments were conducted within 1 month of the introduction of televisions into the homes of these girls, and follow-up assessments were conducted 3 years later with a new cohort of adolescent girls. At baseline, girls reported low levels of body dissatisfaction, dieting, or purging and low endorsement of the importance of being thin. This was consistent with a cultural context that celebrated feeding as an expression of familial care. Within traditional Fijian culture, thinness has been associated with lacking love and the care of family (Becker, 1995). Greater negative associations with thinness and positive associations with fatness have been reported by women in Kenya and Uganda, Africa, compared to women in England (Furnham & Alibhai, 1983; Furnham & Baguma, 1994). Three years later, the new cohort of adolescent Fijian girls endorsed beliefs that success, wealth, and independence were related to being thin and endorsed a desire to be thin. Self-induced vomiting to control weight was reported by 0% of girls at baseline compared to 11% of girls 3 years later. Elevated scores (above 20) on the Eating Attitudes Test increased from 13% to 29%. Thus, this study provides strong evidence that the exportation of Western cultural values may be accompanied by the exportation of Western psychiatric conditions (Becker et al., 2002). Moreover, it provides strong evidence for the role of cultural factors in the emergence of eating pathology. This chapter examines the role of societal factors in the etiology of eating disorders.

CULTURAL IDEAL OF THINNESS

In describing BN as a "new disorder," Gerald Russell (1997) attributed its emergence to the "modern 'cult of thinness'" (p. 23). This represents a model for the development of eating disorders in which societal overvaluation of thinness for women actively promoted throughout print, television, and film media cause eating disorders. According to this model, the idealization of thinness leads girls and women to become dissatisfied with their own body weight and shape and to desire thinner bodies. The desire for a thinner body leads to dieting. If dieting leads to significant and medically dangerous weight loss, then AN has developed. If dieting leads to binge eating, purging may emerge in an effort to avoid weight gain, and then BN has developed. This model proposes that women want thinner bodies because of the very thin models of beauty they see celebrated. Thus, the media play a causal role in the development of body image disturbance—a core feature of eating disorders as defined by the *DSM*. Epidemiological data seem to support this view. As reviewed in Chapter 2, the incidence of AN and BN has increased over recent decades. Coincident with increasing rates has been a change in beauty ideals for women.

Garner, Garfinkel, Schwartz, and Thompson (1980) evaluated trends from 1959 to 1978 for three representations of ideal feminine beauty—Miss America Pageant contestants and winners, *Playboy* centerfold models, and magazines marketed specifically to women. In six popular women's magazines,[1] the average number of articles on weight loss diets increased from 1.4 to 2.5 per month from the first to the second decade of observation. The figures of *Playboy* centerfold models shifted from a voluptuous hourglass to a trimmer "tubular" look in which the waist-to-hip ratio decreased significantly. Percent of average weight among *Playboy* centerfold models also decreased significantly over the 20-year period. Finally, Miss America contestants became increasingly thin in reference to their expected weight for height. Across the period of observation, Miss America contestants weighed less than 100%

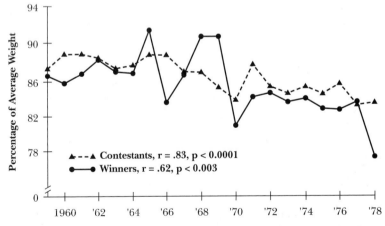

FIGURE 5–1 Percentage of average weight for Miss America Pageant contestants and winners over 20 years.

Source: Reproduced with permission of authors and publisher from: Garner, D. M., Garfinkel, P. E., Schwartz, D., & Thompson, M. Cultural expectations of thinness in women. *Psychological Reports,* 1980, **47,** 483–491. © *Psychological Reports* 1980.

---

[1] *Harper's Bazaar, Vogue, McCall's, Good Housekeeping, Ladies Home Journal,* and *Woman's Day.*

of what would be expected for their height (as did *Playboy* centerfold models). However, before 1968, contestants weighed at least 86% of their expected weight for height (see Figure 5–1). After 1968, their weight remained below 86% of that expected (except for 1971). The relationship between the contestants' weights and the winner's weight was also inconsistent up to 1970. Following 1970, all winners had a lower weight for height compared to the average for contestants. From 1970 on, all Miss America winners weighed less than 85% of that expected for their height. This represents an alarming ideal for feminine beauty considering that weighing less than 85% of that expected for height is the threshold at which AN might be diagnosed. This trend has continued unabated in recent decades (Owen & Laurel-Seller, 2000; Rubinstein & Caballero, 2000; Wiseman, Gray, Mosimann, & Ahrens, 1992).

Patients with eating disorders, like Jean, often point to such ideals in explaining why they are so dissatisfied with their own bodies.

Case Study

When Jean was asked why it was important that she fit into the same size jeans, she replied that it was the only way she would know that she wasn't getting fat. Although she was taller than the average Korean woman, this only contributed to her feeling "big." When she saw women in magazines, she never really saw herself. Models were tall, thin, and blonde or they were very exotic-looking. Jean felt that at 5 feet 4 inches she was still short enough that a very small amount of extra weight would make her look very fat, particularly because she tended to carry weight in her face. In fact, the feature she hated most about herself was her "big, round face." She knew that she would never have high cheekbones like the women in movies or TV shows, but she felt that the least she could do was to have a nice, heart-shaped face. She felt she was too Asian-looking to be an American beauty, and she was too big and "dumpy" to be an Asian beauty.

Echoing observations from Chapter 3, Jean is not protected from the thin ideal by being Asian. Instead, media images of beauty only increase her sense of beauty's being everything she is not. However, of all the attributes she does not possess, a thin body may seem attainable.

WHY IS THIN BEAUTIFUL?

Several explanations exist for the current emphasis on thinness in our culture. Historian Joan Jacobs Brumberg (1989) noted an association between thinness as an aesthetic ideal and periods in which women are encouraged to adopt responsibilities outside of the home and beyond their roles as wives and mothers. For example, the Roaring Twenties represented a time of unprecedented freedom for women following ratification of the 19th Amendment giving women the right to vote. In this period, hemlines rose and flat-chested flappers were in vogue. During the Great Depression of the 1930s, many women worked outside of the home to help feed their families, and during World War II, many women were required to take jobs traditionally held by men. The ideal of feminine beauty during this period was thin (e.g., Katherine Hepburn). The preadolescent figures of flappers represented a direct contrast to the hourglass shape produced by turn-of-the-century Victorian corsets. Following the end of World War II and the return of soldiers to home and jobs, women were expected to return to their roles as mothers and wives. Ideal figures returned to an hourglass shape that emphasized the presence of breasts and hips (e.g., Marilyn Monroe). The next phase of the revolution for women's independence came during the 1960s with the development of birth control pills, the sexual revolution, and the emergence of the feminist movement. Coinciding with demands for women's

Examples of change in ideals of feminine beauty.

Marilyn Monroe picture: Raulin, M. L. (2003). *Abnormal Psychology*. Boston: Allyn & Bacon, 297. Cameron Diaz picture: from http://att.eonline.com/Features/Awards/Golden2003/FashionPolice/index2.htm.

rights and freedom came an ideal of thinness that seemed to demand that women be free of their traditionally feminine shapes. This theory explains the slight U shape in the curve of rates of AN found by Lucas, Beard, O'Fallon, and Kurland (1991) in their review of medical charts in Rochester, Minnesota, from 1935 to 1984. The lowest rates of AN were observed in 1950–1954, not 1934–1939. Indeed, for girls aged 10–19 years, the incidence of AN in 1934–1945 paralleled that from 1965 to 1979. (See Figure 5–2.)

Hsu (1990) has argued that financial prosperity following the Industrial Revolution led to an abundance of food that disrupted the traditional positive correlation between wealth and weight (Nasser, 1988a). Hsu noted that in societies where wealth is associated with fatness, beauty is associated with fatness as well. Conversely, in societies where wealth is associated with thinness, so is beauty. In industrialized nations, there is a significant negative association between socioeconomic status and weight (Rahkonen, Lundberg, Lahelma, & Huchka, 1998; Stunkard, 1996b). Obesity is overrepresented among the poor

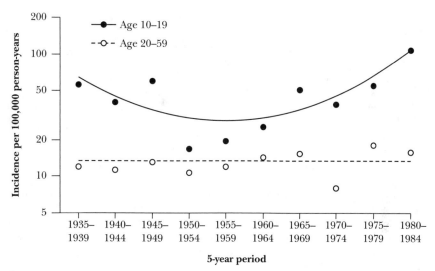

^aPlotted on a log scale.
^bObserved = circles, predicted = lines.

FIGURE 5–2 Age-specific incidence rates[a] for anorexia nervosa, by 5-year periods, in two age groups of female residents of Rochester, Minnesota[b].

Source: Reprinted with permission from the *American Journal of Psychiatry,* Copyright 1991. American Psychiatric Association.

and uneducated, and thinness is more common among the wealthy and well educated in the U.S. This association is particularly strong for women (Ball, Mishra, & Crawford, 2002). This theory may explain the increased prevalence of eating disorders (particularly BN) in industrialized compared to nonindustrialized nations and why rates of eating pathology increase as cultures become more Westernized.

Kilbourn (1987) has argued that a consumer-driven economy requires the constant invigoration of buying. The sole purpose of the multi-billion-dollar advertising business is to encourage people to spend money. One highly successful way to do this is to convince people that there is something they *need* to have. However, basic human needs remain limited—food, shelter, and affiliation. Thus, new "needs" are built upon these basic needs, and affiliation is a good prospect for generating new needs. By creating the impression that one is deficient in some way that will limit prospects for affiliation, advertisements and media can create a need to subscribe to certain beauty ideals (although being beautiful is not a prerequisite for living or procreating). By establishing an unattainable ideal, a constant market for products is created. According to Kilbourn (1987), the presence of body dissatisfaction in the majority of adolescent girls and young adult women is a necessary evil to turn those same women into good consumers. Notably, the quest for thicker eyelashes, luxurious hair, and whiter teeth does not appear to have significant psychiatric consequences. However, the quest for a perfect body may. The alternative view, put forward by members of the media, is that using older or heavier models results in a drop in sales. When a magazine presents a less than "perfect" woman on its cover, the very women this more diverse image of beauty should help do not purchase the magazine. Thus, this may feel both pointless and punishing to the media.

A final possible explanation for why thin is beautiful emerges from the health risks associated with obesity. Thin is beautiful because it represents health and youth—qualities associated with increased reproductive fitness. However, this explanation does not seem particularly compelling because the thin ideal promotes a figure that is associated with loss of reproductive function (amenorrhea). Indeed, an examination of expected weight for a given height reveals that there is more room for weight to go above the expected level, and for the body to remain healthy, than there is room for weight to go below that level while the body remains healthy. For example, at 5 feet 4 inches, a woman with an average frame might be expected to weight 120 pounds (Bray, 1986). BMI for a woman who is 20% above this expected weight would be 24.8 kg/m^2—a weight considered to be within the normal range. However, a woman of that same height whose weight falls 20% below that expected would have a BMI of 16.5 kg/m^2—a weight that both exceeds the requirement for the first symptom of AN and might necessitate inpatient treatment. The extent to which overweight is denigrated appears to go far beyond concerns about the health consequences associated with overweight and may reflect an elaboration of the idealization of thinness—the denigration of fatness (discussed below).

Thus far, this discussion has focused solely on women. This reflects the focus of most research on media portrayals of beauty ideals and body image disturbance. However, recent work has examined media images portraying a male ideal. As reviewed in Chapter 3, Pope, Olivardia, Gruber, and Borowiecki (1999) examined action figure toys that are marketed to prepubescent boys (much as the unrealistically tall, thin Barbie doll is marketed to prepubescent girls). A comparison of action figures for GI Joe and characters from the *Star Wars* movies (Han Solo and Luke Skywalker) revealed significant increases in the chest-to-waist ratio. These authors have argued that unrealistically muscular ideals contribute to excessive exercise and steroid abuse in men, just as unrealistically thin ideals contribute to eating disorders in women. Although the goal for one gender is to reduce overall body size and the goal for the other is to increase overall body size, both ideals promote attempts to reduce body fat and contribute to altered and potentially unhealthy diets. This line of investigation suggests that the media may play a more proactive role in the conception of aesthetic ideals because it is difficult to believe that preadolescent boys would refuse to purchase action toys on the basis of normal waist-to-hip ratios. Thus, time will tell whether men express increased body dissatisfaction in the face of these increasingly unrealistic media images. If no changes emerge, two interpretations could be made. First, media images do not cause population-wide changes in body image. Second, media images of physical appearance have a more powerful effect on women than on men. The latter interpretation has merit because traditional feminine values tend to emphasize physical appearance as a sign of virtue in women (ergo, beauty pageants for women), whereas traditional male values tend to emphasize accomplishments and wealth as signs of virtue in men.

SOCIETAL DENIGRATION OF OVERWEIGHT/OBESITY

In addition to valuing thinness, Western culture denigrates fatness. That is, not only is it good to be thin, it is bad to be fat. Jokes about fat people are tolerated in a society that has eschewed most other forms of physical prejudice. Fat is viewed as bad because obesity is associated with significant health risks; however, when we look at the attitudes toward individuals who are overweight compared to individuals with other health risks, it becomes clear that weight is imbued with moral qualities. For Emily, fat means a loss of control and weakness.

Jokes about fat people are viewed as socially acceptable.

Comer, R. J. (2001). *Abnormal Psychology (Fourth Edition)*. New York: Worth Publishers, 333.

Case Study

Emily denied having any interest in depictions of beauty in magazines, on TV, or in movies. For entertainment, she read novels, and she particularly liked Russian novels. She adamantly refused to accept the idea that her desire to be thin was related to any prepackaged media ideal of beauty. Instead, she pointed to the health risks associated with obesity, the universal preference for symmetry, and her own asymmetrical body. Moreover, Emily was striving for an ideal that was beyond any pedestrian Hollywood image. She was seeking balance in the food she consumed and in her value system and balance in her bodily dimensions. Emily repeatedly stated that she would happily gain weight if she could just do so on her upper body. For this reason, she did not believe that she had an eating disorder because "girls with eating disorders just want to be skinny to look like fashion models," and this was not Emily. Despite her apparent indifference to being thin for the sake of thinness, Emily endorsed an intense fear of becoming fat. She stated that she would rather die than lose control over her eating and her body. When asked what she thought of obese people, Emily said that she felt sorry for those who were obese for medical reasons because there was no way to tell by just looking at a person why he or she was obese. However, she felt repulsed by people who were obese because they could not stop eating; they represented everything that she feared she might become.

Fat persons are viewed as lazy, stupid, lonely, inept, weak, and dependent (Dejong & Kleck, 1986; Tiggemann & Rothblum, 1997). The belief that people can control their weight contributes to a tendency to blame overweight individuals for being overweight

(Crandall & Martinez, 1996; Paxton & Schulthorpe, 1999). Although Emily acknowledges that there is no way to determine why a person is overweight by looking at them, she endorses disgust toward obese people who cannot control their eating. In addition to the virtue associated with refraining from the temptation to eat fattening food, overweight seems to serve as a marker of moral weakness in giving in to temptation too often. Interestingly, women tend to hold more negative stereotypes of the overweight and obese than do men (Tiggemann & Rothblum, 1988), and obese women are viewed more critically than obese men (Harris, Walters, & Waschull, 1991).

These attitudes appear to be somewhat automatic (Grover, Keel, & Mitchell, 2003; Teachman & Brownell, 2001). Alarmingly, negative attitudes toward overweight are held by people regardless of their own weight (Grover et al., 2003) and by the medical professionals responsible for the care of overweight individuals (Teachman & Brownell, 2001). Compared to normal or underweight patients, patients with eating disorders who were overweight (defined by a BMI $> 25 \text{ m/kg}^2$) elicited more fear, more emotional distance, more confrontation, less caring, and less sense of responsibility for therapy from their therapists (Toman, 2002). Unlike the reaction to stereotypes of other aspects of physical appearance (e.g., race), there is little attempt to challenge, alter, or censor these beliefs (Crandall & Biernat, 1990). Further, attempts to reduce antifat prejudice are far less powerful than typical messages that blame fat people for being overweight (Teachman, Gapinski, Brownell, Rawlins, & Jeyaram, 2003).

Longitudinal research suggests that the association between obesity and socioeconomic status may be attributable to an antifat bias and discrimination against individuals who are overweight (Crocker & Major, 1989; Roehling, 1999; Rothblum, Brand, Miller, & Oetjen, 1990). The obese are less likely to be hired (Roe & Eickwort, 1976) and less likely to be promoted (Larkin & Pines, 1979) in comparison to normal-weight individuals with equal qualifications. An alternative explanation for the association between obesity and socioeconomic status comes from a recent study that found more fast-food restaurants in poor compared to wealthy neighborhoods (Reidpath, Burns, Garrard, Mahoney, & Townsend, 2002). Because fast food that is high in fat and calories is inexpensive, it may form a higher proportion of the dietary intake for poor persons. Notably, these two explanations are not mutually exclusive. It is possible that being overweight contributes to lower socioeconomic status and that lower socioeconomic status contributes to the risk of obesity.

Antifat prejudice can be found in children as young as 5 years of age (Lerner & Gellert, 1969). Preadolescent children rate their overweight peers as less likable and least desirable playmates (Strauss, Smith, Frame, & Forehand, 1985). Among elementary school children, the nature of weight biases appears to depend upon the gender of the depicted child, as described in Chapter 3. Among both boys and girls, overweight children are viewed less positively (Kraig & Keel, 2001). Pictures of thin girls are viewed significantly more positively than pictures of either normal-weight or overweight girls (Kraig & Keel). For boys, thin and normal-weight boys are viewed similarly, while overweight boys are held in low regard (Kraig & Keel). These findings suggest that for girls, the salient category may be thinness, whereas for boys, it may simply be a matter of not being fat. This would explain gender differences in drive for thinness and body dissatisfaction.

Ironically, in direct contrast to the increasing value accorded to thinness and the prejudice associated with fatness, the U.S. population has grown increasingly overweight over recent decades (Flegal, Carroll, Ogden, & Johnson, 2002; Flegal & Troiano, 2000; Kuczmarski, Flegal, Campbell, & Johnson, 1994). According to the Centers for Disease Control (CDC), the percentage of Americans who are obese increased from 12% in 1991 to 20% in 2000 (obesity defined as a BMI $\geq 30 \text{ kg/m}^2$). Given the negative social consequences of being overweight, it is not surprising that diet and exercise regimens have become normative New Year's resolutions in Western societies. The large and growing discrepancy between ideal and actual weights for women would be expected to produce significant body image disturbance.

BODY IMAGE

Before considering the impact of societal idealization of thinness on body image, it is important to discuss what is meant by body image. Cash and Deagle (1997) have characterized body image as comprising facets of perception, cognition, and affect. Perception involves both seeing and feeling bodily dimensions such as weight and shape (e.g., "I feel fat" or "I look fat" in the presence of normal weight or underweight). Disturbance in the perception of weight and shape has been documented in women with eating disorders (Altabe & Thompson, 1992; Cash & Deagle, 1997; Smeets, 1999). Interestingly, perceptual disturbance is included as a possible symptom of AN (disturbance in the way one's body weight or shape is experienced—see Chapter 1) but not BN even though perceptual disturbances have not been found to differ between the two disorders (Cash & Deagle, 1997). Notably, perception does not require any particular judgment. A person could perceive herself as fat without making an evaluative statement about what this means. Cognition involves evaluations and thoughts related to body size (e.g., "I weigh more than I should" or "I should lose weight"). Women with eating disorders report greater body dissatisfaction compared to women without eating disorders, and women with BN report greater body dissatisfaction compared to women with AN (Cash & Deagle, 1997). However, the importance given to weight and shape in self-evaluation, and levels of concern with weight and shape (overall importance accorded to the body), have shown the greatest ability to differentiate between women with BN and non-eating-disordered women (Goldfein, Walsh, & Midlarsky, 2000). The undue influence of weight and shape on self-evaluation is included as a possible symptom for AN and as a required symptom for BN (see Chapter 1). Affect involves emotions related to weight or shape (e.g., "I must be thin in order to feel happy" or "When I am unhappy I feel fat"). Most research on body image has focused on perceptual distortions and body dissatisfaction, although neither may represent core features of eating disorders (Cooper & Fairburn, 1993).

An association between societal aesthetic ideals and body image among women has been demonstrated in a number of studies (Groesz, Levine, & Murnen, 2002). Tiggemann and Pickering (1996) found a significant association between body dissatisfaction and time spent watching music videos, soap operas, and movies among adolescent girls. However, this effect has not been universally supported. In a study of the association between time spent reading magazines with high thin ideal images (e.g., a fashion magazine) versus low thin ideal images (e.g., a news magazine), Cusumano and Thompson (1997) found no significant association with disordered eating attitudes or behaviors. One possible explanation for the difference in findings is differences in the age of the participants. Participants in the Tiggemann and Pickering study were adolescent girls, whereas those in Cusumano and Thompson's study were college women. By the time they enter college, women have been adequately exposed to the thin ideal, so further exposure may not substantively alter body dissatisfaction or the risk of developing an eating disorder. Indeed, this study found that measures of awareness of the societal ideal of thinness and internalization of this ideal were significantly associated with disordered eating attitudes and behaviors. A drawback of these correlational studies is their inability to determine the direction of association between media images and body dissatisfaction.

Thus, experimental studies, in which participants can be randomly assigned to media exposure conditions, provide the best evidence of a causal link.

As reviewed in the previous chapter, experimental studies have supported a causal relationship between media images and body dissatisfaction (Groesz et al., 2002; Heinberg & Thompson, 1995; Stice & Shaw, 1994). Thus cultural ideals of beauty can influence the level of body dissatisfaction experienced by girls and women. It is also possible that eating disorders and body image influence perceptions of societal messages. Joiner (1999) stated that individuals with BN may seek confirming evidence that their bodies are unacceptable. In a study of college women, Joiner found that higher levels of bulimic symptoms were correlated with body dissatisfaction and were also associated with interest in receiving negative feedback about the body. King, Touyz, and Charles (2000) investigated the impact of body shape concerns on perceptions of celebrities. Photographs of thin and heavy female celebrities were altered to produce six distorted photographs (three in which the celebrity appeared thinner than they actually were and three in which they appeared heavier). Participants were asked to choose the one photograph that they believed reflected the celebrity's true size. For thin celebrities, college women with higher levels of body concern selected photographs showing thinner than actual bodies, whereas women with lower levels of body concern selected accurate photographs. Regardless of body concern, college women selected photographs of heavy celebrities showing heavier than actual bodies.

Gender differences in body image represent one of the most consistent findings in body image research. High school and college women reliably report greater body dissatisfaction than do men (Barnett et al., 2001; Fallon & Rozin, 1985; Heatherton et al., 1995; Leon et al., 1993). Increased body dissatisfaction in women helps to explain gender discrepancies in rates of eating disorders if body image disturbance translates into disordered eating behaviors. The next section discusses findings concerning one behavioral consequence of body dissatisfaction—dieting.

DIETING

Given that the ideal female body is much thinner than most women's bodies, it is not surprising that most women have attempted to lose weight by dieting. Among high school girls, 63% reported that they are currently attempting to lose weight (Rosen et al., 1987), and 73% reported ever trying to lose weight in the past (Leon, Perry, Mangelsdorf, & Tell, 1989). Among college women, 76% reported dieting at some point and 76% reported desiring weight loss currently, but only 43% described themselves as currently overweight or very overweight (Heatherton et al., 1995).

High school boys are less likely to report a desire for weight loss or weight loss attempts. Only 16% of high school boys reported currently attempting to lose weight (Rosen et al., 1987), and 19% reported ever trying to lose weight (Leon et al., 1989). Notably, high schools girls attempting to lose weight were, on average, normal weight, and high school boys attempting to lose weight were, on average, overweight (Rosen et al., 1987). Among college men, 39% reported dieting at some point and 35% reported desiring weight loss currently, but only 12% described themselves as currently overweight or very overweight (Heatherton et al., 1995).

Interestingly, the percentage of college students desiring weight loss exceeds the percentage describing themselves as overweight. Further, the percentage describing themselves as overweight, far exceeds the percentage who are actually overweight (3% of college women and 4% of college men) (Heatherton et al., 1995). Thus, many people who are normal weight, and even view their weight as normal, attempt to lose weight by dieting.

The physiology of weight control is a balance between energy intake (eating) and energy expenditure (**resting metabolic rate** + activity level). So, weight loss should be imminently attainable by reducing food intake and increasing exercise. The ability to lose weight is the essential claim of the multi-billion-dollar weight loss industry. From organized programs to commercially available liquid diets to specific food regimens (the Zone, the high protein diet, etc.), multiple promises are made and accepted each year by individuals attempting to attain the "right" body. The average financial investment in these programs has increased steadily, without evidence that rates of obesity are declining or even slowing. Across different weight loss programs, initial weight loss appears to be attainable. However, maintaining the weight loss is much more difficult.

As noted in Chapter 4, one possible explanation for the failure of most diets to produce lasting weight loss is that dieting may contribute to binge eating. In the first half of the 20th century, Ancel Keys and colleagues (1950) conducted a study of the consequences of starvation and methods for safe refeeding in preparation for the return of prisoners of war after World War II. Physically and psychologically healthy young men who had been conscientious objectors to the war were recruited for the study. Participants were placed on a diet and exercise regimen designed to produce weight loss to 75% of their previous weight. The results of this study (known as both the *Conscientious Objector's Study* and the *Minnesota Starvation Study*) have provided important insights for the field of eating disorders concerning the consequences of food restriction and significant weight loss.

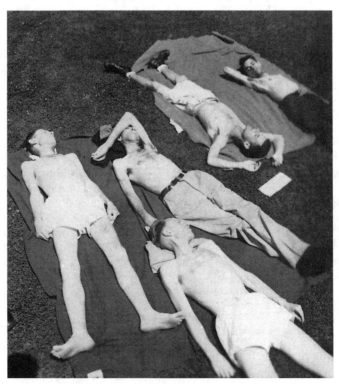

Subject Nos. 26, 20, 111, and 101 sun-bathing during the final week of semistarvation.

Initially, participants lost weight quickly. However, as the study continued, weight loss slowed and analyses of the men's physiological functioning revealed a significant drop in their basal metabolic rate (BMR), which accounts for approximately 70–75% of energy expenditure (depending upon age, gender, body weight, muscle mass, and activity level). Decreased BMR was associated with slowed pulse, decreased respiration, lowered blood pressure, and decreased temperature, among other physical changes (all noted physiological consequences of AN). By diminishing the amount of energy expended in maintaining the body, the men became more efficient in their use of calories. In addition to these physiological changes, the men experienced increases in depression, introversion, apathy, and food-related obsessions and rituals. Finally, in 29% of the men, binge-eating episodes began. That is, when the diet ended, participants reported episodes in which they consumed large amounts of food and experienced a loss of control over their eating. For some men this overconsumption led to vomiting, and one man required hospitalization after excessive food intake. These observations showed evidence of physiological mechanisms that prevented weight loss and contributed to the hypothesis that binge eating might represent a behavioral mechanism to prevent weight loss. Following a series of animal studies, **set-point theory** emerged to explain why organisms resist weight change (Keesey, 1986). According to this theory, our bodies have evolved weight-defending mechanisms in order to withstand periods of famine. Such mechanisms could be triggered by dieting and make weight loss more difficult than portrayed by weight loss programs.

Appealing as this model is, it has received only partial support in research examining weight loss among overweight individuals. The onset of binge eating may be specific to individuals who go from a normal weight to underweight rather than individuals who go from overweight to normal weight. However, many adolescent girls begin to diet at essentially a normal weight at a time when the body is still growing. Thus, weight loss from normal weight during a period when weight gain is supposed to occur may be adequate to trigger the same weight-defending mechanisms observed in the Conscientious Objector's Study.

An association between dieting and disordered eating attitudes and behaviors has been demonstrated in prospective longitudinal studies. Patton, Johnson-Sabine, Wood, Mann, and Wakeling (1990) found that girls who dieted were eight times more likely to develop an eating disorder than girls who were not dieting. Most modern cases of AN in Western cultures begin when the person begins a weight loss diet. Several studies have supported a specific link between dieting and binge eating. In longitudinal studies, dieting most often precedes and predicts binge eating among adolescent girls (Patton et al., 1990; Stice, 2002). Most patients with BN recall going on a diet before experiencing their first binge episode (Bulik, Sullivan, Carter, & Joyce, 1997a; Mussell et al., 1997). Experimental studies demonstrating an association between dieting status and the propensity to eat larger amounts of food were described in Chapter 4.

In contrast to studies suggesting that dieting contributes to eating pathology, Presnell and Stice (2003) found that individuals placed on diets lost weight in conjunction with a decrease in bulimic symptoms. Further, Lowe and colleagues (1998) found that greater dietary restraint was associated with lower rates of binge eating among patients with BN. This latter finding makes some sense because recurrent binge-eating episodes reduce overall dietary restraint. Indeed, women with ANR demonstrate high levels of dietary restraint without experiencing binge-eating episodes. However, this does not mean that dieting is not contributing to their eating pathology.

Among women and men with BED, 55% reported binge-eating onset before their first diet (Spurrell et al., 1997) compared to only 9% (Mussell et al., 1997) to 17% (Bulik et al., 1997) of women with BN. Of note, the absence of dieting before binge eating in some individuals does not preclude dieting from increasing the risk of binge eating. It simply points to additional risk factors for binge-eating episodes (Grilo & Masheb, 2000), particularly for individuals with BED.

CONCLUSION

The increasing idealization of thinness provides one explanation for the increasing rates of eating disorders in Western cultures in the second half of the 20th century. This ideal (see the figure on page 62) contrasts sharply with the actual appearance of most women's bodies, leaving most women wanting to lose weight. Marketing the promise that body weight can be controlled makes being overweight a sign of personal weakness. The final step of this equation is linking weight loss diets to the core feature of AN—significant weight loss—as well as to the core feature of BN—binge eating.

Despite its coherence and supporting evidence, this explanation of the etiology of eating disorders is far from complete. First, there is evidence of AN outside of the modern cult of thinness (see Chapter 2)—suggesting that this explanation may be less relevant for AN than for BN. Second, there is evidence that in a small but reliable percentage of women with BN, binge eating precedes the first diet (Bulik et al., 1997a; Mussell et al., 1997). Among individuals with BED, the percentage reporting that binge eating precedes dieting nearly equals the percentage reporting that dieting precedes binge eating (Spurrell et al., 1997). Finally, to the extent that the thin ideal has led to body dissatisfaction and attempts at weight loss in a majority of American women, eating disorders affect only a very small minority. Thus, this explanation seems neither necessary nor sufficient to understand the etiology of eating disorders. Cultural ideals provide an important part of the explanation for the emergence of eating disorders, but they are only part of the picture. Chapter 6 discusses another sphere of social influence: the family. As reviewed in Chapter 4, the family environment appears to contribute to the risk of developing BN and BED. The next chapter examines family attributes that may be important in producing this risk.

KEY TERMS

Resting metabolic rate
Set-point theory
Socioeconomic status

CHAPTER 6

Family Factors in the Development of Eating Pathology

Eating disorders often begin during adolescence when families provide a primary social context. Thus, early hypotheses on the etiology of eating disorders focused on the families from which patients came. Chipley (1860) attributed self-starvation to a desire to gain attention, and a common therapeutic recommendation of the late 19th century was to remove afflicted individuals from their family environment. Gull (1874) recommended that patients be surrounded by "persons who would have moral control over them; relations and friends being generally the worst attendants" (p. 26). A focus on the family environment also reflected the dominant theoretical models for mental disorders when AN emerged—namely, **psychoanalytic** and, later, psychodynamic models.

Because different theoretical orientations have contributed to different explanations of the family's role in the etiology of eating disorders, this chapter presents a review of family factors within different theoretical models. Supporting evidence for each model is reviewed as well. Historically, psychoanalytic models provided the first description of how parents contributed to the development of eating disorders in children.

PSYCHOANALYTIC MODEL OF FAMILY INFLUENCE

Building on the emergence of AN symptoms near the onset of puberty and a view of neurotic illnesses as stemming from unconscious sexual conflicts, psychoanalytic theory interpreted AN as a fear of sexual maturity. This arose in families in which the father was kind but passive and the mother was aggressive and *castrating* (a psychoanalytic term meaning disempowering). Because mothers provided unfit models of femininity, girls in these families feared becoming women like their mothers. (See Figure 6–1.) This fear became symbolized as a fear of oral impregnation.

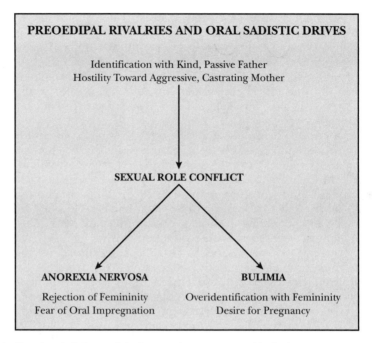

FIGURE 6–1 Psychoanalytic model of anorexia nervosa and bulimia.
From Boskind-Lodahl (1976). *Signs: Journal of Women in Culture and Society.* Copyright © The University of Chicago.

Szyrynski (1973) provided the following summary of the fear of oral impregnation thought to underlie AN:

> Fear of pregnancy often dominates the picture; pregnancy being symbolized by food, getting fat means becoming pregnant. Such fantasies are also quite often formulated as oral impregnation. The girl, after kissing a boy for the first time, gets panicky lest pregnancy should follow. She pays particular attention to her gaining weight and not infrequently a casual remark of a visitor, a relative, or a friend, that she is looking well and probably has gained some weight will unleash the disastrous ritual of self-starvation.
>
> *(Quoted in Boskind-Lodahl, 1976, p. 344. Signs: Journal of Women in Culture and Society. Copyright © The University of Chicago.)*

Girls suffering from AN were thought to have an unconscious hatred of femininity stemming from their unconscious preoedipal mother conflict. The physical signs of AN seemed to confirm this interpretation, as starvation led to a loss of both secondary sex characteristics and menstrual function. Thus, AN was an attempt to regress to the safety of childhood. For girls, treatment involved (as it did in the psychoanalytic care of most women suffering from mental disorders) "putting an end to that hatred of femininity by helping the woman learn to accept and to act out the traditional female role" (Boskind-Lodahl, 1976, p. 345).

Maturity Fears is a subscale on the Eating Disorders Inventory (EDI; Garner, Olmstead, & Polivy, 1983), a frequently used measure of attitudes and behaviors characteristic of patients with AN and BN. Lower Maturity Fears predicted recovery among patients with AN (Fassino et al., 2001; Van der Ham, Van Strien, & Van Engeland, 1998), and higher Maturity Fears predicted increased bulimic symptoms among women followed 10 years after graduating from college (Joiner, Heatherton, & Keel, 1997). These longitudinal studies suggest that a fear of adulthood may contribute to the presence of eating disorders. However, Hurley, Palmer, and Stretch (1990) found that Maturity Fears did not differ between patients with AN, patients with BN, and patients with other psychiatric disorders, suggesting that such fears may not be specifically associated with eating disorders.

In contrast to the psychoanalytic model described above, studies of gender role identification have found a positive association between endorsement of the feminine gender role and the presence of eating pathology that is particularly salient for patients diagnosed with AN (Murnen & Smolak, 1997). Eating pathology also has been associated with lower levels of masculinity (Murnen & Smolak, 1997). Thus, women with eating disorders are actually more likely to accept the traditional female role when they are actively ill than are women without eating disorders. These results are consistent with Boskind-Lodahl's (1976) feminist psychoanalytic interpretation of AN.

According to Boskind-Lodahl (1976), eating disorders emerged in a family context in which mothers were both powerless and controlling, while fathers were absent but idealized. Her portrayal of parents bears a strong resemblance to the characterization of a kind, passive father and an aggressive, castrating mother proposed by traditional psychoanalytic models. However, in the traditional psychoanalytic model, girls identified with their fathers and experienced hostility toward their mothers because their fathers modeled more appropriate behaviors for their gender. In the feminist psychoanalytic model, families reinforced patriarchal devaluation of women and emphasized that women's value was to be found in their relationship with men. Thus, the mother was controlling precisely because she lacked power in relationships outside the family. However, achieving this position required forming a relationship with a man in order to have children. This led girls to overvalue traditional feminine roles and acceptance by men as a means of evaluating self-worth. In an appearance-obsessed society in which women are viewed as objects rather than agents, the main quality for being valued by a man is physical appearance. Girls who experienced either real or imagined rejection by a male felt worthless and sought to improve their self-worth through weight loss. (See Figure 6–2.)

If the best way to a man's heart was through *his* stomach in the first half of the 20th century, then the best way to a man's heart was through control of *her* stomach in the second half of the century. Boskind-Lodahl (1976) interpreted the perfect childhood of eating-disordered women as reflecting social demands encouraging them to be physically attractive and submissive and discouraging them from being independent, self-reliant, or assertive. Thus, adolescence served as a trigger for girls because it introduced demands to interact with men outside of the family and the potential for failure in achieving validation from men.

Cauffman and Steinberg (1996) examined menarcheal status and opposite-sex socializing in 89 adolescent girls (ages 12 to 13 years). Disordered eating was significantly greater in girls involved in more mixed-sex social activities, girls who were dating, and girls who were more physically involved with their boyfriends. This association was particularly strong among girls who had reached menarche. However, the association may not be specific to relationships with boys (Paxton, 1996). McVey and colleagues (2002) found that the importance of social acceptance by peers was significantly associated with disordered eating in seventh- and eighth-grade girls.

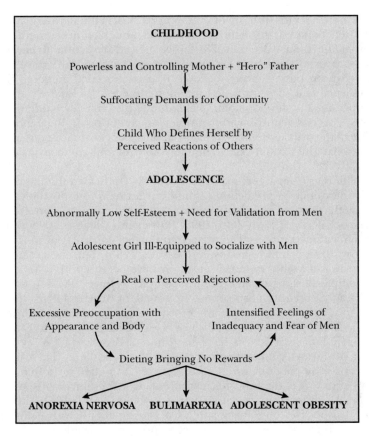

FIGURE 6–2 Development of bulimarexic behavior.
From Boskind-Lodahl (1976). *Signs: Journal of Women in Culture and Society.* Copyright © The University of Chicago.

PSYCHODYNAMIC MODEL OF FAMILY INFLUENCE

Bruch (1978) posited that girls who later developed AN had difficulty identifying and interpreting their internal states because, when they were infants, their mothers had difficulty accurately identifying and appropriately responding to their baby daughters' needs. For example, the mother may have responded to the baby's hunger with holding, sleepiness with food, and distress with naps. This mismatch between the infant's needs (or drive states) and her mother's responses impaired the development of the girl's ability to interpret her own internal states—what Sifneos (1972) has termed *alexythymia* (inability to read emotional states) and others (e.g., Garner et al., 1983) have termed *interoceptive awareness.* In an attempt to adjust to an environment that did not reflect their internal states, these girls learned to adapt their needs to what they perceived as being provided by their environments—thus becoming the perfect daughters. However, these girls suffered from feelings of profound ineffectiveness because their environments neither perceived nor responded to child-initiated cues (Bruch, 1978).

Parents of girls with AN often reported to Bruch that their daughters had been especially well behaved throughout childhood and had never demonstrated defiance of parental limitations (Bruch, 1978). Thus, the sudden refusal to eat represented a marked departure from the docile, accommodating daughters the parents had congratulated themselves on raising. Bruch believed that adolescence triggered the rebellion because adolescence is a stage in which autonomy emerges. However, an anorexic girl was ill equipped for this developmental stage due to her inability to identify her own needs and desires. This crisis contributed to a rebellion centering on the symbolically meaningful rejection of the primary source of maternal nurturance—food. This was also the sole point at which a daughter could assert complete control and combat her feelings of inadequacy (Bruch, 1978).

Findings from a 4-year prospective study confirmed the importance of poor interoceptive awareness in predicting eating disorder symptoms in adolescents but did not support ineffectiveness as a predictor of disordered eating (Leon et al., 1993, 1999; Leon, Fulkerson, Perry, & Early-Zald, 1995). Other investigators have found high alexythymia scores in eating-disordered compared to normal control groups (Bourke, Taylor, Parker, & Bagby, 1992; Schmidt, Jiwany, & Treasure, 1993). Further, greater problems in interoceptive awareness but not ineffectiveness have been reported for eating-disordered samples compared to psychiatric control samples (Hurley, Palmer, & Stretch, 1990). Thus, empirical research supports some, but not all, of Bruch's (1978) theory.

Although research supports an association between poor interoceptive awareness and the development of eating disorders, evidence that poor interoceptive awareness is a result of infant experiences has been limited. Bruch's (1978) evidence came from the lack of conflict over infant feeding that mothers recalled: "The early feeding histories of many anorexic patients, when reconstructed in detail, are often conspicuously bland" (p. 43). Still, it is unclear that early rearing experiences of daughters who go on to develop AN differ from those of daughters who do not. This is a difficult hypothesis to test with retrospective follow-back studies because patients with eating disorders would be unable to recall such early experiences, and parents would have been unaware that they were not responding to their infant's needs appropriately.

Several studies have examined parental patterns concerning feeding in high-risk and low-risk populations—that is, children of mothers who have suffered from eating disorders (high-risk group) and children of mothers who have never suffered from eating disorders (low-risk group) (Agras, Hammer, & McNicholas, 1999; Russell, Treasure, & Eisler, 1998; Stein, Woolley, & McPherson, 1999; Waugh & Bulik, 1999). Much of this work followed the observation that children of women who had suffered from AN were at an increased risk for **nonorganic failure to thrive** (Brinch, Isager, & Tolstrup, 1988; van Wezel-Meijler & Wit, 1989). Nonorganic failure to thrive is a condition in which children do not gain adequate weight, and no medical reason can be found for low weight. Women with eating disorders had more anxiety, rigidity, and conflict about feeding their children compared to women who had never suffered from an eating disorder. This was related to lower weight in children of women with eating disorders (Stein et al., 1994, 1999; Stein, Murray, Cooper, & Fairburn, 1996).

Stein et al. (1994) videotaped mother–infant interactions during mealtimes and play times. Index mothers in the study included women who had experienced a partial or full eating disorder during the year following the birth of their child (index infants). They were compared with sociodemographically matched control mothers from the community. Videotapes were rated on several dimensions by raters who were blind to mothers' eating disorder status. No differences were observed during play times. During mealtimes, index mothers were more intrusive, made more critical and derogatory comments, and were more concerned with avoiding a mess compared to controls. Significantly greater conflict emerged during mealtimes between index mothers and infants, and this resulted in significantly less food intake. Index infants weighed significantly less than control infants, and weight was significantly inversely associated with conflict.

In a related study, Stein et al. (1999) examined specific antecedents to potential conflicts and maternal and infant responses to these antecedents. Three types of antecedents were identified and coded by blind raters:

1. The infant indicated a desire to feed itself, while the mother indicated a desire to feed the infant.
2. The mother expressed concern over the manner of the infant's eating (usually about the mess).
3. The infant refused offered food.

Three potential responses that might prevent conflict were also coded:

1. The mother acknowledges the infant's cues.
2. The mother puts aside her own desires.
3. The infant disengages.

Finally, three types of episodes were coded:

1. Antecedents end in conflict in the index group.
2. Antecedents do *not* end in conflict in the index group.
3. Antecedents do *not* end in conflict in the control group.

Episodes of antecedents leading to conflict were not coded in the control group because these episodes occurred too infrequently. The following is an excerpt from a meal presented by Stein et al. (1999, p. 458):

> The mother is feeding her infant, holding the food dish out of his reach. The infant cries and tries to get hold of the food in the dish, indicating wish to feed himself. The mother then pulls the dish further away and says, "Ooh, we don't want you in here." The infant whimpers and tries to reach the food again. The mother responds in a critical tone, "No, you'll only get it all over the place" (avoiding mess).
>
> The mother now offers the infant another spoonful of food and the infant refuses and tries to put his hand in the dish again.
>
> The mother, ignoring the infant's signals, keeps the dish out of reach and then puts a spoon of food to the infant's lips which he refuses; he also cries.
>
> The mother says, "Oh, you've had enough then?" (describing refusal as satiety).
>
> After a brief pause, the mother then continues to offer food which the infant refuses. The mother then tries to divert the infant with a game, using the spoon as an aeroplane coming in to land in the infant's mouth. The infant repeatedly refuses the mother's attempts, crying increasingly in protest, with the mother eventually looking on in puzzlement at his distress. Very little food was consumed at this mealtime.
>
> (*Source:* Reprinted by permission of the Royal College of Psychiatrists.)

Within the index group, antecedents were less likely to lead to conflict when mothers acknowledged infants' cues, mothers set aside their own concerns, or infants disengaged. Compared to control mothers, index mothers were less likely to acknowledge infants' cues or put aside their own concerns. Compared to control infants, index infants were significantly more likely to disengage. Indeed, *no* control infant disengaged in response to an antecedent.

It is unclear from these studies whether index infants will develop AN or any other eating disorder as a consequence of early feeding difficulties. However, these data provide some evidence that infants avoid conflict by becoming passive when mothers fail to recognize or respond to their cues. Such a pattern could contribute to the illusion of a "perfect baby."

FAMILY SYSTEMS MODEL OF FAMILY INFLUENCE

Minuchin, Rosman, and Baker (1978) developed a **family systems model** to explain eating disorders as a manifestation of disturbed family relationships. According to this model, all families are made up of subsystems (e.g., spousal, parental, and sibling) in which different roles and responsibilities occur. Boundaries between subsystems can range from **enmeshed** (too weak) to **disengaged** (too strong). Enmeshment represents poorly differentiated boundaries. For example, children are invited to take part in transactions that would typically remain between husband and wife (spousal subsystem). Disengagement represents boundaries that create isolation among family members. Clarity of boundaries may differ across family members and may change within a family over time. Indeed, family systems are required to change in response to the normal processes of development (i.e., as children grow to adulthood) and in response to external events (e.g., the family moves).

Minuchin and his colleagues (1978) posited that families in which AN arose were marked by the following characteristics: enmeshment within the family; overprotection of children, resulting in rigid boundaries separating family members from extrafamilial relationships; conflict avoidance; and a concern for bodily functions including physical symptoms, eating, and diets. According to this model, family conflict had no means for outlet because distress was suppressed behind a façade of closeness. The lack of boundaries among family members triggered conflict as girls approached adolescence. Girls in enmeshed families were stifled in their attempts to achieve independence and establish relationships outside the family. Because there was no viable option for expressing interpersonal conflict, conflicts were **somaticized.** That is, they were expressed as physical conditions. Within Minuchin et al.'s (1978) framework, the conflict could be revealed in a variety of physical maladies within any member of the family. Applied to AN, the daughter represented the "identified patient"; her symptoms were not evidence of **intrapsychic** conflict, as proposed by Boskind-Lodahl (1976) and Bruch (1978), but of intrafamilial conflict.

A number of studies have examined the quality of family relationships of individuals with eating disorders and have generally supported elevated levels of dysfunction (Haudek et al., 1999; Laliberte, Boland, & Leichner, 1999; McDermott, Batik, Roberts, & Gibbon, 2002; Neumark-Sztainer, Story, Hannan, Beuhring, & Resnick, 2000; Rorty, Yager, Rossotto, & Buckwalter, 2000; Wade, Bulik, & Kendler, 2001). Compared to families of normal controls, families of patients with BN or ANBP have been characterized as expressing less nurturance, support, understanding, and empathy and more conflict, hostility, blame, neglect, rejection, and isolation (Humphrey, 1986, 1988, 1989; Humphrey, Apple, & Kirschenbaum, 1986). Families of patients with BN have been characterized as more intrusive (Rorty et al., 2000), and families of patients with ANBP have been characterized by worse communication and emotional expression (Casper & Troiani, 2001). In contrast, families of patients with ANR have self-reported no differences from controls

(Casper & Troiani, 2001; Humphrey, 1988) but have been rated by blind observers as expressing a contradictory message of nurturance/affection and neglect of the daughter's need for self-expression (Humphrey, 1989). Patients have endorsed this contradiction in reporting more compulsive care-seeking *and* more compulsive self-reliance attachment styles compared to controls (Ward, Ramsay, Turnbull, Benedettini, & Treasure, 2000). Notably, these studies have examined concurrent associations between eating pathology and family relationships. Thus, the direction of these associations is unclear. It is possible that family interactions were normal before the eating disorder developed and became dysfunctional only in response to the eating disorder.

Shoebridge and Gowers (2000) used a retrospective follow back design to examine evidence of overprotective parenting prior to the onset of AN. Compared to mothers of matched controls, index mothers were more likely to report providing near-exclusive child care (defined as 95% or more of child care to the exclusion of fathers), infant sleep difficulties, distress at first separation, higher trait anxiety, and later age for daughter's first sleepover. In explaining the source of anxieties, examination of obstetric records revealed that 25% of the index mothers experienced a severe obstetric loss (e.g., miscarriage) compared to only 7.5% of the control mothers. In 90% of the cases of obstetric loss in index mothers, the daughter with AN was the next-born female child. Not surprisingly, more index mothers reported significant worry about miscarriage during their pregnancy compared to control mothers. Of interest, no significant differences were reported for child eating difficulties in the first 5 years of their children's lives (Shoebridge & Gowers, 2000).

Byely, Archibald, Graber, and Brooks-Gunn (2000) used a prospective design to evaluate the relationship between dieting and body image disturbance and girls' perceptions of family relationships. Over a 1-year follow-up period, girls ages 10–14 reported increased problems in family relationships. Further, negative family relationships predicted dieting at follow-up even after controlling for dieting at baseline. Nevertheless, family relationships did not predict changes in body image. In addition to examining the quality of family relationships, Byely et al. evaluated maternal modeling of dieting behaviors as a potential predictor of dieting and body image disturbance in girls and found no association.

Laliberte et al. (1999) examined family relationships in two ways: "traditional family process variables (conflict, cohesion, expressiveness)" and "'family climate for eating disorders' . . . Family Body Satisfaction, Family Social Appearance Orientation, and Family Achievement Emphasis" (p. 1021). Disordered eating attitudes and behaviors in college women were significantly predicted by both types of family relationship variables, with the family climate for eating disorders demonstrating a stronger relationship. In comparisons of eating-disordered patients, depressed controls, and healthy controls, the family process variables distinguished both patient groups from controls but not from each other (Laliberte et al., 1999). Conversely, the family climate for eating disorders differentiated the eating-disordered group from both the psychiatric and healthy controls (Laliberte et al., 1999).

Examination of the theorized role of family factors thus far demonstrates some similarities. First, most theories with empirical support suggest a role for parental criticism. Second, most theories acknowledge that concerns with food, eating, and weight may shape the content of criticisms. The following section examines the extent to which disordered eating may represent a learned behavior. Potentially, the emergence of eating pathology within poorly functioning families is more directly related to the presence of disordered eating attitudes and behaviors within these families.

SOCIAL LEARNING MODEL OF FAMILY INFLUENCE

From a social learning perspective, disordered eating attitudes and behaviors might be learned from family members just as many other attitudes and behaviors are learned. Indeed, food preferences are highly influenced by culture and rearing environment, as can be seen in Jamie's case.

Case Study

One problem that Jamie had with all weight loss diets was the emphasis on eating more fresh fruits and vegetables. He felt that if the number of calories he could eat was restricted, he wanted to use as many calories as possible for the foods he liked and not waste any calories on foods he didn't like. Jamie's favorite foods were those that reminded him of his mother's cooking. His mother had grown up in the South and made wonderful chicken fried steak with gravy, biscuits, and fried okra. Thinking that okra was a vegetable he liked, Jamie once tried to prepare stewed okra on a diet. However, the consistency of stewed okra was that of "snot with boogers." It was slimy and slightly sticky, and the okra seeds were tasteless little blobs suspended in the goop. Like his father, Jamie felt that a meal without red meat was not a "real" meal.

Supporting a social learning model, eating disorders have been found to run in families (Lilenfeld et al., 1998; Strober, Lambert, Morrel, Burroughs, & Jacobs, 1990). Pike and Rodin (1991) demonstrated that daughters with high scores on the EDI were more likely to have mothers who reported higher levels of disordered eating. In addition, mothers of high-EDI-scoring daughters were more likely to be critical of their daughters' weights and state that their daughters needed to lose weight compared to the mothers of low-EDI-scoring daughters. This occurred despite no differences in body weight between the two groups of daughters.

One explanation for associations between parental concerns about eating and weight and disordered eating in daughters is that biological relatives share not only their environments but also their genes. This issue will be covered in greater depth in Chapter 8. One population-based twin study will be reviewed here. Klump, McGue, and Iacono (2000c) examined EDI scores in 680 11- and 602 17-year-old female twin pairs. In the 11-year-old cohort, EDI correlations within twin pairs were similar between MZ and DZ twins. Conversely, EDI correlations were significantly higher for MZ compared to DZ twins in the 17-year-old cohort. Reflecting this pattern, shared environmental factors explained the EDI scores in the 11-year-old twins, while genetic factors explained the EDI scores in the 17-year-old twins. These results suggest that the rearing environment may significantly impact disordered eating attitudes and behaviors in pre- and peripubertal children.

The following section will explore whether children learn disordered eating attitudes and behaviors from parents who model such eating attitudes and behaviors or from parents who directly instruct their children to be concerned about weight and eating. In these ways, parents may amplify cultural expectations about being thin by emphasizing these values within the home and personally endorsing them (Garfinkel & Garner, 1982).

Eating-Disordered Mothers and Their Infants

Waugh and Bulik (1999) investigated health, nutrition, and mealtime interactions (assessed by blind ratings of videotaped meals) in young children of women with current or past eating disorders compared to children of controls. In contrast to previous studies, only one difference was found. Women with current or past eating disorders made significantly more positive comments about eating compared to control mothers (e.g., "'this is yummy potato soup'"; p. 130).

Agras et al., (1999) conducted a prospective longitudinal study with 41 women with current or past eating disorders (ED mothers) and 153 non-eating-disordered controls and their infants. Several differences emerged specifically for daughters of ED mothers. ED mothers reported finding daughters, but not sons, to be more difficult to wean from the bottle. In addition, daughters of ED mothers vomited more frequently. Similarly, there was a significant association in ED mothers between eating disorder symptoms and attitudes toward the weight or shape of daughters but not sons. Regardless of the child's gender, ED mothers reported using food to reward or calm a child more often than did control mothers, used a less regular feeding schedule for their children, and reported that their children dawdled more while eating. Overall, weight and shape concerns were highest when reported by ED mothers for their daughters. No differences in caloric intake or weight were found between infants of ED mothers versus control mothers, and no differences in child BMI emerged over the course of follow-up.

Stice, Agras, and Hammer (1999) examined rates and predictors of childhood eating disturbances from the study of Agras et al. (1999). Childhood eating disturbances over the course of follow-up emerged in 34% of participants. These included inhibited eating, secretive eating, overeating, and overeating-induced vomiting. Interestingly, no significant gender differences were found for rates of these disturbed eating patterns with the exception of overeating-induced vomiting, which was more common in boys than girls. Eating disturbances in children were predicted by various maternal variables, including mother's BMI, body dissatisfaction, bulimic symptoms, and dietary restraint. These results support a prospective relationship between parental disordered eating attitudes and behaviors and the emergence of eating disturbance in young children.

Adolescent Daughters and Parents: Modeling or Instruction?

Similar to the results of Byely et al. (2000) reported above, a number of studies have failed to support an association between parental modeling and the development of dieting and disordered eating in daughters. Keel, Heatherton, Harnden, and Hornig (1997b) found no correlation between daughters' Restraint Scale scores and those reported by their mothers and fathers. Sanftner, Crowther, Crawford, and Watts (1996) found no significant association between EDI scores for mothers and their prepubertal daughters. Although significant correlations for body weight and BMI existed between mothers and daughters (Ogden & Steward, 2000), no significant correlation was found for body dissatisfaction or restrained eating. Garfinkel et al. (1983) found that parents of children with AN, as a group, did not differ from parents of controls regarding weight or eating concerns or in judging their daughter's current or ideal weight. Similarly, Steiger, Stotland, Ghardirian, and Whitehead (1995) found no significant increase in eating or weight concerns in the first-degree relatives of women with eating disorders compared with normal dieters and nondieting controls.

In contrast to these results, MacBrayer, Smith, McCarthy, Demos, and Simmons (2001) found significant associations between adolescent girls' perceptions of their mothers' eating attitudes and behaviors and their own scores on the Bulimia Test-Revised. Woodside et al. (2002) found significantly elevated weight and shape concerns among parents of eating-disordered probands compared to controls. Gershon et al. (1983) found that mothers of eating-disordered adolescents had a history of dieting more frequently than mothers of controls. Additionally, mothers and daughters have been shown to share similar attitudes about diet and weight (Hill, Weaver, & Blundell, 1990; Pike & Rodin, 1991).

A hidden variable in studies finding a significant association may be the extent to which family members make direct comments to their daughters concerning weight and eating. Striegel-Moore and Kearney-Cooke (1994) found a strong relationship between mothers' dieting and the extent to which they encouraged their children to diet. Strong and Huon (1998) reported that high school girls' perceptions of parental encouragement to diet was a significant predictor of dieting behavior even after controlling for girls' BMI and body dissatisfaction. Twelve-year-old dieters are more likely to report that their parents discourage eating between meals, eating too much, or eating sweets (Edmunds & Hill, 1999). Keel et al. (1997b) reported that adolescent girls were more likely to diet when their mothers described them as overweight and commented on their weight, and that girls' body dissatisfaction was related to fathers' dissatisfaction with their own weight and comments on daughters' weight.

Smolak, Levine, and Schermer (1999) examined the influences of mothers' and fathers' direct comments about their children's weight and modeling of concerns about their own weight on children's body image and weight loss behaviors. For girls, body dissatisfaction and weight loss behaviors were correlated with mothers' comments on daughters' weight, complaints about mothers' own weight, weight loss attempts, and fathers' complaints about their own weight. For sons, the only consistent predictor of both body dissatisfaction and weight loss behaviors was mothers' comments on sons' weight. Overall, direct parental comments had greater effect than did parental modeling, and mothers had a greater effect than fathers on children's body image and weight control behaviors (Smolak et al., 1999).

This work suggests that modeling alone may not explain the familial aggregation of eating disorders. Instead, criticism of children's weight or shape may create a particularly pernicious environmental risk factor for the development of eating pathology. This is consistent with findings reviewed in Chapter 4 of Fairburn and colleagues (1997, 1998). Jean's case demonstrates how such criticism can coincide with the stress of pubertal development in creating shame.

Case Study

Jean knew that a lot of her weight concerns came from her mother. When Jean reached puberty, her mother expressed shock and dismay. Jean's menstrual cycle began when she was 11 years old. Her mother had not expected her daughter to start menstruating until she was 13, the age when her own menses had begun. Jean's mother felt that this had happened because Jean was "too fat." As with all girls, Jean's weight increased during puberty, but her mother refused to buy her new clothes until the beginning of the next academic year. So, Jean was forced to wear shirts and pants that were too tight. Boys at school started commenting on her development, and one boy kept trying to touch her breasts and buttocks. Jean started wearing a coat throughout the school day to hide her body.

CONCLUSION

Although it is easy to focus on the differences among various theoretical explanations for the role of family factors, it may be more useful to focus on their similarities. Compared to the families of individuals without eating disorders, families of individuals with eating disorders have more problems. These include problems in general interaction style and specific problems related to eating disorder attitudes and behaviors.

Rearing environments that do not recognize or respond to child-initiated cues may increase the pressure on individuals to conform to external demands. As a consequence, these individuals may be particularly vulnerable to messages concerning how they should behave and how they should look. The mismatch between child needs and parental responses may contribute to difficulties in identifying and differentiating internal drives and may reinforce the futility of attempting to do so. It is unclear what transpires between infancy and the onset of adolescence. However, at the beginning of adolescence, the thin ideal may provide a road map for achieving social acceptance, particularly if family members subscribe to attitudes that contribute to eating pathology, such as the importance of being thin.

A review of family factors in the development of eating disorders demonstrates that families do not starve their children or force them to binge eat. Instead, families influence children's thoughts, behaviors, and personality styles in ways that may increase the risk of eating disorders. Thus, environmental vulnerability influences personal vulnerability. The role of psychological factors is discussed in the next chapter.

KEY TERMS

Alexythymia
Disengagement
Enmeshment
Family systems model

Intrapsychic
Nonorganic failure to thrive
Psychoanalytic
Somaticize

CHAPTER 7

Psychological Factors in the Development of Eating Disorders: The Contributions of Personality, Behavior, and Cognition

Chapters 5 and 6 covered two spheres of social influence—society and family. Although other spheres of social influence (e.g., specific professions, athletic teams, and peer groups) may impact the development of eating disorders, this chapter shifts the focus to psychological factors that may contribute to the etiology of eating disorders. These are factors that occur within the individual and explain individual differences in the susceptibility to develop an eating disorder. Chapter 4 introduced some psychological factors in the context of risk factor research, and Chapter 6 included psychological factors in the context of psychoanalytic, psychodynamic, and learning models. This chapter reviews the roles of personality, behavior, and cognition in the development and maintenance of eating disorders.

PERSONALITY

Personality has been defined as a stable way in which individuals perceive, react to, and interact with their environments that is influenced by both biology and experience (Phares, 1988). **Temperament** has been defined as a biologically based predisposition to experience certain emotional and behavioral responses (Cloninger, Svrakic, & Przybeck, 1993). Temperament is the building block upon which personality develops. Although considerable debate surrounds the definitions of temperament and personality (Craik, Hogan, & Wolfe, 1993), this section will review models that have been applied to understanding the development of eating disorders.

Cloninger (1987, 1993) has described four dimensions of temperament: **novelty seeking, harm avoidance, reward dependence,** and **persistence.** Novelty seeking represents a tendency to pursue rewards. Harm avoidance represents a tendency to avoid punishment by inhibiting behavior. Reward dependence represents a tendency to continue rewarded behavior. Persistence represents a tendency to continue behavior that is no longer rewarded. On self-report measures, AN has been associated with low novelty seeking, high harm avoidance, and high persistence (Bulik, Sullivan, Weltzin, & Kaye, 1995; Fassino et al., 2002a; Klump et al., 2000a). In contrast, BN has been associated with high novelty seeking and high harm avoidance (Bulik et al., 1995; Fassino et al., 2002a). These findings map onto the behaviors typical of these disorders. In AN, low novelty seeking would contribute to decreased eating, and high harm avoidance would contribute to avoiding weight gain. High persistence would enable women to reach and maintain extremely low weights. The combination of high novelty seeking and high harm avoidance in BN captures the conflict between engaging in rewarding behavior (increased eating) and wanting to avoid punishing weight gain (inappropriate compensatory behaviors).

Tellegen (1982) described three personality dimensions: **positive emotionality, negative emotionality,** and **constraint.** Positive emotionality represents the tendency to enjoy and be actively engaged in work and social interactions. Negative emotionality represents the tendency to experience negative mood states (dysphoria, anxiety, anger). Constraint represents the tendency to inhibit impulses and show caution, restraint, and conventionalism. Consistent with results regarding temperament, AN has been associated with high levels of constraint, low levels of positive emotionality, and high levels of negative emotionality (Casper, Hedeker, & McClough, 1992; Pryor & Wiederman, 1996). Women with BN also have reported low levels of positive emotionality and high levels of negative emotionality compared to controls, and BN has been associated with lower constraint compared to AN (Casper et al., 1992; Pryor & Wiederman, 1996).

Research findings on temperament and personality in patients with eating disorders map onto early clinical descriptions of patients suffering from eating disorders. Bruch (1978) characterized patients with AN as having a high level of **perfectionism.** Her patients tended to be straight-A students with many accomplishments. In addition, they were less likely to drink alcohol, use illicit substances, or be sexually active—suggesting higher levels of constraint. Prior to the onset of their illness (premorbid state), they were characterized by hiding negative feelings. In contrast to their happy external appearance, Bruch's (1978) patients experienced significant anxiety, sadness, and concern about disappointing others. Many of these features can be seen in Emily's case study.

Case Study

Emily's eating disorder came as a shock to her family because she always seemed so in control of her life and destiny. The idea that she might have a problem beyond her control did not make sense to them or to Emily. Even as a small child, Emily had always managed to keep things in perfect order. She had alphabetized her books by author and then title as soon as she learned the alphabet. She organized her dresser drawers so that her white ribbed socks were kept separate from her white terry socks and both were kept separate from her colored socks. Emily recalled always wanting things to be perfect. She said she could even remember that on her first day of school she had decided that she would always do everything exactly as it should be done. In elementary school, she cried the first time she received a grade of less than 100%. She was a straight-A student throughout school; however, this came at a slight cost. Because she feared ruining her perfect grade point average, Emily started avoiding classes in which she thought she might not do well. She took advanced placement (AP) courses in English and history, but she decided against taking AP biology and math. Although she had been interested in becoming a doctor, she feared that these classes might be too hard for her and that she might receive less than an A. In contrast to her outward appearance of confidence and success, Emily constantly feared that people would realize that she actually wasn't very smart. The need for perfect grades was as much a defense against discovery as a means to achieve entry into a top college.

———•◆•———

Emily's story provides a classic picture of ANR. Long before her eating disorder emerged, Emily cared deeply about achieving perfection and avoiding failure, as if perfection and failure were the only two options in life. Her eating disorder seems to reflect another manifestation of an unrelenting drive to achieve and surpass all external standards. If the ability to control eating and weight is viewed as evidence of moral superiority (see Chapter 5), then Emily's behavior asserted her ability to surpass all others. Reflecting on the case of St. Veronica (see Chapter 2 for a discussion of medieval fasting saints), this drive is mirrored in St. Veronica's belief that she "was in a race against all the other novices to show who loved God the most," so she "carried more water and chopped more wood than anyone else" (Bell, 1985, p. 71).

In contrast to early clinical descriptions of AN, Gerald Russell (1979) characterized his patients with BN as having antisocial behaviors (abusing drugs, stealing, and being sexually promiscuous), as well as social anxiety, depression, and poor social adjustment. The early clinical observations of Bruch (1978) and Russell characterize patients with AN as perfectionistic, rigid, and inhibited (consistent with high persistence, high constraint, and low novelty seeking) and characterize patients with BN as impulsive (consistent with low constraint and high novelty seeking). Both patient groups have been characterized as depressed and anxious (consistent with high negative emotionality).

Others have reported that constricted/overcontrolled personality is characteristic of restricting AN, while impulsive/emotionally dysregulated personality is characteristic of binge eating in both AN and BN (Steiger, Puentes-Neuman, & Leung, 1991; Westen & Harnden-Fischer, 2001). This suggests that the symptoms of restricting versus binge-eating/purging may be more closely related to personality function than the effects of symptoms on weight. However, Westen and Harnden-Fischer (2001) reported that a high-functioning/perfectionistic personality style was present in both AN and BN. Thus, perfectionism may increase the risk of developing both eating disorders. Perfectionism combined with inhibition may contribute to the development of ANR. Perfectionism combined with impulsiveness may contribute to the development of bulimic symptoms.

One concern in the interpretation of results from correlational studies (such as comparisons of personality between women with and without eating disorders) is the influence of state of illness on personality measures (Vitousek & Manke, 1994). As was discussed in Chapter 5, starvation in the absence of AN can have a significant impact on functioning. In Ancel Keys et al.'s study of starvation (1950), changes in participants' **Minnesota Multiphasic Personality Inventory (MMPI)** scores were observed as a consequence of significant weight loss. Several participants demonstrated significant deviations from normal personality and behavioral functioning. For example, some participants demonstrated impulsive behaviors that had never occurred before starvation (e.g., stealing food). Other participants became preoccupied with food and developed eating rituals that never occurred before starvation. In the most extreme example of starvation-induced disturbance, participant No. 20 engaged in self-mutilation and chopped off three fingers of his left hand with an axe. Personality changes normalized after weight gain in most participants, and even No. 20 showed a "slow return toward normality" toward the end of nutritional rehabilitation (p. 897). These observations highlight the importance of using caution in interpreting personality function among individuals with current eating disorders.

Eating rituals such as licking a plate may be a consequence of starvation, as demonstrated by a participant in Keys et al.'s (1950) study.
Oltmanns, T. F., & Emery, R. E. (2001). *Abnormal Psychology (3rd ed.)*. Upper Saddle River, N. J.: Prentice Hall.

Given concerns about the potential influence of eating disorders on personality function, results from prospective studies are particularly valuable. Vohs et al. (1999) evaluated perfectionism, self-esteem, and perceived weight status as predictors of increases in bulimic symptoms in a prospective longitudinal study. Baseline measures were evaluated in the spring of participants' senior year in high school (after participants had accepted admission to a specific college). Follow-up measures were taken during participants' freshman year of college. High school seniors who scored high on perfectionism, reported that they were overweight, and had low self-esteem experienced an increase in bulimic symptoms at follow-up assessment. Notably, none of these three factors alone (perfectionism, perceived weight status, or self-esteem) predicted changes in bulimic symptoms. This finding has been replicated (Bardone, Vohs, Abramson, Heatherton, & Joiner, 2000).

In addition to results from prospective longitudinal studies, several studies have demonstrated that personality disturbances persist after women have recovered from eating disorders. Casper (1990) found elevated constraint in women recovered from ANR compared to controls. Srinivasagam et al. (1995) reported that women recovered from AN reported significantly greater levels of perfectionism and obsessions with symmetry and exactness compared to controls. Similar to these results, von Ranson, Kaye, Weltzin, Rao, and Matsunaga (1999) reported that women recovered from BN reported high levels of obsessions with symmetry and exactness that were similar to those reported by women with current BN and greater than those reported by controls. In contrast, Keel et al. (1999) found that women who recovered from BN were less impulsive than women who remained ill. Further, overall levels of impulse control did not differ between women 10–15 years after diagnosis with BN and a comparison sample (Keel, 1998).

In summary, research examining the temperament and personality features of patients with AN support early clinical descriptions. Women with ANR appear to be characterized by high levels of perfectionism and constraint. This personality seems consistent with the overt behaviors of AN patients—an unrelenting pursuit of thinness through self-denial of food in the modern era or an unrelenting pursuit of moral purity through self-denial of food in past historical periods (see Chapter 2). These characteristics do not appear to result from starvation because they persist after weight recovery. In contrast to findings for ANR, ANBP and BN have been associated with high levels of impulsiveness and poor emotional regulation. Difficulties in controlling impulses have been implicated in the chaotic symptoms of women with bulimic symptoms—the oscillation between dietary restraint and binge episodes followed by purging. However, recovery from BN is associated with improved impulse control.

Both AN and BN patients experience high levels of dysphoria characterized by feelings of depression and anxiety. As described in Chapter 4, higher levels of negative emotionality predicted the development of new-onset eating pathology in a prospective longitudinal study (Leon et al., 1999). Although negative emotions tend to be more muted in patients with AN compared to patients with BN, the intensity of affect often increases as patients with AN gain weight. This has led some eating disorders experts to speculate that weight loss serves as an effective numbing mechanism. Similarly, among patients with BN, binge-eating episodes appear to produce temporary reprieves from intensely negative emotions by allowing women to "zone out" (Heatherton & Baumeister, 1991). A tendency to experience increased negative emotions could increase the likelihood of using extreme methods to regulate emotions. A tendency to experience changes as particularly stressful could explain the disorders' onset during adolescence (Leon et al., 1999; Leon, Keel, Klump, & Fulkerson, 1997). From this perspective, personality and temperament explain the tendency to experience certain emotional states, and eating disorder symptoms represent a behavioral response to these experiences.

BEHAVIOR

This section discusses the role of behavioral mechanisms in the development of eating disorder symptoms. Chapter 6 discussed how disordered eating might be learned through modeling or direct instruction within families. Another type of learning, **operant conditioning,** may play an important role in the acquisition and maintenance of eating-disordered behaviors. Operant conditioning is a form of learning in which learned associations between behaviors and their consequences influence the likelihood that those behaviors will recur.

Positive Reinforcement

Positive reinforcement is a desirable consequence of behavior that increases the likelihood that behavior will recur. For most individuals, dieting is accompanied by initial success in weight loss. This may produce considerable positive social reinforcement in the form of compliments and attention. Branch and Eurman (1980) conducted a survey of friends and relatives of patients with AN to understand social attitudes toward the patients' appearance and behaviors. Although all respondents expressed concern, 50% reported envy of the patient's self-control and discipline concerning food. Further, friends and relatives were more likely to endorse positive than negative statements concerning the patient's appearance: slender (58%), neat (83%), well groomed (100%), and fashionable (100%) versus skinny (8%), haggard (8%), and emaciated (8%). The authors concluded that even in their emaciated state, patients with AN experienced more approval than disapproval.

Compliments and attention serve as positive reinforcers of food restriction. Like weight loss, binge eating may be highly positively reinforcing. Indeed, the foods typically consumed during binge episodes (e.g., ice cream, cookies, candy) often are used by parents as rewards for good behavior. Although patients find binge-eating episodes very upsetting, patients in treatment also express a sense of loss when they realize that they may never have binge episodes again after treatment. In Jamie's case, binge episodes are experienced as highly pleasurable.

Case Study ●◆●

Jamie wished he could take a pill instead of eating food. He complained that diet pills were fine for curbing appetite, but the perfect diet pill would replace food altogether so that, in addition to not feeling hungry, he would not need to eat. This would be his perfect diet pill because he could not imagine ever being able to stop eating once he started. The food always tasted too good to stop. Interestingly, moderation was missing in other areas of Jamie's life as well. As an athlete in school, he had always worked out harder and longer than everyone else on the team. He loved the "high" he got from exercising. Because of this work ethic, he became a star member of the team and eventually its captain. Jamie's tendency to persist was also an asset in his job. More than any other employee, Jamie would persist in pursuing clients until he landed the deal. The bonuses that Jamie received for signing new clients allowed him to purchase new "toys"— Jamie was a self-described technophile. He loved computers, computer games, big-screen TVs, and DVDs. Jamie described his apartment as a shrine to an electronics department.

●◆●

Clearly, one reason Jamie has binge episodes is that he enjoys them. However, eating disorders do not consist solely of pleasurable/rewarding behaviors. Thus, to understand the full array of symptoms, one must examine both the consequences of a given behavior and the consequences that would result from *not* engaging in the behavior.

Negative Reinforcement

Like positive reinforcement, **negative reinforcement** increases the likelihood of a behavior. However, negative reinforcement increases a behavior by removing an undesirable consequence of *not* engaging in the behavior. In this case, the behavior is designed to prevent an undesirable consequence or terminate an undesirable experience. For example, binge eating may be negatively reinforced by the escape it offers from negative feelings when it enables patients to zone out (Heatherton & Baumeister, 1991). Although feeling nothing is not necessarily pleasurable, it is preferable to feeling distress. However, when a binge-eating episode ends, anxiety typically arises about how the binge will affect weight. Purging offers a means to avoid this negative consequence. Although purging is not an effective form of weight control, it does cause an immediate decrease in anxiety. This decrease in anxiety provides powerful negative reinforcement for purging.

In many cases, negative reinforcement is more powerful in maintaining a behavior than positive reinforcement. Each time a person engages in the behavior, he or she experiences both the actual and the perceived consequences. In positive reinforcement, the pleasurable consequence is experienced exactly as it exists. In negative reinforcement, the consequence is experienced as the absence of something that is prevented. Thus, each time people engage in a negatively reinforced behavior, they can conclude that they would have been worse off had they not engaged in the behavior. For example, a person who purges may be dissatisfied with her weight. However, she may believe that if she did not purge, she would weigh even more and be even more dissatisfied with her weight. The only way to challenge this assumption is to stop purging so that the person can learn that purging does not prevent weight gain. However, given the person's intense fear of weight gain, this may seem to be too great a risk to take.

Punishment

Punishment is a negative consequence that inhibits behavior. For example, eating can be very punishing for patients with AN. It can trigger anxiety, gastrointestinal discomfort, and water retention. Similarly, shame over eating may prevent patients with eating disorders from eating in the presence of others, and shame over body weight/shape may prevent them from joining activities in which their bodies will be exposed. In eating disorders, it is often easy to perceive all of the behaviors in which patients engage. The behaviors in which they do not engage frequently remain hidden. However, many of these inhibited behaviors contribute to significant psychosocial maladjustment.

Like negative reinforcement, behavioral responses to punishment are driven by a desire to avoid negative consequences. The primary difference is that a negative reinforcer increases a behavior (e.g., increased purging), while a punishment decreases a behavior (e.g., decreased eating). In both cases, a temperamental/personality style that predisposed an individual to experience negative emotions would increase the power of these consequences.

Researchers are beginning to examine how individual differences in responsiveness to rewards and punishments may be correlated with eating disorder symptoms. Bulik et al. (1995) found that women with AN reported higher reward dependence compared to women with BN on a self-report measure. As described above, reward dependence represents a tendency to continue rewarded behavior. This result suggests that ANR may be associated with a higher need for and sensitivity to praise and reward and may tend to "persist in previously rewarded behavior even to the point of exhaustion" (Bulik et al., 1995, p. 257). Several authors have reported an association between reward sensitivity and eating disorders (Davis & Woodside, 2002; Farmer, Nash, & Field, 2001; Loxton & Dawe, 2001).

Farmer et al. (2001) examined the association between reward sensitivity and specific bulimic symptoms (binge eating, self-induced vomiting, and purging). In order to measure reward sensitivity, participants (13 individuals with BN and 21 individuals with an EDNOS) engaged in a verbal learning task. An experimenter presented participants with 80 index cards. A verb (e.g., *run*) appeared in the middle of the card, and six pronouns (*I, we, she, he, they, you*) appeared in the lower left corner. (See Figure 7–1.) The

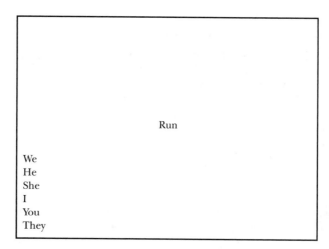

FIGURE 7–1   Depiction of card used in Farmer et al. (2001) study.

order of the pronouns was randomized across cards. For each card, participants made up a sentence using the verb and one of the six pronouns. For the first 20 cards, experimenters gave no response to sentences. After the 20th card, the experimenter rewarded the participant for sentences that used either of the first two listed pronouns from the previous card. Rewards consisted of giving the participant 5 cents and saying "good." Reward sensitivity was measured as the increase in the use of rewarded words over baseline use of these words (measured during the first 20 cards). Results showed a significant positive association between reward sensitivity and frequency of vomiting and purging but not frequency of binge-eating episodes. This result was somewhat surprising and awaits replication.

Craighead, Allen, Craighead, and DeRosa (1996) examined the differential influence of reward versus punishment on learning in three groups of women: women with BN and past depression, women with past depression, and healthy control women. Participants were randomized into a learning task in which they either received positive social feedback for correct responses (reward) or negative social feedback for errors (punishment). Subjects with BN and past depression receiving punishment for errors learned the task more quickly than those receiving reward for correct responses. Subjects with BN and past depression in the reward condition did not differ on time needed to learn the task from the other two groups. These results suggest that patients with BN may be particularly responsive to negative feedback.

Given that eating disorders lead to distress, impairment, and an increased risk of medical complications, it can be difficult to understand why individuals continue such self-destructive patterns. In fact, many of the symptoms of eating disorders may be understood by their *immediate* or *perceived* consequences. Eating disorders become a trap for many individuals because the harmful long-term consequences are overshadowed by the immediate consequences of their behaviors. As the disorders lead to problems and distress, patients may be pushed further into disordered eating behaviors in an attempt to cope. Differences in vulnerability to develop eating disorders may be related to how salient immediate consequences are, which in turn is related to how individuals with eating disorders think about their behaviors.

COGNITION

Cognition involves processes related to thinking and includes attention, perception, learning, and memory (Roediger, Capaldi, Paris, & Polivy, 1991). As described in Chapter 5, body image disturbance is a cognitive feature of eating disorders. Specifically, Chapter 5 reviewed attitudes and perceptions common to body image disturbance in eating disorders. The following section reviews other findings related to cognitive function in individuals with eating disorders.

Attention

Cognitive research in eating disorders has demonstrated that women with AN and BN demonstrate attentional biases associated with food and body-related cues. That is, women with eating disorders pay more attention to information about food and body weight/shape than do women without eating disorders. Although some of this difference may be deliberate (i.e., a woman who is worried about becoming fat may choose to weigh herself more frequently than a woman who is unconcerned with weight), food- and body-related information may be more salient to women with eating disorders. This may help to explain the bases of their preoccupations with food, weight, and shape and why negative consequences in regard to weight and shape seem so much more salient than negative consequences in other aspects of life.

The **Stroop Test** has been used to evaluate attentional processes in women with eating disorders. In the classic Stroop Test, a participant is asked to name the color of ink that words are printed in when the words are names of different colors. For example, the word *green* may be printed in red ink, and the correct response is "red." This task is difficult because information about the meaning of the word competes with information about the color of the ink for attention. In order to evaluate the salience of food and body-related words, this task has been modified. Words such as *thighs, hips, stomach, candy,* and *chocolate* are printed in different colors, and the speed with which participants can name the colors is assessed. Although results of these studies have been somewhat mixed, they do provide evidence of attentional biases (Cooper & Todd, 1997; Flynn & McNally, 1999; Formea & Burns, 1996; Jones-Chesters, Monsell, & Cooper, 1998; Lovell, Williams, & Hill, 1997). Women with eating disorders, but not controls, are slower to name the color of ink for words that name food or body parts compared to words that name neutral objects. Similar results have been shown in women recovered from AN (Lovell et al., 1997) but not in women recovered from BN (Flynn & McNally, 1999; Lovell et al., 1997).

Viken, Treat, Nosofsky, McFall, & Palmeri (2002) recently examined attentional and perceptual differences between women with high versus low scores on a measure of bulimic symptoms recruited from an introductory psychology class (note: this is an analogue study, as the groups did not necessarily represent women with and without eating disorders). Participants viewed pictures of women in which emotional expressions (happy to sad) varied across different body sizes (light to heavy). In one task, pictures were paired randomly, and participants were asked to rate the similarity between the pictures in each pair. These ratings allowed researchers to determine whether facial expression, body size, or neither was more influential in similarity ratings. In another task, participants were asked to sort pictures into two categories. One category was marked by a picture of a thin, happy woman, and the other category was marked by a picture of a heavy, sad woman. No other information was given to identify either the pictures or the categories. Because the pictures to be sorted included all possible combinations (e.g., thin happy, heavy happy, thin sad, heavy sad), the "correct" answer was ambiguous when pictures matched one dimension (e.g., expression) but not the other (e.g., size). Thus, researchers could determine whether facial expression, body size, or neither was more influential in participants' sorting decisions for ambiguous matches. The second task was also reversed, so that participants were later asked to sort pictures according to a category depicted by a thin, sad woman and a category depicted by a heavy, happy woman.

Viken et al. (2002) found that participants with high scores on the bulimia measure showed greater attention to and use of information on size and less attention to and use of information on emotion compared to participants with low scores. In addition, salience of body size on the first task was correlated with salience of body size on the second task. Such results are interesting because they suggest that in a society filled with images of successful thin women and super-sized fries, these messages may be particularly powerful in women who develop eating disorders.

Cognitive Distortions

Cognitive distortions are thoughts that do not adequately reflect reality. Both AN and BN are characterized by numerous cognitive distortions (Peterson & Mitchell, 2002). For example, **dichotomous thinking** (also known as *black-and-white* thinking) is a cognitive distortion expressed in many of the features common to eating disorders. For example, foods become classified as either good or bad. One's pattern of eating is categorized the same way. Many diets encourage dichotomous thinking about foods— pizza, potato chips, cookies, and ice cream all represent bad foods to someone interested in losing weight. Conversely, foods such as celery, carrots, and diet sodas represent foods that are safe and therefore good. In reality, no edible food is inherently good or bad. This lack of inherent food value can be observed in noting that different diet plans create different bad foods. For example, on a low-fat diet, bacon is a bad food and grapefruit is a good food. However, on a low-carbohydrate diet, bacon is good and grapefruit is bad. (The role of different nutrients, such as fat and carbohydrates, will be reviewed in more detail in Chapter 9.)

Dichotomous and rule-bound thinking can be seductive for individuals in significant distress because it greatly simplifies the world. Research has demonstrated that when individuals experience increased stress, their ability to handle complex information diminishes (Vedhara, Hyde, Gilchrist, Tyrtherleigh, & Plummer, 2000). Unfortunately, dichotomous thinking does not adapt to changes in context. For example, losing weight is good and gaining weight is bad even when weight loss becomes dangerous. Similarly, bad foods are bad even when the social context and the initial portion size make consumption of those foods normal and desirable.

Cognitive rigidity in individuals with eating disorders reveals itself as a perseverative approach to problems. The patient with AN has a rigidly held belief that weight loss will bring happiness and freedom from the fear of becoming fat. However, as patients lose more and more weight, they tend to become more depressed and more terrified of weight gain. Patients with eating disorders engage in a behavior motivated to achieve a specific end, and exactly the opposite result occurs (weight loss leads to increased fear of becoming fat). However, these individuals do not reevaluate the usefulness of their behaviors according to the consequences; they simply persist in believing that somehow they "just haven't done enough" or "just haven't done it right." Cognitive rigidity has been observed in neuropsychological testing of patients with ANR compared to controls; cognitive rigidity was uncorrelated with starvation in this study (Fassino et al., 2002b).

Patients with BN often come to treatment with the hope of eliminating binge-eating episodes so that they can successfully lose weight through dieting. As in Jean's case, dieting is rarely viewed as the problem.

Case Study

Jean believed that her binge eating and purging were caused by her decision to move in with her boyfriend and the availability of forbidden foods that followed. She contemplated asking him to stop buying these foods, but she was afraid of having to explain why. At first, she tried to talk him into going on a diet with her "to be more healthy." However, Jean's boyfriend was completely unconcerned about his weight or eating habits. He was able to eat a few cookies at a time, and a package of cookies would last a month (at least as far as he knew). Jean did not understand how he could show so much self-control. However, when asked, Jean was able to acknowledge that before her weight-loss diet, she had also been able to have one dessert after dinner at a restaurant and not lose control of her eating later on. She had always thought that this was because the restaurant controlled how much food she was given. However, she had to admit that the restaurant did not keep her from going to a store and buying a package of cookies or a gallon of ice cream after leaving. So, she too was probably able to eat some dessert without losing control.

Jean's loss of control appears to be related, in part, to her beliefs about her ability to eat "forbidden foods" in moderation. Although she has been able to eat just one dessert, she has convinced herself that this is not possible when she is alone. Therefore her only choices are to eat nothing or eat everything (dichotomous thinking). Interestingly, individuals with bulimic symptoms have demonstrated significantly greater cognitive impulsivity compared to controls (Ferraro, Wonderlich, & Zeljko, 1997). Thus, unlike a patient with ANR who will rigidly maintain abstinence, patients with bulimic symptoms shift back and forth between eating nothing and everything.

As a short-term approach, abstinence from forbidden foods may provide some success because it may be easier to avoid some foods altogether than to eat a small amount of those foods. Still, abstinence is not a flexible approach. Consistent with dichotomous thinking, one is either abstinent or not. Thus, eating one piece of cake on a special occasion would be viewed as a failure. Beyond the potential for dieting to trigger physiological weight-defending mechanisms that contribute to binge eating (see the discussion of Keys et al. 1950, in Chapter 4), it is likely that the cognitive processes involved in dieting contribute to binge eating. Indeed, would it even be possible to experience a loss of control over eating if one weren't attempting to control eating in the first place?

Polivy and Herman (1985) proposed that the introduction of cognitive regulation of dietary intake (eating in response to rules about when to eat and what to eat rather than eating in response to hunger) introduces opportunities for loss of control over eating **(disinhibition).** Disinhibition could occur in response to a cognitive trigger, an affective trigger, or a pharmacological trigger. An example of a **cognitive disinhibitor** is attending a friend's birthday party and being offered a piece of birthday cake that is not allowed on a weight loss diet. After having the cake, dieters might conclude that they have "blown" their diet and might as well eat whatever they want for the rest of the evening. An example of an **affective disinhibitor** is a fight with a loved one leading to frustration and sadness. In this case, cognitive resources that would normally be employed to restrict food intake are used to cope with distress. In addition, eating may be used as a source of comfort and justified as a special treat. An example of a **pharmacological disinhibitor** is becoming intoxicated and losing track of what or how much was eaten. In each case, the cognitive control of food intake is interrupted, resulting in a loss of control over eating. Polivy and Herman argued that individuals who become chronic dieters (or *restrained eaters*) lose the ability to determine when they feel hungry or full. Thus, sensations of hunger and satiety (physiological control of food intake) cannot take the place of cognitive control, resulting in the consumption of an unusually large amount of food (Ruderman, 1986). According to this explanation (also known as the *restraint hypothesis*), Jean's binge-eating episodes are caused by her weight loss diet. Jean's diet creates the rule that she should eat no junk food. When Jean is alone in the apartment and eats a cookie, she has failed, and there is no reason for her to stop eating. In addition, her dieting has disrupted her ability to eat in response to hunger and stop in response to satiety. Thus, what was interpreted as alexythymia or poor interoceptive awareness (see Chapter 6) has been described as a consequence of weight-loss dieting.

A series of experimental studies have supported hypotheses concerning the influence of dieting-related cognitions concerning food intake. Two studies are reviewed in detail here. Spencer and Fremouw (1979) divided participants into restrained eaters and unrestrained eaters based on scores on a self-report measure of dietary restraint. Participants were then brought into a laboratory for a "taste test" (see Chapter 4 for a description of the basic taste test study design). Prior to the taste test, all participants were asked to consume a milkshake. However, participants were randomized into one of two conditions. In one condition, they were told they were consuming a low-calorie milkshake. In the other condition, they were led to believe they were consuming a high-calorie milkshake. The milkshake did not differ in actual nutritional content so that no physiological differences in satiety would be produced. During the subsequent taste test, restrained eaters consumed significantly more in the "high-calorie" compared to the "low calorie" condition. This pattern was not observed in unrestrained eaters. (See Figure 7–2.) Thus,

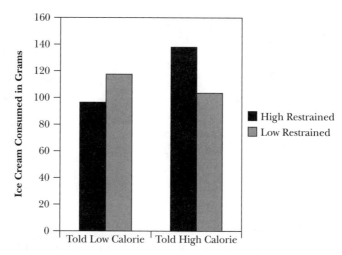

FIGURE 7–2 Average grams of ice cream consumed by high- and low-restrained subjects given high- and low-calorie instructions.

Source: Spencer, J. A., & Fremouw, W. J. (1979). Binge eating as a function of restraint and weight classification. *Journal of Abnormal Psychology, 88,* 262–267.

the extent to which restrained eaters *believe* that they have broken their diets predicts subsequent food consumption during the taste test. Further, rather than compensating for the high-calorie shake by eating less (which would help them adhere more closely to their diets), restrained eaters eat more.

Urbszat, Herman, and Polivy (2002) investigated the impact of anticipating a 1-week diet on food consumption in restrained and unrestrained eaters. Participants characterized as restrained or unrestrained eaters were randomly assigned to one of two conditions: being told they would be placed on a 1-week diet (diet condition) or being told they would not be placed on a diet (no-diet condition). Table 7–1 presents details provided to participants concerning what they would be allowed to eat in the diet condition. There was a significant interaction between dietary restraint and experimental condition in predicting cookie consumption during a taste test. (See Figure 7–3.) Restrained eaters consumed significantly more cookies when anticipating a 1-week diet than did restrained eaters in the no-diet condition. Conversely, experimental condition (diet or no diet) did not influence cookie consumption among unrestrained eaters. Restrained eaters in the diet condition also ate significantly more than unrestrained eaters in either condition, and restrained eaters in the no-diet condition ate significantly less than unrestrained eaters in the no-diet condition. Because no actual dieting took place, it was the expectation of dieting that altered food consumption in restrained eaters. Interestingly, the absence of this effect in unrestrained eaters suggests that experience with dieting might be required to produce overeating in anticipation of food restriction. Alternatively, it is possible that restrained and unrestrained eaters differ in how desirable or tempting forbidden or bad foods seem. This could result in differences in the perceived need to exert external control over food intake and contribute to differences in dietary restraint.

Selective abstraction occurs when one part comes to represent the whole (Beck, 1970). For example, Emily was able to acknowledge that several areas of her body were not fat (e.g., her shoulders and arms) and even expressed the desire to build muscle

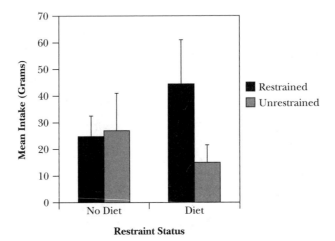

FIGURE 7–3 Mean intake of restrained and unrestrained subjects given diet- and no-diet instructions.

Source: Urbszat, D., Herman, C. P., & Polivy, J. (2002). Eat, drink, and be merry, for tomorrow we diet: Effects of anticipated deprivation on food intake in restrained and unrestrained eaters. *Journal of Abnormal Psychology, 111,* 396–401.

TABLE 7–1   Content of Diet Presented to Participants Randomized to Diet Condition

Breakfast—1 Slim-Fast breakfast shake
Lunch—1 serving each of lean protein, starch, fruit or vegetable, 6 oz skim milk
Dinner—1 prepackaged frozen Lean Cuisine

Lean Protein Suggestions	Starch Suggestions
30 g (2 slices) cooked turkey/chicken breast (no skin)	1 slice of white sandwich bread
1/2 can of tuna or salmon	1 1/2 slices of whole wheat bread
1 vegetarian meat patty	10 wheat or vegetable crackers
25 g (one slice) cooked ham	3 rice cake patties
25 g (one chop) pork	50 g of cooked white rice
20 g (one patty) lean ground beef	1 raw potato
40 g tofu (one half of any above portions with 20 g of cheddar cheese)	1/2 cooked potato
2 egg whites (no yolks)	250 ml of macaroni

Snack Suggestions	Prohibited Foods
Rice cakes	Added fats (butter, margarine)
Low-fat yogurt (no fruit)	Ice cream
Apple, banana, orange, pear, plum	Chocolate
2 carrot sticks	Baked goods (cookies, cakes, pie)
3 celery sticks	Potato chips
Whole wheat or vegetable crackers	Candy
One small wheat or bran muffin	Fried foods (fries, chicken fingers)
Popcorn (no butter)/pretzels	Soft drinks
	Submarine sandwiches
	Cheese slices
	Oils (cooking, salad dressing)
	Cream sauces
	Hamburgers
	Cream, whole fat or 2% milk
	Bacon
	Egg yolks
	Pizza
	Exotic cheeses

Source: Urbszat et al. (2002).

mass in her upper body. However, because she perceived fat on her thighs, this one region of her body carried the evaluation of her whole body as being in danger of becoming fat. Similarly, a patient with BN may describe himself as a vegetarian who believes it is wrong to eat animals because he has eliminated meat from his diet. However, he will ignore his consumption of fast food hamburgers during binge-eating episodes. In this case, selective abstraction provides a moral justification for dietary rules that may increase the risk of binge-eating episodes. Selective abstraction is particularly likely to occur among perfectionists because if something would be perfect if not for one specific flaw, then this one flaw carries undue importance in evaluating the worth of the whole.

In summary, societal messages that contribute to disordered eating, such as the importance of being thin, may be particularly salient to individuals who develop eating disorders. In addition, the way that information is used and evaluated likely contributes to disordered eating. Rather than feeling good about both small and large successes, people with eating disorders have cognitive distortions that leave them vulnerable to suffer innumerable failures in terms of their eating, their bodies, and their lives. The extent to which general dysphoria gets funneled into dissatisfaction with weight or shape has been proposed as an etiological factor in the development of BN (Keel, Mitchell, Davis, & Crow, 2001). For adolescents, controlling weight and shape may seem like a manageable solution to alleviate distress; however, for many, it becomes a trap. A vicious cycle develops in which general threats to self-evaluation are funneled into a need to obtain or maintain a specific body weight or shape, as if this will lead to contentment. The few successes and numerous failures to control body weight and shape negatively influence self-evaluation and lead to increased efforts to alleviate distress through weight control (Heatherton & Baumeister, 1991). One limitation in this line of reasoning is that the cognitive features characteristic of eating disorders may or may not have predated the onset of an eating disorder. Instead they may reflect an aspect of having an eating disorder or even a consequence. For example, binge eating is always associated with BN, but this does not make it a cause of BN. To the extent that some research has suggested cognitive differences in women recovered from eating disorders, this may reflect thought processes that predated and contributed to the onset of the eating disorder. However, caution is warranted with this reasoning as well. A consequence of having an eating disorder could remain after the eating disorder remits, much as a scar remains after a wound has healed.

CONCLUSION

Review of psychological contributions to the development of eating disorders reveals a high degree of overlap across cognition, behavior, and personality. This overlap may be explained by the role of personality in shaping how individuals perceive, react to, and interact with their environments. Thus, an individual who is highly perfectionistic, constrained, and demonstrates high persistence and reward dependence may show a cognitive style that is marked by rigidity, dichotomous thinking, and selective abstraction and may be particularly sensitive to rewards that would encourage the learning of certain associations. This person would be more vulnerable to social messages concerning the importance of being thin. He or she also may be more likely to persist in the pursuit of this ideal, even when the rewards diminish in intensity. Conversely, an individual who is impulsive and disinhibited may show cognitive disinhibition more easily. He or she might find it more difficult to resist the rewarding aspects of food and eating, and higher reward and punishment sensitivity may contribute to a vicious cycle of binge eating and purging. These patterns provide a fairly coherent explanation for the symptomatic differences between ANR and both ANBP and BN.

High levels of negative emotionality are characteristic across eating disorder subtypes. Disordered eating symptoms may serve as a maladaptive solution to problems that elicit intense negative emotional states. The failure to recognize that the symptoms do not actually solve the problem may result from a combination of cognitive distortions and the salience of immediate consequences over long-term consequences. Thus, negative emotionality may be a common factor in different types of eating disorders.

KEY TERMS

Affective disinhibitor
Cognition
Cognitive disinhibitor
Cognitive distortions
Constraint
Dichotomous thinking
Disinhibition
Harm avoidance
Minnesota Multiphasic Personality
  Inventory (MMPI)
Negative emotionality
Negative reinforcement
Novelty seeking

Operant conditioning
Perfectionism
Persistence
Personality
Pharmacological disinhibitor
Positive emotionality
Positive reinforcement
Punishment
Reward dependence
Selective abstraction
Stroop Test
Temperament

CHAPTER 8

⬥•⬥

Biological Bases, Correlates, and Consequences of Eating Disorders

This chapter introduces some of the biological bases, correlates, and consequences of eating disorders. Just as eating disorders impact psychological function, they impact biological functions, and, as discussed in Chapter 4, it would be unethical to directly test factors believed to cause eating disorders in humans. Thus, this chapter reviews these areas together because much of the research concerning the biological bases of eating disorders cannot disentangle causes from consequences.

The first section of this chapter reviews the biological bases of appetite and weight regulation, as well as associations between the functions of different neurochemicals and eating disorders. Importantly, this review reveals how the brain influences hunger and satiety. No one would argue that eating can be explained fully as a response to hunger and satiety, as people often eat for reasons completely unrelated to biological needs. However, it would be equally unwise to completely discount the role of such mechanisms in the etiology or maintenance of eating disorders.

The second section of this chapter discusses the contribution of genes to the etiology of eating disorders. This review begins with an examination of data from family and twin studies (see Chapter 4 for a full discussion of twin study methods). It then reviews results of studies designed to identify specific genes that increase the risk of eating disorders (molecular genetic studies).

The third section reviews known consequences of eating disorders. Because eating is a basic biological function required to sustain life, disruption of eating has profound consequences for biological function. This fact explains the ambiguity associated with results of studies attempting to reveal the biological bases of eating disorders.

BRAIN FUNCTION AND EATING DISORDERS

Appetite and Weight Regulation

The **hypothalamus** is a structure in the brain responsible for appetite and weight control. It can be divided into different sections named by their location in relation to each other, and these different sections are associated with different effects on appetite and weight. Specifically, surgically damaging the **ventromedial** hypothalamus produces increased food intake and significant obesity (Hetherington & Ranson, 1942). In contrast, surgically damaging the **lateral** hypothalamus produces dramatic decreases in food intake and weight loss (Anand & Brobeck, 1951; Teitelbaum & Stellar, 1954). Electrical stimulation of these brain regions produces the opposite effect (Kandel, Schwartz, & Jessell, 1991). This suggests that the ventromedial hypothalamus is responsible for inhibiting appetite and food intake and that the lateral hypothalamus is responsible for increasing them. These areas appear to work together in healthy individuals to maintain a balance in weight and appetite and are thought to be important in understanding satiety function as it may relate to eating pathology.

In addition to regulating eating, the hypothalamus regulates other body functions such as sexual activity and drinking. The hypothalamus is located near the pituitary gland at the base of the brain. The hypothalamus and pituitary gland are involved in two systems—the **hypothalamic-pituitary-adrenal (HPA) axis** and the **hypothalamic-pituitary-gonadal (HPG) axis.** The HPA axis has been implicated in responses to stress, and the HPG axis is involved in the release of sex hormones and the process of maturation. Both

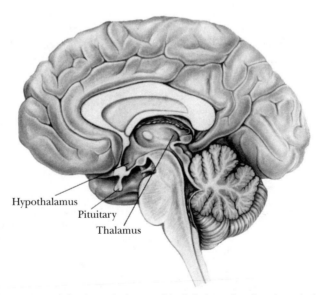

The location and structure of the hypothalamus. Medial view showing the relationship of the hypothalamus to the pituitary and thalamus.

Kandel, E. R., Schwartz, J. H., & Jessell, T. M. (1991). *Principles of Neural Science (Third Edition)*. New York, NY: Elsevier Science Publishers, 738.

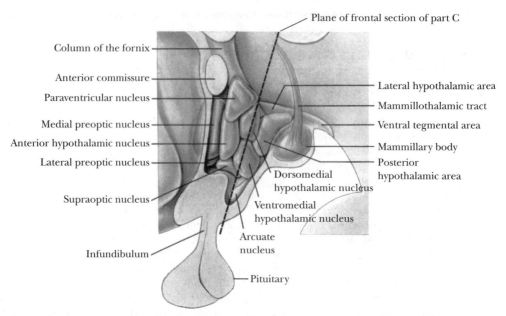

Column of the fornix

Anterior commissure

Paraventricular nucleus

Medial preoptic nucleus

Anterior hypothalamic nucleus

Lateral preoptic nucleus

Supraoptic nucleus

Infundibulum

Plane of frontal section of part C

Lateral hypothalamic area

Mammillothalamic tract

Ventral tegmental area

Mammillary body

Posterior hypothalamic area

Dorsomedial hypothalamic nucleus

Ventromedial hypothalamic nucleus

Arcuate nucleus

Pituitary

The location and structure of the hypothalamus. Medial view showing positions of the main hypothalamic nuclei. Some nuclei are visible only in the frontal view in part C.

Kandel, E. R., Schwartz, J. H., & Jessell, T. M. (1991). *Principles of Neural Science (Third Edition)*. New York, NY: Elsevier Science Publishers, 738.

Obesity caused by surgical destruction of the ventromedial hypothalamus.

Roediger, H. L., Capaldi, E. D., Paris, S. C., & Polivy, J. (1991). *Psychology* (3rd ed.). New York, NY: HarperCollins Publishers, p. 440.

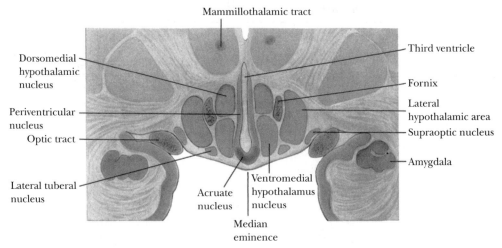

Mammillothalamic tract

Third ventricle

Fornix

Lateral hypothalamic area

Supraoptic nucleus

Amygdala

Dorsomedial hypothalamic nucleus

Periventricular nucleus

Optic tract

Lateral tuberal nucleus

Acruate nucleus

Ventromedial hypothalamus nucleus

Median eminence

The location and structure of the hypothalamus. Frontal view of the hypothalamus (section along plane shown in part A).

Kandel, E. R., Schwartz, J. H., & Jessell, T. M. (1991). *Principles of Neural Science (Third Edition)*. New York, NY: Elsevier Science Publishers, 738.

functions seem to be altered in patients with eating disorders, who also demonstrate perturbations of weight and appetite regulation.

Table 8–1 provides a list of neurochemicals, their site of action in the hypothalamus, and their effects on eating as an overview to the rest of this section. A great deal of research on the biological bases of eating disorders has focused on neurophysiology—specifically, the function of **neurotransmitters** and **neuropeptides** that are related to appetite, weight, and mood.

Neurotransmitters and Eating Disorders

Neurotransmitters are chemicals that facilitate communication between brain cells (**neurons**). Examples of neurotransmitters include **serotonin** (also called *5-hydroxytryptamine, 5-HT*), **norepinephrine,** and **dopamine.** Importantly, food intake is associated with the release of these three neurotransmitters in the hypothalamus (Fetissov, Meguid, Chen, & Miyata, 2000). Activity of 5-HT in the medial hypothalamus decreases food intake (Fetissov et al., 2000), suggesting that 5-HT is important to the role of the ventromedial hypothalamus in reducing appetite and weight. Activity of dopamine and norepinephrine in the hypothalamus inhibits the normal function of the hypothalamus (Fetissov et al., 2000). Thus, activity of dopamine and norepinephrine in the lateral hypothalamus decreases food intake, whereas their activity in the medial hypothalamus increases food intake.

Serotonin

Animal and human studies have demonstrated that 5-HT plays an important role in the regulation of mood, appetite, and impulse control. Diminished 5-HT function is

TABLE 8–1   Overview of Neurochemicals That Influence Eating

Neurochemical	Site of Action	Effect on Eating	Level in Patients with Eating Disorders			
			AN, Ill	AN, Rec	BN, Ill	BN, Rec
Serotonin (5-HT)	Paraventricular nucleus	Decrease	Mixed	High	Low	Normal
	Medial hypothalamus	Decrease				
Dopamine	Lateral hypothalamus	Decrease	Mixed	Low	Low	Normal
	Medial hypothalamus	Increase				
Norepinephrine	Lateral hypothalamus	Decrease	Low	Low	Low	
	Medial hypothalamus	Increase				
Cholecystokinin	Ventromedial hypothalamus	Decrease	Mixed		Low	Normal
Leptin	Paraventricular nucleus	Decrease	Low	Normal	Low	Mixed
Neuropeptide Y	Lateral hypothalamus	Increase	High	Mixed		Normal
Melonocortin-stimulating hormone	Paraventricular nucleus	Decrease	Low	Normal		

associated with dysphoria, increased appetite, and decreased impulse control. Because these three domains are altered in patients with eating disorders, 5-HT became a prime candidate in attempting to understand the biological correlates (and potentially causes) of AN and BN. Specifically, research on BN has focused on the hypothesis of inadequate 5-HT function to explain binge eating, and recent research on AN has focused on over-function of 5-HT to explain self-starvation.

An early hypothesis proposed that inadequate 5-HT function produced "carbohydrate craving" that caused binge-eating episodes (Wurtman & Wurtman, 1986). Dieting was thought to contribute to carbohydrate craving because many weight-loss diets of the 1970s emphasized restricted carbohydrate intake. 5-HT is not found in food, and it cannot cross from the blood into the brain. However, **tryptophan,** an amino acid required to make 5-HT, is found in food and can cross the blood-brain barrier. So, diets that diminish tryptophan intake could lead to diminished 5-HT production. The process that enables tryptophan to cross the blood-brain barrier also transports other large neutral amino acids (LNAAs), and tryptophan competes with LNAAs to enter the brain. High-carbohydrate meals increase the tryptophan/LNAA ratio as an indirect effect of insulin causing decreased levels of the LNAAs (Fernstrom, 1994). This effectively increases the amount of tryptophan entering the brain that can then be used to create 5-HT. Conversely, when individuals eat low-carbohydrate/high-protein meals, they limit the transport of tryptophan into the brain and limit the brain's ability to make 5-HT. Thus, binge-eating episodes that typically consisted of high-carbohydrate foods (e.g., cookies, cakes, chips) were thought to represent an attempt at self-medication for low 5-HT function. Low 5-HT function would certainly explain the dysphoric mood and large appetites demonstrated by women with BN.

Supporting the 5-HT hypothesis, Kaye and colleagues (1988a) found that cessation of binge-purge episodes among women with BN appeared to be related to the extent to which binge episodes produced an increase in the tryptophan/LNAA ratio in their blood. Concentrations of tryptophan, LNAA, insulin, and glucose were repeatedly measured in nine women with BN who were allowed to binge and purge at will. Women who reached their "desired effect" spontaneously stopped within one to three binge-purge cycles and demonstrated greater increases in tryptophan/LNAA ratios compared to women who did not stop their binge-purge cycles spontaneously.

In contrast to the 5-HT hypothesis, studies comparing fasting concentrations of tryptophan/LNAAs in women with BN to those of non-eating-disordered controls have found no differences (Brewerton et al., 1992; Lydiard et al., 1988; Weltzin, Fernstrom, Fernstrom, Neuberger, & Kaye, 1995). Thus, although women with BN reported higher levels of dietary restraint, this did not appear to impact their fasting blood concentrations of tryptophan and therefore should not have resulted in a deficit of the building block for 5-HT in their brains. Similarly, macronutrient analysis of binge-eating episodes suggests that when individuals binge, they eat from too many food groups to effectively increase the tryptophan/LNAA ratio in their blood (Jansen, van den Hout, & Griez, 1989). Thus, binge-eating episodes may be an ineffective means of increasing central 5-HT function.

More recent research has examined emotional and behavioral responses to changes in blood tryptophan levels. This kind of study was described in Chapter 4. Briefly, individuals were given a liquid meal that caused a significant *decrease* in the tryptophan/LNAA ratio. This diminishes the brain's resources to create 5-HT. Although experimental manipulations of 5-HT levels in participants with BN and controls demonstrated similar changes in blood concentrations of tryptophan and LNAAs, only participants with BN reported significant increases in dysphoria, anxiety, and the urge to eat following tryptophan depletion (Smith et al., 1999; Weltzin et al., 1995). Thus, dieting may cause binge eating in people whose brains react differently to decreased tryptophan. However, this may not be observable as a difference in the blood concentration of tryptophan.

Several lines of investigation have suggested diminished 5-HT function in the brains of patients with BN. One line of investigation has examined the by-product of 5-HT use in the brain. When 5-HT is used in the brain, 5-hydroxyindoleacetic acid (5-HIAA) is a leftover product that is washed out into cerebrospinal fluid. For example, if you wanted to measure how many candy bars a person ate without directly observing the person, you could count the number of candy wrappers in the trash. Examining 5-HIAA in the cerebrospinal fluid is a very similar approach. Although no overall differences in cerebrospinal fluid 5-HIAA concentrations have been reported between patients with BN and controls (Jimerson, Lesem, Kaye, & Brewerton, 1992; Kaye et al., 1990a), cerebrospinal fluid 5-HIAA concentrations are lower in patients who binge more frequently (Jimerson et al., 1992).

A second line of investigation has examined the ability of 5-HT to facilitate communication between cells. In order for 5-HT to function, it must be released from one brain cell and bind to a **receptor** of another brain cell. Each neurotransmitter functions by fitting like a key into a lock that is the receptor. Decreased 5-HT receptor function has been reported for platelet cells in patients with BN compared to controls (Marazziti, Macchi, Rotondo, Placidi, & Cassano, 1988). Although platelet cells exist in the bloodstream, not in the brain, they may reflect how 5-HT receptors work in the brain. Goldbloom and colleagues (1990) reported increased 5-HT reuptake. This means that the brain cell releasing 5-HT reabsorbed the 5-HT before it could bind to a receptor of another brain cell. This finding may explain the success of selective-5-HT reuptake inhibitors (such as Prozac) in treating BN. These medications prevent the brain cell releasing 5-HT from reabsorbing it **(reuptake)** and give 5-HT more opportunity to bind to receptors of another brain cell. Finally, brain imaging research has reported diminished binding at the 5-HT$_{2A}$ receptor in patients who have recovered from BN compared to controls (Kaye et al., 2001a). Thus, differences in 5-HT receptor function cannot be attributed to the presence of bulimic symptoms (although they could be a consequence of a history of these symptoms).

A third line of investigation has examined brain 5-HT function by studying its hormonal consequences. Increased 5-HT function in the brain increases **prolactin** release in the blood. Fenfluramine, meta-chlorophenylpiperazine (m-CPP), and L-tryptophan (L-TRP) are all 5-HT **agonists** (agents that increase 5-HT function). When given a 5-HT agonist, patients with BN have shown lower prolactin release compared to controls (Brewerton, Brand, Lesem, Murphy, & Jimerson, 1990; Brewerton et al., 1992; Halmi, McBride, & Sunday, 1993; Jimerson et al., 1997). Lower prolactin release suggests that 5-HT is less responsive to agonists in patients with BN compared to controls. However, this difference appears to be related to the state of the illness. Women recovered from BN do not differ from healthy controls on their prolactin response to a 5-HT agonist (Wolfe et al., 2000).

Jimerson et al. (1992) have suggested a model to explain 5-HT findings in BN. In this model, periodic binge-eating episodes cause sudden increases in 5-HT in the brain. This causes 5-HT receptors to become less sensitive (a process known as **down-regulation**). When a patient with BN resumes dietary restriction, 5-HT levels normalize or decrease. Because of decreased receptor sensitivity, the patient's 5-HT receptors are less responsive to even normal levels of 5-HT. This would explain the different response to tryptophan depletion observed in BN patients compared to controls. Although sustained low concentrations of 5-HT could lead to increased sensitivity of 5-HT receptors (**up-regulation**), down-regulation occurs more readily than up-regulation in neurotransmitter systems. For example, down-regulation of opioid receptors in response to heroin (i.e., tolerance) can occur over hours or days; by contrast, up-regulation of opioid receptors to previous levels of function can take over 3 weeks to complete (i.e., the end of the withdrawal period). Thus, if binge-eating episodes are occurring several times per week, then there may be repeated insult to 5-HT receptors that cannot be reversed by interepisode periods of dietary restriction. Thus, Jamie's experience of his binge episodes as representing an addiction may be accurate (see Chapter 1).

Research on 5-HT function in AN has produced mixed findings. Patients with AN demonstrate diminished concentrations of 5-HIAA in their cerebrospinal fluid compared to controls (Kaye, Ebert, Raleigh, & Lake, 1984b, 1988b), and Kaye, Ebert, Gwirtsman, & Weiss (1984a) reported lower cerebrospinal fluid concentrations of 5-HIAA among weight-recovered ANBP patients compared to weight-recovered ANR patients and controls. However, concentrations of cerebrospinal fluid 5-HIAA appear to be related to weight in AN (Demitrack et al., 1993; Gerner et al., 1984; Kaye et al., 1984b, 1988b). Thus, both weight loss and decreased 5-HT production may be a consequence of not eating, as food is a primary source of tryptophan for 5-HT production. Like patients with BN, patients with AN show diminished platelet 5-HT receptor function compared to controls (Weizman, Carmi, Tyano, & Rehavi, 1986). Patients with AN also demonstrate a diminished prolactin response to a 5-HT agonist (Brewerton et al., 1990; Golden & Shenker, 1994; Monteleone, Brambilla, Bortolotti, & Maj, 2000b).

Monteleone et al. (2000b) compared prolactin responses to a 5-HT agonist in women in four diagnostic groups: AN, BN, BED, and healthy controls. Women with BN with frequent binge episodes and women with AN demonstrated a lower prolactin response, suggesting decreased 5-HT function. In contrast, women with BN and infrequent binge episodes and women with BED did not differ from healthy controls on their prolactin response. Thus, diminished 5-HT function appears to be associated with low weight in AN and high binge-purge frequency in BN.

In contrast to findings with BN, Kaye, Gwirtsman, George, and Ebert (1991a) found that levels of 5-HIAA are *higher* in patients with AN following weight recovery compared to controls. This has led to the hypothesis that AN may be marked by premorbidly high concentrations of 5-HT that contribute to overcontrol and undereating (Kaye, 1997). Self-starvation has been interpreted as a form of self-medication that helps to reduce 5-HT to more tolerable levels. The problem with this hypothesis is that patients with AN, like the participants in the Keys et al. (1950) study, tend to become more rigid and over-controlled as they lose weight—presumably as their 5-HT levels decrease to a normal and then a subnormal range. Unlike the 5-HT hypothesis for BN, in which vacillations between dietary restriction and binge-eating episodes could create a vicious cycle, continued dietary restraint motivated by elevated levels of 5-HT should resolve as the 5-HT level normalizes. This should be all the more true among patients with AN who binge (if binge episodes reduce the sensitivity of 5-HT receptors). Thus, it is difficult to reconcile the finding of diminished 5-HT function as a contributor to both binge-eating episodes in BN and sustained food refusal in AN. However, it would be naive to expect the function of a single neurotransmitter to explain any complex mental disorder.

Dopamine

As described earlier in this chapter, dopamine appears to inhibit food intake by acting on dopamine receptors in the lateral hypothalamus, and dopamine activity in the medial hypothalamus increases food intake. In addition, it is possible that diminished dopamine function may reduce the rewarding effects of a normal amount of food (Jimerson et al., 1992). Thus, decreased dopamine function may be associated with binge eating because normal amounts of food may be less satisfying. **Homovanillic acid (HVA)** is the by-product of dopamine use in the brain. Research has demonstrated decreased concentrations of HVA in the cerebrospinal fluid (Jimerson et al., 1992; Kaye et al., 1990a) and plasma (Kaplan, Garfinkel, Warsh, & Brown, 1989) of women with BN compared to controls, and studies have shown an inverse relationship between the frequency of binge-eating episodes and HVA concentration (Jimerson et al., 1992; Kaye et al., 1990a). That is, women who binged more frequently had lower HVA concentrations. However, HVA concentrations did not differ between women recovered from BN and healthy controls (Kaye, Frank, & McConaha, 1999).

Similar to findings in BN, decreased HVA concentrations have been found in women with AN (Kaye et al., 1984b), which may persist after weight recovery in ANR (Kaye et al., 1999). Brambilla, Bellodi, Arancio, Ronchi, and Limonta (2001) found evidence of decreased dopamine receptor sensitivity in women with AN (both subtypes) compared to women with BN and healthy controls. These authors further postulated that this result reflected increased dopamine availability in the brains of patients with AN, causing receptors to become less sensitive (similar to Jimerson et al.'s 1992 explanation of decreased sensitivity of 5-HT receptors). Although this seems to contradict results suggesting decreased dopamine activity in the brains of patients with AN (Kaye et al., 1984b, 1999), decreased HVA concentrations could reflect decreased dopamine levels, decreased dopamine use, decreased clearance of HVA into the cerebrospinal fluid, or any combination of these. Returning to the analogy of using candy wrappers in a trash can to assess how many candy bars a person has, a decreased number of wrappers could indicate that the person simply has fewer candy bars, or that the person has plenty of candy bars but hasn't eaten any, or that the person has eaten plenty of candy bars but is keeping the wrappers. Another complication in interpreting results concerning the HVA concentration is that this reflects dopamine use throughout the brain. As noted earlier in the chapter, the effect of dopamine on food intake depends upon where in the brain it is acting.

Like findings for 5-HT function in AN, findings for dopamine function in AN are mixed. Overfunction of dopamine in the lateral hypothalamus would make more sense for explaining the decreased food intake characteristic of AN. However, several studies have produced results that show similarity between patients with AN and patients with BN. To some extent, this could reflect the inclusion of patients with AN who binge.

Norepinephrine

As described earlier in this chapter, norepinephrine can both increase and decrease food intake, depending upon where in the hypothalamus it is acting. Studies of norepinephrine and its by-product (methoxy-hydroxy-phenylglycol, or MHPG) indicate reduced levels in the brain and body in patients with eating pathology (Koo-Loeb, Costello, Light, & Girdler, 2000) compared to controls, with lower levels found in both AN and BN (Pirke, 1996). Kaye et al. (1984b) reported diminished norepinephrine concentrations in the cerebrospinal fluid of weight-recovered anorectic patients compared to controls. Because norepinephrine may stimulate carbohydrate intake (Carlson, 1994), diminished norepinephrine function could contribute to successful food restriction in AN. However, in a later report by Kaye et al. (1999), the norepinephrine levels did not differ among controls, women recovered from BN, or women recovered from AN.

In summary, the majority of research on neurotransmitter function in eating disorders has focused on 5-HT function. Across studies, the most consistent evidence has pointed to decreased 5-HT function in women with BN. However, it remains unclear whether differences between women with BN and healthy controls reflect 5-HT's role in causing BN or the effect of BN on 5-HT function. Results of neurotransmitter function in AN are more mixed, likely reflecting the significant impact of starvation on neurotransmitter production in the brain.

Neuropeptides and Eating Disorders

Neuropeptides function similarly to neurotransmitters but are physically larger. Examples of neuropeptides include **cholecystokinin, leptin,** and **neuropeptide Y.** As depicted in Table 8–1, cholecystokinin and leptin both work to decrease appetite through activation of the medial hypothalamus. In contrast, neuropeptide Y increases appetite by stimulating the lateral hypothalamus.

Cholecystokinin

Cholecystokinin is a neuropeptide that is released in the small intestine following food ingestion (Gibbs, Young, & Smith, 1972). Like 5-HT, cholecystokinin does not cross the blood-brain barrier. However, it binds to its receptors on the **vagus nerve** in the stomach (Gibbs & Smith, 1977; Robinson, McHugh, Moran, & Stephenson, 1988). The vagus nerve is a cranial nerve that sends signals directly to the brain, and stimulation of this nerve activates the ventromedial hypothalamus (Peiken, 1989). In addition to binding to cholecystokinin receptors on the vagus nerve, cholecystokinin causes contraction of the **pyloric sphincter** (a muscle that controls the rate at which food passes from the stomach to the small intestine; Moran, Robinson, & McHugh, 1985). As the person eats, the food in the stomach causes the stomach to expand. This triggers gastric stretch receptors that also stimulate the vagus nerve. Cholecystokinin enhances this process by slowing the rate at which food can pass from the stomach into the small intestine.

A series of studies have demonstrated a reduced cholecystokinin response to food in women with BN compared to normal controls (Devlin et al., 1997; Geracioti &

Liddle, 1988; Pirke, Kellner, Friess, Krieg, & Fichter, 1994). Thus, another reason that women with BN may have large binge episodes is that a larger quantity of food is required to produce satiety. In one study, cholecystokinin function normalized after symptom remission in BN (Geracioti & Liddle, 1988). Studies of cholecystokinin function in AN have produced inconsistent results (Pirke et al., 1994; Phillipp, Pirke, Kellner, & Krieg, 1991).

Leptin

Leptin is a neuropeptide that provides a negative feedback loop in the brain's control of weight and food intake. Leptin receptors have been found in the **paraventricular nucleus** and ventromedial hypothalamus. Leptin is released from fat tissue in the body. Thus, the more fat that is in the body, the more leptin is circulating in the blood, and higher levels of leptin produce decreased food intake. Leptin is produced by the *ob* gene. Mice with a mutated *ob* gene (known as *ob/ob* mice) are obese, weighing three times more than normal mice and having five times the amount of body fat. Injections of leptin produce weight loss in these mice (Friedman & Halaas, 1998), and leptin decreases weight in both animals and humans by reducing food intake (Friedman & Halaas, 1998; Heymsfield et al., 1999; Schwartz, Baskin, Kaiyala, & Woods, 1999).

Not surprisingly, several studies have demonstrated decreased leptin concentrations in patients with AN compared to controls (Di Carlo et al., 2002; Hebebrand et al., 1997; Lear, Pauly, & Birmingham, 1999; Mantzoros, Flier, Lesem, Brewerton, & Jimerson, 1997; Monteleone, Di Lieto, Tortorella, Longobardi, & Maj, 2000c; Tolle et al., 2003). This is likely a consequence of weight loss rather than a cause because diminished concentrations of leptin should increase food intake and promote weight gain (Gendall, Kaye, Altemus, McConaha, & La Via, 1999). Some studies of women recovering from AN have found that leptin concentrations normalize before weight reaches a normal level in AN (Hebebrand et al., 1997; Mantzoros et al., 1997). Thus, it is possible that women with AN receive physiological signals indicating the presence of normal weight before they actually reach a normal weight. If this is true, it would explain their ability to maintain a weight below normal. However, this hypothesis has not been supported in other studies of weight recovery in AN (Gendall et al., 1999; Pauly, Lear, Hastings, & Birmingham, 2000; Tolle et al., 2003).

Given the association between body weight and leptin concentration, one would expect normal-weight women with BN to have normal concentrations of leptin. However, several studies have demonstrated diminished concentrations of leptin in women with BN compared to healthy controls (Brewerton, Lesem, Kennedy, & Garvey, 2000; Jimerson, Mantzoros, Wolfe, & Metzger, 2000; Monteleone et al., 2000a, 2000c). One study has reported diminished leptin concentrations in women recovered from BN compared to healthy controls (Jimerson et al., 2000), but another study (Gendall et al., 1999) has not. Diminished leptin in BN may contribute to binge-eating episodes by increasing the physiological drive to eat. This effect may be mediated by leptin's influences on neuropeptide Y function and **proopiomelanocortin (POMC)** gene expression.

Neuropeptide Y

Neuropeptide Y increases food intake and is inhibited by leptin. Kaye, Berrettini, Gwirtsman, and George (1990b) found elevated concentrations of neuropeptide Y in patients with AN and in anorectic patients with short-term weight recovery compared to controls. However, no significant differences were found between long-term weight-recovered anorectic patients and healthy controls (Gendall et al., 1999; Kaye et al., 1990b). Similarly, no significant differences in neuropeptide Y concentrations were found between controls and women recovered from BN (Gendall et al., 1999).

Proopiomelanocortin

POMC is the precursor of **melanocyte-stimulating hormone (MSH).** MSH and its receptor (melanocortin-4 receptor) appear to be necessary for a response to increased leptin concentrations. MSH agonists decrease food intake in humans, and MSH antagonists decrease it in animals (Friedman & Halaas, 1998). Kaye et al. (1987) examined three peptides derived from POMC in three groups: patients with AN both before and after short-term weight recovery, patients with long-term weight recovery from AN, and healthy controls. When underweight, patients with AN had significantly lower concentrations of all POMC-related peptides. These concentrations normalized with weight recovery, and no differences were observed between the long-term recovered and normal control groups (Kaye et al., 1987). Thus, at least while underweight, patients with AN may have decreased POMC function. This should lessen their response to leptin and facilitate weight gain.

Summary of Brain Function and Eating Disorders

The hypothalamus is responsible for the regulation of food intake and weight. The lateral hypothalamus increases eating and weight, and the paraventricular and ventromedial hypothalami are associated with decreased eating and weight. However, these basic functions can be activated or inhibited, depending upon what neurochemical is active in a given area. For example, 5-HT in the paraventricular nucleus of the hypothalamus and medial hypothalamus enhances the activity of this area in reducing food intake, but dopamine and norepinephrine in the medial hypothalamus inhibit its activity, resulting in increased food intake. Given these complex associations, it is not surprising that inconsistent results have been found for neurochemical correlates of eating disorders. Further, given that many of the observed differences disappear after recovery, studies of neurophysiological function in patients with eating disorders may represent consequences of the illness more than causes. However, evidence of postrecovery differences in leptin concentrations in BN, and of 5-HIAA concentrations in AN, provide some hints to conditions that might predate and contribute to the onset of eating disorders.

GENETIC CONTRIBUTIONS TO EATING DISORDERS

As described briefly in Chapter 6, eating disorders run in families. In family studies, the individual affected with an eating disorder is referred to as a **proband.** Biological relatives of eating disorder probands are 5 to 12 times more likely to have an eating disorder compared to individuals in the general population or relatives of individuals without eating disorders (Lilenfeld et al., 1998; Stein et al., 1999; Strober et al., 1990; Strober, Freeman, Lampert, Diamond, & Kaye, 2000; Strober, Morrell, Burroughs, Salkin, & Jacobs, 1985; Woodside, Field, Garfinkel, & Heinmaa, 1998). **First-degree relatives** (e.g., mothers, sisters, and daughters) are more likely to suffer from eating disorders than **second-degree** (e.g., aunts, grandmothers, and granddaughters) or **third-degree relatives** (e.g., cousins) (Strober, Freeman, Lampert, Diamond, & Kaye, 2001; Woodside et al., 1998). Chapter 6 discussed how children may learn disordered eating behaviors and attitudes in their rearing environment. However, families share **genes** as well as environments. In order to differentiate the influence of genes from the influence of environment, twin studies have been conducted (see Chapter 4 for a full discussion of the basic design and logic of twin study methods).

Twin Studies

Population-based twin studies in Virginia, Minnesota, Australia, and Denmark indicate that genes play an important role in the development of eating disorders. These investigations found high rates of concordance in MZ compared to DZ twins and reported high **heritability estimates** (a percentage representing how much genes contribute to the development of an eating disorder in a given group of people). Heritability estimates have ranged up to 76% for AN (Klump, Miller, Keel, Iacono, & McGue, 2001) and up to 83% for BN (Bulik, Sullivan, & Kendler, 1998b). Supporting these results, high heritability estimates have also been reported for disordered eating attitudes and behaviors (Rutherford, McGuffin, Katz, & Murray, 1993; Sullivan et al., 1998b; Wade et al., 1999).

Questions have been raised about whether findings from twin studies can be taken at face value. Fichter and Noegel (1990) posited that being a member of a twin pair, particularly an MZ twin pair, might decrease the development of independence and, consequently, increase the risk of eating disorders. If this is true, then twins would not be representative of the general population (a violation of the **representativeness assumption**), and findings from twin studies would not accurately reflect how eating disorders develop in nontwins. Supporting this concern, Waters and colleagues (1990) reported clinical differences between eating disorders in twins and nontwins. Similarly, Klump, Keel, Leon, and Fulkerson (1999) found that twins may be at increased risk for disordered eating compared to nontwins. This was particularly true for DZ twins in this small school-based study. Studies using larger population-based twin samples have found that twins and nontwins were at equal risk for several different types of psychopathology, including eating disorders, and no differences in clinical presentation have been reported in these investigations (Kendler, Martin, Heath, & Eaves, 1995; Klump, Kaye, & Strober, 2001a).

As described in Chapter 4, an assumption of twin models is that members of twin pairs reared together (whether MZ or DZ) share 100% of their home environment (**equal environments assumption**). Nevertheless, members of an MZ twin pair may be treated more similarly than members of a DZ twin pair, particularly in relation to comments about their appearance. A greater similarity in environment, rather than a higher percentage of shared genes, might explain why MZ twins are more similar in eating disorders compared to DZ twins. Supporting this concern, physical similarity (Hettema, Neale, & Kendler, 1995) and socializing with cotwins (Kendler & Gardner, 1998) are significantly greater in MZ compared to DZ twins and are significant predictors of BN concordance in twins. However, Klump, Holly, Iacono, McGue, and Willson (2000b) found that neither general physical similarity nor body size/shape similarity was significantly associated with twin similarity for eating attitudes and behaviors. Thus, although violations of the representativeness and equal environments assumptions have been found, they do not fully account for the greater similarity in eating disorders between MZ compared to DZ twins.

In attempting to understand what inherited factor increases the risk of eating disorders, researchers have examined several possible traits. Family, twin, and adoption studies have yielded significant heritability estimates for BMI (Allison, Heshka, Neale, Lykken, & Heymsfield, 1994; De Castro, 1999; Koeppen-Schomerus, Wardle, & Plomin, 2001) and daily diet (De Castro, 1999). It is possible that most people lack the genetic makeup that would enable them to develop AN. This could explain the relatively low prevalence of AN despite a ubiquitous cultural idealization of an extremely thin ideal.

Similar to studies of body weight, studies of personality traits suggest substantial genetic influence, including those traits hypothesized to contribute to the risk of developing an eating disorder (see Chapter 7). Using a population-based twin sample, Klump, McGue, and Iacono (2002) found that associations between personality and disordered eating were best explained by shared genetic factors (rather than shared environment). However, only a limited proportion (2–22%) of the genetic influence on disordered eating was shared with personality. Thus, although significant associations between personality traits and eating pathology have been found, and although these associations are best explained by shared genetic factors, the majority of genetic influences on disordered eating appear to be independent of personality (Klump et al., 2002).

In summary, twin studies have yielded impressive estimates of heritability for eating disorders. Although adoption studies have been used to evaluate the heritability of body weight and personality traits (Plomin, DeFries, McClearn, & McGuffin, 2001), this design has yet to be employed in examining eating disorders. Such research could provide useful insights into the ways genes and environment act together to increase the risk of eating disorders. While twin studies provide compelling evidence of a genetic contribution to eating disorders, they cannot reveal the influence or action of specific genes. Following advances in human genome mapping, an exciting avenue of research examines specific genetic loci associated with the increased risk of eating disorders.

Molecular Genetic Studies

A gene is a sequence of **deoxyribonucleic acid (DNA)** that is transcribed into a specific sequence of **ribonucleic acid (RNA)** that assists in building a chain of amino acids into proteins. For example, a gene could code for a neurotransmitter receptor. An **allele** is one of several forms of the same gene. For a given gene, children receive a single allele from each parent. The resulting combination of alleles for a given gene is called a **genotype.** For some genes, there are only two possible forms of an allele. For other genes, there are numerous different forms an allele can take. When the alleles received from each parent are the same, the result is a **homozygous** genotype. When the alleles received from each parent differ, the result is a **heterozygous** genotype. (See Figure 8–1.) The effects of different genotypes (i.e., different combinations of alleles for a given gene) can range from differences in eye color, to the ability to curl one's tongue into a U shape, to the risk of developing an eating disorder. The observable manifestation of a genotype is referred to as a **phenotype.** Thus, in the search for specific genes that increase the risk of an eating disorder, eating disorders represent phenotypes.

Unlike results from family and twin studies, well-replicated results have yet to emerge from studies examining the specific genes that increase the risk of developing an eating disorder. Most molecular genetic research has involved **association studies** in which the frequency of alleles for specific genes (*candidate genes*) are compared between individuals affected with a disorder and those unaffected. For example, several **candidate gene studies** have examined allele frequencies for the gene that codes for building the 5-HT$_{2A}$ receptor. There are two possible alleles for this gene, A and G, that can be combined into three distinct genotypes (A/A, A/G, or G/G; note: A/G and G/A are

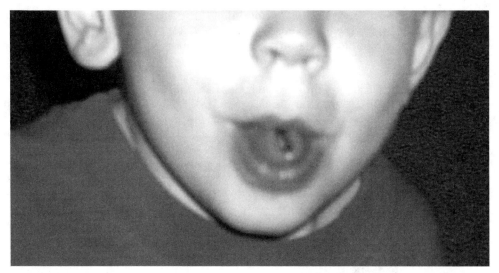

Ability to curl tongue into a U-shape is determined by a single dominant gene.

functionally the same genotype). If individuals with eating disorders are more likely than controls to have a specific allele (for example, A) or genotype (for example A/A), then this supports an association between the given gene and its function in the risk of developing an eating disorder.

In **transmission disequilibrium tests (TDT),** the frequency of allele transmission from heterozygous parents to affected offspring is compared to that expected if there is

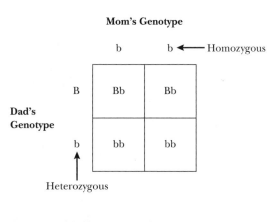

Genotype = bb, Phenotype = Blue eyes
Genotype = Bb, Phenotype = Brown eyes
Genotype = BB, Phenotype = Brown eyes

FIGURE 8–1 Punnett square for eye color.

Four squares represent possible genotypes for children of a Mom with the bb genotype and Dad with the Bb genotype.

no association between the allele and the disorder. For example, in a sample of parents who all have the heterozygous A/G genotype for the 5-HT_{2A} receptor gene, approximately 25% of children should receive the homozygous A/A genotype, 25% should receive the homozygous G/G genotype, and 50% should receive the heterozygous A/G phenotype by chance (because 25% should receive A/G and 25% should receive G/A, and these are functionally the same genotype; see the Punnett square on page 113). If it is found that children with an eating disorder who all have heterozygous parents are more likely to have a specific allele (e.g., A) or genotype (e.g., A/A) than predicted by chance, this supports an association between that gene and the risk of developing an eating disorder.

Both candidate gene studies and TDT studies rely on identifying a specific gene to examine. In contrast, a **genome-wide linkage study** evaluates alleles at several **genetic markers.** Genetic markers are places in the **genome** where known genes reside, regardless of the specific function of the gene. This analysis looks at all genes in relatives who have an eating disorder to detect alleles that are shared more frequently than would be expected by chance. These various approaches have produced a number of interesting leads.

Candidate Gene Studies

Genes that impact 5-HT function represent prime candidates for understanding the genetic etiology of eating disorders. Particular attention has been given to the gene for the 5-HT_{2A} receptor. In 1997, Collier and colleagues reported an increased frequency of the A allele and the A/A genotype of the 5-HT_{2A} receptor gene in patients with AN compared to controls. Thus, genes that code for the receptors may influence changes in 5-HT receptor function discussed earlier in the chapter. Five studies have reported this finding, and one study indicated an association between bulimic symptoms and the G allele (see Table 8–2). In contrast, six other studies did not find an association between eating disorders and the 5-HT_{2A} receptor gene (see Table 8–2).

Substantial differences in eating disorder phenotypes may account for inconsistent findings. For example, three studies (Nacmias et al., 1999; Ricca et al., 2002; Sorbi et al., 1998) have suggested that the A allele and A/A genotype for the 5-HT_{2A} gene are more common in ANR than in ANBP. Less consistent findings surround less frequently studied components of the serotonergic system, including the 5-HT_{2C} receptor gene (Hu et al., 2003; Karwautz et al., 2001; Nacmias et al., 1999; Westberg et al., 2002) and the 5-HT transporter gene (Di Bella, Catalano, Cavallini, Riboldi, & Bellodi, 2000; Hinney et al., 1997a; Lauzurica et al., 2003; Sundaramurthy, Pieri, Gape, Markham, & Campbell, 2000; see Table 8–2).

As can be seen in Table 8–3, no other candidate genes have produced findings to equal those associated with the 5-HT_{2A} receptor. Of interest, two studies have reported an association between the estrogen beta receptor gene and AN (Eastwood, Brown, Markovic, & Pieri, 2002; Rosenkranz et al., 1998). This result may explain observed developmental changes in heritability for disordered eating attitudes and behaviors. As described in Chapter 6, Klump and colleagues (2000c) found that 17-year-old twins exhibited a greater genetic influence on eating attitudes and behaviors than 11-year-old twins. In a subsequent investigation, Klump and colleagues (2003) reported increased heritability of disordered eating in postpubertal compared to prepubertal 11-year-old twins. The authors hypothesized that the release of estrogen during puberty may activate genes that increase the risk of eating disorders. This would explain why eating disorders usually begin after the onset of puberty and provides another possible explanation for the increased prevalence of eating disorders in women compared to men.

TABLE 8–2   Candidate Genes Studies of Serotonin System

Study	Candidate Gene	Result
Collier et al. (1997)	5-HT_{2A} receptor	AN > controls for A allele and A/A genotype
Enoch et al. (1998)	5-HT_{2A} receptor	AN > BN, controls for A allele and A/A genotype
Sorbi et al. (1998)	5-HT_{2A} receptor	ANR > ANP, controls for A allele and A/A genotype
Nacmias et al. (1999)	5-HT_{2A} receptor	ANR > ANP, BNP, controls for A allele and A/A genotype on 5-HT_{2A} receptor gene
	5-HT_{2C} receptor	No difference for 5-HT_{2C} receptor gene
Nishiguchi et al. (2001)	5-HT_{2A} receptor	ANB, BN > ANR, controls for G allele
Kipman et al. (2002)	5-HT_{2A} receptor	AN, controls no difference
		AN (mean age at onset = 15.28) > AN (mean age at onset = 14.01) for A allele
Ricca et al. (2002)	5-HT_{2A} receptor	Obese BED, obese non-BED, controls no difference
	5-HT_{2A} receptor	AN, ANR, BN > controls for A allele and A/A genotype
	5-HT_{2A} receptor	ANP, controls no difference
Hinney et al. (1997c)	5-HT_{2A} receptor	AN, obese controls, underweight controls no difference
Campbell et al. (1998)	5-HT_{2A} receptor	AN, controls no difference
Hinney et al. (1999a)	5-HT_{1DB} receptor	AN, obese controls, underweight controls no difference
	5-HT_7 receptor	
Karwautz et al. (2001)	5-HT_{2A} receptor	AN, unaffected sisters no difference
	5-HT_{2C} receptor	
Ziegler et al. (1999)	5-HT_{2A} receptor	AN, BN, controls no difference
Ando et al. (2001)	5-HT_{2A} receptor	AN, controls no difference
Hu et al. (2003)	5-HT_{2C} receptor	AN > controls for Ser 23 allele and Ser 23/Ser 23 genotype
Hinney et al. (1997a)	5-HT transporter gene	AN, obese controls, underweight controls no difference
Sundaramurthy et al. (2000)	5-HT transporter gene	AN, controls no difference
Di Bella et al. (2000)	5-HT transporter gene	BN > controls for s allele and s/s genotype
	5-HT transporter gene	ANR, ANBP, controls no difference
Lauzurica et al. (2003)	5-HT transporter gene	BN, BN with prior AN, controls no difference

Note: Participants in the study of Nacmias et al. (1999) are included in the study of Ricca et al. (2002).

Transmission Disequilibrium Test Studies

Gorwood et al. (2002) examined transmission of the A and G alleles of the 5-HT_{2A} receptor gene from heterozygous (A/G genotype) parents of offspring with AN. The distribution of the A and G alleles did not differ significantly from that expected by chance. However, a follow-up investigation analyzing a subset of patients with an older age of onset demonstrated increased transmission of the A allele for the 5-HT_{2A} receptor gene (Kipman et al., 2002). Kipman and colleagues suggested that the 5-HT_{2A} receptor gene may contribute to the etiology of AN in patients who develop the eating disorder in mid-adolescence or later. Most studies of other candidate genes using the TDT have not

TABLE 8–3   Candidate Genes Studies of Other Systems

Study	Study Groups	Candidate Gene	Difference Between Groups
Bruins-Slot et al. (1998)	AN Controls	Dopamine$_{D3}$ receptor	No
Hinney et al. (1999b)	AN Obese controls Underweight controls	Dopamine$_{D4}$ receptor	No
Karwautz et al. (2001)	AN Unaffected sisters	Dopamine$_{D4}$ receptor	No
Hinney et al. (1998)	AN BN Obese controls Underweight controls Healthy controls	Section of gene that controls leptin gene function	No
Hinney et al. (1997b)	AN Obese controls Underweight controls Healthy controls	β-andronergic receptor (influences leptin function)	No
Vink et al. (2001)	AN Controls	Melanocortin 4-receptor	Yes
Branson et al. (2003)	Severely obese Controls (examined association between gene mutation and binge eating)	Melanocortin 4-receptor	Yes
Rosenkranz et al. (1998b)	AN Obese Underweight	Neuropeptide Y_1 receptor Neuropeptide Y_5 receptor	No
Eastwood et al. (2002)	AN Controls	Estrogen$_2$ receptor Estrogen$_1$ receptor	Yes No
Rosenkranz et al. (1998a)	AN BN Obese controls Underweight controls	Estrogen$_2$ receptor	Yes

reported significant findings for eating disorders (Hinney et al., 1997b, 1999b; Rosenkranz et al., 1998b; Sundaramurthy, Pieri, Gape, Markham, & Campbell, 2000; Urwin, Bennetts, Wilcken, Beumont, Russell, & Nunn, 2003).

Genome-Wide Linkage Study

Because genome-wide linkage studies examine alleles at multiple **genetic markers** across the genome, study results are interpreted according to locations on chromosomes that may hold genes that contribute to the etiology of eating disorders. One genome-wide linkage study found that alleles on chromosome 4 were more likely to be similar in AN probands and their eating-disordered relatives than expected by chance (Grice et al., 2002). When analyses were restricted to relatives who both had ANR, a more significant result was found on chromosome 1 (Grice et al., 2002). A recent follow-up study of this result (Bergen et al., 2003) suggested that genes for the 5-HT$_{1D}$ receptor and the opioid delta receptor on chromosome 1 might contribute to the risk of AN. A genome-wide linkage analysis of BN probands and their eating-disordered relatives in which all individuals engaged in self-induced vomiting suggested that genes on chromosome 10p may contribute to the risk of developing BN (Bulik et al., 2003).

Overall, the most promising findings have emerged for genes related to the function of 5-HT. Although candidate gene and TDT studies are theoretically informed and have yielded interesting results, they represent a somewhat limited approach for exploring potential genetic loci compared to a genome-wide linkage study. Both candidate gene and TDT studies rely on a good working knowledge of the biological antecedents (versus consequences) of eating disorders in order to identify candidate genes. Given the nature of eating disorders, it is difficult to disentangle such factors. As can be seen from Tables 8–2 and 8–3, most molecular genetic studies have investigated AN and not BN or BED. Thus, little is known about the genes that may increase the risk of these disorders.

Conclusions about Genetic Contributions to the Risk of Eating Disorders

Behavioral genetic studies have clearly supported a genetic diathesis to eating disorders, but molecular genetic studies have yet to clearly identify the specific genes that increase the risk. This is likely a reflection of the early stage of molecular genetic research in this area as well as the etiologic complexity of these disorders. As with most psychiatric disorders, the genetic diathesis to eating disorders is likely to involve **complex inheritance** rather than **Mendelian inheritance** (Risch & Merikangas, 1993). Mendelian inheritance refers to the action of a single gene on the expression of a phenotype (such as eye color). Complex inheritance refers to the combined action of many genes on the expression of a phenotype. Notably, all candidate gene studies examine the association between phenotypes and a single gene as if a single gene will account for the genetic risk for eating disorders.

Two epidemiological patterns suggest that it is unlikely that a single gene could account for the genetic risk for eating disorders. First, eating disorders are associated with a higher prevalence than typical Mendelian diseases. This is because diseases that are associated with decreased ability to survive and have children (decreased **reproductive fitness**) tend to be quickly eliminated from the gene pool, as individuals with those genes die without reproducing. Second, the risk of eating disorders to first-degree relatives of eating-disordered probands (risk ratio) is far below that expected in Mendelian diseases with a dominant gene (5000:1) or a recessive gene (2500:1). Although **reduced penetrance** (the genotype does not lead to the phenotype), **variable expressivity** (the genotype leads to variable phenotypes), and **phenocopies** (the phenotype occurs in the absence of the genotype) diminish the risk the ratios for Mendelian diseases, these ratios remain well above those reported for eating disorders (5:1 to 12:1). In complex inheritance, each gene contributes a small amount to developing a disorder, and a large number of research participants is needed to show a reliable effect of a specific gene. Thus, some inconsistencies in research findings may be caused by inadequate sample sizes. An additional challenge in the search for genetic susceptibility loci is difficulty defining eating disorder phenotypes. Unlike eye color, where it is reasonably easy to conclude that brown and blue represent different colors (and different phenotypes), it remains unclear whether ANR and ANBP represent one or two disorders. Thus, more research on the definition of eating disorders is necessary to identify valid phenotypes. This research will, in turn, allow more efficient progress toward establishing the genetic underpinnings of eating disorders.

Given the challenges facing molecular genetic research, the findings suggesting an association between the 5-HT$_{2A}$ receptor and AN are quite promising. It is also important to acknowledge an advantage that molecular genetic research has in the search for the biological bases of eating disorders. Unlike other potential biological contributors, gene sequences do not alter as a function of the presence or absence of an eating disorder. Thus, it is possible to examine candidate genes among individuals with eating disorders without worrying that an association between a specific genotype and the presence of an eating disorder reflects the effect of the eating disorder on the genome. This represents a significant advantage because eating disorders produce profound effects on the body.

PHYSICAL CONSEQUENCES OF EATING DISORDERS

For many studies of neurotransmitter and neuropeptide function in individuals with eating disorders, it is not possible to determine whether the dysfunction predated the presence of the eating disorder or represents a consequence of the eating disorder. When the body has inadequate resources to maintain body weight and must revert to fat stores, other physical changes necessarily follow. This section discusses known physical consequences of eating disorders that are not believed to have a role in the onset or maintenance of eating disorders. As an overview to this section, Table 8–4 presents the medical complications frequently associated with eating disorders.

Neuroanatomical Changes

Patients with AN have increased ventrical size compared to healthy controls (Katzman, Zipursky, Lambe, & Mikulis, 1997; Kingston, Szmukler, Andrewes, Tress, & Desmond, 1996; Krieg et al., 1989; Swayze et al., 1996). Ventricles contain cerebrospinal fluid, and relative increases in ventrical size reflect relative decreases in brain mass (loss of gray and white matter). Thus, in addition to triggering the breakdown of fat, muscle, and bone, starvation triggers the breakdown of brain matter. Some of the lost brain matter is regained with recovery (Kingston et al., 1996; Swayze et al., 1996); however, evidence of diminished gray matter persists after recovery from AN (Katzman et al., 1997).

Bone Mineral Density

Several studies have demonstrated decreased bone mineral density and increased rates of osteoporosis in patients with AN compared to controls (Grinspoon et al., 1999; Hotta, Shibasaki, Sato, & Demura, 1998). Bone mineral loss has been attributed to a combination of starvation and hormonal changes that result from starvation—notably decreased concentrations of sex hormones such as estrogen and progesterone and increased concentrations of cortisol. In addition, the diets of patients with AN are often nutritionally imbalanced, with overconsumption of caffeine and underconsumption of calcium-rich foods (Newman & Halmi, 1989). Like Emily, many patients with eating disorders learn about the effects of starvation on bone mineral density through research participation.

TABLE 8–4   Medical Complications of Eating Disorders (by Major Organ System)

A	B	C	Medical Complication	Definition
Cardiovascular				
A	B	C	Orthostatis/hypotension	Low blood pressure
A			Bradycardia	Slow heart beat
A		C	Congestive heart failure	Loss of heart function
A	B	C	EKG abnormalities	Abnormal heart beat patterns
A			Refeeding cardiomyopathy	Loss of heart tissue
A			Refeeding edema	Swelling/water retention
		C	Arrythmias	Irregular heart beat
A	B	C	Sudden cardiac death	Sudden heart attack leading to death
Renal/Electrolytes				
A	B	C	Dehydration	Decreased body fluid
A	B	C	Decreased glomerular filtration rate	Decrease in kidneys' ability to filter and remove waste products from blood
A	B	C	Abnormal electrolytes	Abnormal concentrations of electrically charged substances in blood
A	B	C	Kaliopenic nephropathy	A condition of the kidneys that causes insufficiency of potassium in the body
A			Refeeding edema	Swelling/water retention
		C	Reflex edema (after cessation of laxatives/diuretics)	Swelling/water retention
Endocrine				
A			Growth Retardation	Delayed maturation
A			Delayed onset puberty	Delayed menarche
A	B		Abnormal HPG axis function	Disrupted sex hormones
A			Abnormal HPA axis function	Disrupted stress hormones
A			Abnormal thyroid function	Disrupted mood and appetite hormones
Gastrointestinal				
	B		Parotid gland swelling	Swelling of salivary glands
	B		Hyperamylasemia	Elevated blood concentrations of salivary gland enzyme that helps to digest glycogen and starch
	B		Esophageal tear	Tear in the esophagus
	B		Mallory-Weiss tears	Tears in the esophagus' mucus between esophagus and stomach
A	B	C	Delayed gastric emptying	Slowed digestion of food in stomach
A			Superior mesentery artery syndrome	Partial obstruction of the intestine by the superior mesenteric artery
	B		Gastric dilation/rupture	Enlargement of and tear in stomach
A			Refeeding pancreatitis	Infection/irritation of pancreas
A	B	C	Constipation	Inability to pass solid waste
		C	Melanosis coli	Dark discoloration of colon's mucus after long-standing use of certain laxatives
		C	Steatorrhea/protein-losing gastroenteropathy	Fecal matter that is frothy, foul-smelling, and floats due to high fat content
		C	Cathartic colon	Anatomic and physiologic change in the colon following use of stimulant laxatives
A	B	C	Hypokalemic ileus	Temporary immobility of intestine, preventing the passage of solid waste caused by low blood potassium levels

(continued)

TABLE 8–4 *(continued)*

A	B	C	Medical Complication	Definition
Metabolic				
A			Osteoporosis/osteopenia	Loss of bone mass
A	B	C	Trace mineral deficiencies	Decreased minerals
A	B	C	Vitamin deficiencies	Decreased vitamins
A			Hypercholesterolemia	Increased blood cholesterol
	B	C	Obesity	Overweight
Pulmonary				
	B		Subcutaneous emphysema	Presence of air beneath skin
	B		Pneumomediastinum	Rupture of alveoli of lungs
	B		Aspiration pneumonitis	Lung infection/irritation caused by inhaling Vomit
Dermatological				
A			Hair loss	Balding
A			Lanugo-like hair growth	Fine, downy hair covering body
A			Dry skin, brittle hair, nails	Caused by lack of fat in diet
A			Petechia, purpura	Discolorations in the skin caused by small bleeding vessels near skin surface
	B		Finger calluses/abrasions	Caused by friction against teeth while gagging
Hematological/Immunological				
A			Anemia	Decreased iron in blood
A			Leukopenia with relative lymphocytosis	Decreased white blood cells with unusually high number of normal lymphocytes
A			Thrombocytopenia	Decreased platelets in the blood, resulting in decreased clotting/increased bleeding
A			Abnormal CD4/CD8 counts	
A			Abnormal cytokines	Disrupt cell-cell communication; thought to directly act on hypothalamic neurons
Neurological				
A			Enlarged ventricles	Loss of gray matter in the brain
A	B		Sleep disorders	Disrupted sleep patterns
A	B		Abnormal position emission tornography scans	Disrupted brain use of glucose
Other				
	B		Dental complications	Increased cavities and gum infections
A			Impaired thermoregulation	Low body temperature
	B	C	Vitamin K–deficient coagulopathy	Defect in the blood clotting
		C	Skeletal muscle myopathy	Loss of muscle

Note: Column A indicates conditions that are due to the starvation of AN. Column B indicates conditions that are due to the binge/purge symptoms of BN and BP. PAN. Column C indicates conditions that are due to other symptoms of eating disorders.

Source: Adapted from Pomeroy (2001).

Case Study

As part of Emily's participation in the research study, the results of her bone scan were given to her doctor. The doctor shared them with Emily. The scan indicated that Emily's bone mineral density was 35% lower than expected for her age. When asked what this meant, the doctor explained that because of Emily's diet and weight loss, her body had begun to feed on itself. This was the process that produced weight loss; however, the weight loss was not restricted to a loss of fat. It included a loss of muscle and bone. A consequence of decreased bone mineral density was an increased risk of bone fractures. Essentially, Emily at 20 years of age had the bone structure of a woman past menopause. Her doctor prescribed calcium supplements to help Emily regain bone tissue. However, Emily was told that the best way to reverse this damage was to gain weight.

Consequences of Purging

Purging through self-induced vomiting and severe laxative and diuretic abuse has been associated with electrolyte imbalances in the bloodstream (Mitchell, Pyle, Eckert, Hatsukami, & Lentz, 1983; Mitchell, Seim, Colon, & Pomeroy, 1987). Specifically, the loss of stomach acid in vomit decreases the presence of positively charged ions such as potassium (K^+). In addition, patients with eating disorders can have decreased blood concentrations of magnesium (Mg^+) and calcium (Ca^+). Electrolyte imbalances can contribute to fluid retention (**edema**) when patients attempt to reduce disordered eating patterns (Mitchell, Pomeroy, Seppala, & Huber, 1988).

Self-induced vomiting can also contribute to significant dental problems because the stomach acid in vomit erodes tooth enamel. This leaves teeth vulnerable to plaque and bacteria (Milosevic, 1999; Simmons, Grayden, & Mitchell, 1986). Although this is not a life-threatening consequence, it can cause tooth loss and the need for dentures at a young age. Esophageal tears represent a rare, but serious, consequence of using fingers or instruments to produce vomiting by inducing a gag reflex (Mitchell, 1990). Use of fingers to induce vomiting can also cause calluses to develop on the hand (known as *Russell's sign*). Self-induced vomiting also can lead to swelling of the salivary (parotid) glands. Because of the location of the parotid glands near the face, this side effect sometimes results in increased frequency of self-induced vomiting, as patients misinterpret this symptom as a "fat face." This consequence of purging may have increased Jean's dislike of her face described in Chapter 5.

Case Study

Jean was startled when a dental hygienist asked if Jean had ever had an eating disorder. Jean lied and said that she had not. Later, she asked the hygienist the reason for the question. The hygienist explained that Jean had some tooth enamel erosion that was consistent with purging. In addition, she commented that self-induced vomiting was associated with swelling of the salivary glands, and she had noticed that Jean's cheeks appeared a little swollen. Jean said that she had always had round "chipmunk" cheeks. However, later that day, Jean looked at pictures of herself in her photo album. She realized that her face did look more round than it had when she wasn't purging.

Mortality

Finally, eating disorders can lead to death. Mortality as an outcome will be reviewed in more detail in Chapter 11. AN can lead to death by starvation. At a certain point, the body cannot function without fuel, and multiple organ failure occurs. The body can be substantially weakened by prolonged starvation, and death can occur as a consequence of an infection that would not normally be life-threatening. For example, pneumonia is a rare cause of death in healthy young women. However, for a young woman physically weakened by AN, pneumonia becomes a more significant threat to life. Consequences of specific symptoms can interfere with organ function on a cellular level. For example, low potassium concentrations (known as *hypokalemia*) can contribute to heart failure and kidney failure, particularly in individuals whose organs have been weakened by a sustained state of starvation.

CONCLUSION

The contribution of biology to the etiology of eating disorders is indisputable. Studies of 5-HT function in individuals with eating disorders indicate several abnormalities; however, many of these normalize upon recovery. Of interest, there has been a finding of decreased 5-HT function following recovery in women with BN (Kaye, 2001a) and increased 5-HT function following recovery in patients with AN (Kaye et al., 1991a). These results await replication. Clear evidence supports the role of genes in increasing the risk of developing an eating disorder. Mirroring results from physiological studies, preliminary results suggest that genes involved in 5-HT function may increase the risk of eating disorders.

Many of the studies of biological function in patients with eating disorders likely represent correlates or consequences of the disorder. To the extent that biological indices are directly correlated with the severity of symptoms in terms of low weight or binge frequency, studies may be indexing state rather than trait qualities. Further, the influence of eating disorders on biological function has long been appreciated. It is difficult to dramatically alter food intake without causing significant alterations in the biological function of an organism. Understanding the biological consequences of eating disorders is an important area of inquiry, as it may improve our understanding of the treatment and long-term outcome associated with these disorders.

KEY TERMS

Agonist
Allele
Association studies
Candidate gene study
Cholecystokinin
Complex inheritance
Deoxyribonucleic acid (DNA)
Dopamine
Down-regulation
Edema
Equal environments assumption
First-degree relative
Gene

Genetic markers
Genome
Genome-wide linkage study
Genotype
Heritability estimate
Heterozygous
Homovanillic acid (HVA)
Homozygous
Hypothalamic-pituitary-adrenal (HPA) axis
Hypothalamic-pituitary-gonadal (HPG) axis
Hypothalamus

Lateral
Leptin
Melanocyte-stimulating hormone (MSH)
Mendelian inheritance
Neuron
Neuropeptide Y
Neuropeptides
Neurotransmitters
Norepinephrine
Paraventricular nucleus
Phenocopy
Phenotype
Proband
Prolactin
Proopiomelanocortin (POMC)
Pyloric sphincter

Receptor
Reduced penetrance
Representativeness assumption
Reproductive fitness
Reuptake
Ribonucleic acid (RNA)
Second-degree relative
Serotonin (5-HT)
Third-degree relative
Transmission disequilibrium test (TDT)
study
Tryptophan
Up-regulation
Vagus nerve
Variable expressivity
Ventromedial

CHAPTER 9

Treatment

This chapter covers interventions designed to remedy eating disorders. Use of different types of treatment will be reviewed to provide an overview of the amount, type, and cost of treatments received by patients with eating disorders (treatment use). Following this, a discussion of the rationale and specific techniques associated with different methods of intervention will be presented. In addition, evidence of success associated with different types of treatment will be reviewed. Long-term effects of treatment will be reviewed in Chapter 11.

TREATMENT USE

As reviewed in Chapter 8, AN is associated with serious medical complications. Thus, many individuals with the disorder require medical as well as psychological treatment. This increases both the amount and the cost of treatment associated with AN. In the United States, Striegel-Moore, (Leslie, Petrill, Garvin, and Rosenheck 2000a) reported that female patients with AN averaged 26 days of inpatient care and 17 days of outpatient care during 1 year. Costs associated with this care were $19,728 per female patient per year. In contrast, male patients with AN averaged 16 days of inpatient care and 9 days of outpatient care per year.

Among individuals who had received inpatient care for AN in Germany, Fichter and Quadflieg (1999) reported that 63% of women received further inpatient treatment. Levels of outpatient care were also high, with approximately 89% of women receiving some form of outpatient care during follow-up. This treatment comprised an average of 69 individual sessions, 5 group sessions, and less than 1 family session per patient. Thus, patients with AN often require extensive and costly treatment for their eating disorder.

Although most women who suffer from BN may never seek treatment (Fairburn, Cooper, Doll, Norman, & O'Connor, 2000; Fairburn et al., 1996), treatment use is high among those who do. In the United States, Striegel-Moore et al. (2000a) reported that female patients with BN averaged 15 days of inpatient care and 16 days of outpatient care during 1 year. Costs associated with this care were $10,970 per female patient per year. Male patients averaged 22 days of inpatient care and 9 days of outpatient care per year.

Among individuals who had received inpatient treatment for BN in Germany, Fichter and Quadflieg (1997) reported that 67% of women received additional inpatient treatment. Levels of outpatient care were also high, with approximately 83% of women receiving some form of outpatient care following hospital discharge. This treatment comprised an average of 59 individual sessions, 11 group sessions, and 1 family session per patient.

Women with AN spent significantly more days and money in inpatient treatment compared to women with BN. This likely reflects the increased need for medical care in AN. However, no significant differences in days or cost of outpatient treatment existed between women with AN compared to women with BN (Keel et al., 2002a; Keel & Herzog, 2004). Similarly, treatment with antidepressants or anxiolytics did not differ between AN and BN (Keel et al., 2002a). Although inpatient care did not differ between female and male patients in Striegel-Moore et al.'s (2000a) study, women received significantly more outpatient care. This may reflect reluctance among male sufferers to seek treatment for a disorder strongly associated with women. It may also reflect reduced recognition of eating disorders in individuals who do not match the stereotype for an eating disorder (see Chapter 3 for a discussion of eating disorder stereotypes). Other predictors of increased treatment use in eating disorders included a combination of greater symptom severity, worse psychosocial function, and the presence of personality disorders and mood disorders (Keel et al., 2002a). Thus, more severe problems lead to increased treatment use. This may reflect the role of personal suffering in motivating the search for treatment. It may also reflect the extent to which an individual with a more severe disorder may take longer to recover and therefore need continued treatment.

Fewer data are available for treatment use among individuals with BED. Given the prevalence of BED among individuals seeking weight loss, it seems likely that many individuals with the disorder may seek treatment for their weight problems rather than traditional psychological treatment for their eating behaviors. Fichter, Quadflieg, and Gnutzmann (1998) reported that 66% of patients with BED received additional inpatient treatment following discharge from an inpatient program, suggesting that treatment use for BED is comparable to that for AN and BN in Germany. In contrast, Fairburn and colleagues (2000) reported that as few as 8% of individuals with BED ever received any treatment for an eating disorder compared to 40% of individuals with BN in England.

Notably, studies of treatment use do not provide a direct measure of treatment needs. In Striegel-Moore et al.'s (2000a) study, only 0.06% of female patients in the National Insurance Claims database were treated for eating disorders. This rate is much lower than the prevalence of eating disorders, suggesting that the majority of women with eating disorders may not receive treatment. Individuals may not receive the treatment they need because of lack of money, lack of access, lack of interest, or any combination of these factors. Specific problems with lack of insurance coverage for the level of care needed to treat eating disorders have been noted (Franko & Erb, 1998; Silber & Robb, 2002).

Review of treatment use reveals that most individuals with eating disorders may never receive any form of treatment. To some extent, this reflects the imbalance between the large number of individuals who suffer from eating disorders and the small number of clinicians available to help them (Levine & Smolak, 2001). This imbalance has led many researchers to argue for the importance of prevention (Austin, 2000; Levine & Smolak, 2001), which will be discussed in the next chapter. However, for patients with access to treatment, a wide range of options may be available. The following section discusses different types of treatment that are used for eating disorders.

TREATMENT MODALITIES

Inpatient Treatment

Inpatient treatment represents the most expensive treatment and, for many patients like Emily, the least desirable form of treatment for eating disorders. The primary rationale for inpatient treatment is to achieve medical safety in a controlled environment. For individuals who seem unable to interrupt their eating-disordered behaviors despite imminent health risks, inpatient treatment provides a safe environment where they will be prevented from hurting themselves. Most often, inpatient treatment is used for individuals with AN who are dangerously underweight because of the severe medical consequences related to starvation (see Chapter 8). Inpatient treatment is also employed for patients who purge very frequently because of the dangerous electrolyte imbalances that accompany this symptom.

Case Study

In addition to seeing a doctor to monitor her medical condition, Emily began seeing a psychologist and a nutritionist. However, she continued to lose weight over the first 4 weeks of treatment. In therapy, Emily admitted that she was afraid of becoming fat as a result of treatment and that she had been increasing her weight loss efforts to protect against this potential outcome. However, Emily's weight was now critically low, and her treatment team feared that she might go into cardiac arrest. They informed her that she needed inpatient treatment. Emily pleaded that she would be able to gain weight on her own and that she had not been "truly trying." However, her treatment team informed her that this would be unsafe because the process of regaining weight could be dangerous once weight dropped below a certain point. Reluctantly, Emily agreed to enter an inpatient eating disorders treatment program. She hated the program, hated the loss of autonomy, hated the nursing staff, hated the other patients, hated being monitored all the time, being forced to eat, and being forced to take part in "stupid groups." However, Emily slowly gained weight. As this happened, she found that it was easier to read and concentrate on conversations, and that some of the other patients and nursing staff were actually "nice" and "interesting." As she neared her target weight for discharge, Emily felt a combination of eagerness to be free from the antiseptic environment of the inpatient unit and fear of leaving what had become a safe place where it didn't matter whether she wanted to eat or not because it was not her decision.

In order to achieve a controlled environment, inpatient eating disorder treatment programs share several features. These include medical monitoring of pulse, blood pressure, body temperature, and blood electrolyte levels, as well as daily weight checks to determine whether underweight individuals are gaining weight. As in Emily's case, weight gain toward a specific goal is often a condition of discharge. Another shared feature of inpatient programs is monitored meals. These can occur in groups or with a nurse present in the room during mealtime for patients who have been put on bed rest. Patients may also be monitored during their use of the bathroom in order to prevent purging. In addition to monitoring eating, activity level, and potential opportunities to purge, inpatient treatment programs often include group sessions for patients to discuss feelings about

Daily record. A teenager with anorexia nervosa writes in her journal as part of an inpatient treatment program. The writing helps her identify the fears, emotions, and needs that have contributed to her disorder.

Kosslyn, S. M. & Rosenberg, R. S. (2001). *Psychology: The Brain, The Person, The World.* Needham Heights, MA: Allyn & Bacon, 502.

eating, their bodies, gaining weight, and recovery. Patients may be asked to keep a journal to help them understand their feelings and to facilitate communication of these feelings with others. Group sessions can include any of the methods described below in the section titled "Psychotherapy Content and Theoretical Orientations."

Inpatient treatment programs vary significantly in their level of success. Some of this variation appears to be attributable to the nature of the patient populations treated. Moreover, it is difficult to assess whether the outcomes reported for hospitalized patients are worse than what would have occurred had these patients not received inpatient care. Given the medical emergency represented by most hospitalized cases, it would be unethical to randomly assign some patients to inpatient care and others to a waitlist control. At the very least, inpatient care delays death for some patients; for many, it may save their lives and give them the opportunity to achieve eventual recovery.

Because inpatient treatment is employed for patients who are medically unstable, an added benefit of this treatment is the structured environment it provides. As described in Emily's case, this environment relieves many patients of their internal battles about eating by taking the decision to eat or purge away from them. However, patients are usually discharged once they reach medical stability, regardless of whether they have achieved full recovery or are responding well to a structured environment. Residential treatment programs offer the benefits of a structured environment to patients who are medically stable.

Residential Treatment Programs

The Renfrew Center of Philadelphia was the first residential treatment clinic for eating disorders in the United States. The program advertises "a safe, non-institutional, nurturing environment" that provides therapy from trained clinicians who specialize in the treatment

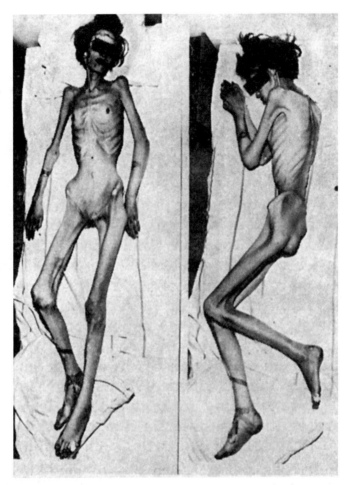

Patient hospitalized for anorexia nervosa in attempt to prevent her death.
Valanne, E. H., Taipale, V., Larkio-Miettinen, A. K., Moren, R., and Ankee, M. (1972). Anorexia Nervosa:
A follow-up study. *Psychiatria Fennica*, 267.

of eating disorders. The Renfrew Center has expanded since opening in June 1985 and in-cludes a second residential center in Florida, as well as outpatient clinics in other locations. It hosts conferences in which nationally known researchers and clinicians provide contin-ued education and clinical training to health professionals who work with eating-disordered patients. In addition to the expansion of the Renfrew Center, several other residential treatment programs have emerged across the United States over the past two decades. These centers treat many of the most severe and chronic cases of eating disorders.

One of the most famous residential treatment clinics for AN in recent history was the Montreux Clinic established in 1993 in British Columbia, Canada. The director of this clinic, Peggy Claude-Pierre, was featured in popular television shows and magazines as having developed a cure for hopeless cases. In *The Secret Language of Eating Disorders*, Claude-Pierre (1998) described the development of her treatment program based on her experience caring for her two daughters, who developed AN. She viewed AN as a symptom of a "Confirmed Negativity Condition" in which individuals with eating disorders perceive themselves as without value. Because they do not feel they have value, they believe they do not deserve life or food to sustain life. According to Claude-Pierre, her program offered patients unconditional love and nurturance.

In December 1999, the Montreux Clinic was closed after allegations that it was in conflict with British Columbia's licensing laws, employed former patients as staff without adequate training, force-fed patients, and illegally treated a 4-year-old child for AN. Moreover, concerns that medically unstable patients were being admitted without adequate medical supervision led to the Canadian government's conclusion that the clinic was putting patients at risk. The clinic was briefly reopened while it appealed the decision; the appeal was unsuccessful.

A source of concern about the Montreux Clinic was the high cost of care. Residential treatment programs can be private, nonprofit or commercial, for-profit enterprises. Thus, they can be very expensive, and access to such care is limited by what insurance carriers are willing to pay or by patients' ability to pay personally for treatment. The costs of residential treatment programs are similar to those of inpatient treatment. Providing health care 24 hours a day is very expensive. Another feature common to both inpatient and residential treatment programs is limited ability to determine the success of treatment compared to that of no treatment or alternative treatment. Residential treatment centers are designed to provide a service. Thus, they do not randomly assign patients to different treatment conditions. Instead, they attempt to ensure that each patient receives whatever form of treatment is deemed necessary.

Outpatient Treatment

Outpatient care is less expensive than inpatient or residential care because outpatients do not require room and board. Outpatient treatment can occur at different levels of intensity/frequency, including day programs, evening programs, intensive group therapy, and intensive individual therapy, weekly, biweekly, or even monthly sessions. If inpatient treatment represents spending 24 hours per day in treatment, then day programs represent spending 40 hours per week in treatment. In day treatment programs, patients attend treatment in a manner that is similar to going to work. They receive a level of therapeutic intervention similar to that offered by inpatient programs, as well as a controlled environment for eating two or three meals plus snacks during the day. In contrast, they do not receive the same level of medical monitoring, and they spend their evenings and nights at home. Evening programs allow patients to work during the day or care for children and then enter a controlled environment for their evening meal. For some individuals, their jobs provide adequate control over behaviors such as binge eating and purging, and an evening treatment program helps to sustain that structure. For others, the need to work or care for children restricts their ability to participate in a day program. Intensive group and individual therapy occurs several times per week, and sessions may last for up to 2 hours. Thus, they fill neither the entire day nor the entire evening. Weekly, biweekly, and monthly outpatient sessions are appropriate for patients with medical stability and the ability to modify their behaviors in response to therapeutic interventions. A traditional schedule for outpatient therapy would be one 50-minute session per week. Regardless of treatment duration or frequency, the content of treatment that occurs during sessions depends upon the theoretical orientation and treatment goals.

PSYCHOTHERAPY CONTENT AND THEORETICAL ORIENTATIONS

This section reviews the logic and content of the different approaches to treating eating disorders that a patient may encounter. Different theoretical orientations emphasize different treatment goals and methods for reaching these goals. These orientations are not specific to eating disorders, nor are they related to any particular treatment modality discussed above. Instead, they reflect ways of understanding mental disorders in general and have been applied to the treatment of several different problems. This section also reviews the demonstrated success (or lack thereof) of treatments from each theoretical orientation. The success of treatment in producing desired changes is referred to as treatment **efficacy.**

Psychoeducation

When patients first seek treatment for their eating disorder, they often have several questions about the disorder. Thus, **psychoeducation** is included in most forms of intervention and shapes the content of psychotherapy. However, psychoeducation alone is not often thought of as a distinct psychotherapy, and it is not viewed as an adequate intervention (Fairburn, Kirk, O'Connor, & Cooper, 1986).

The basic rationale behind psychoeducation as an aspect of intervention is that for patients to recover from eating disorders, they must understand what the disorders are, what factors are thought to contribute to or exacerbate problem eating, what approaches are thought to decrease problem eating, and the consequences of continued disordered eating. In addition, psychoeducational approaches often include a fair amount of information on weight regulation. This is used to combat the wealth of misinformation on weight regulation provided by popular culture. The role of popular culture in promoting specific and unobtainable aesthetic ideals is also covered. Some specific forms of information that might be shared with patients with eating disorders follow.

The idea that thin is beautiful is a relatively recent belief that one may or may not choose to adopt. Images presented in popular media do not represent people as they actually look because of postproduction techniques. In addition to the arbitrary nature of the thin ideal, this ideal is not obtainable by most individuals. The body is designed to defend itself against significant weight loss. When caloric intake drops and weight loss begins, the BMR decreases as well, and the BMR accounts for the majority of calories consumed by the body. Thus, a diet that initially allows a patient to lose weight will eventually stop working because of the resulting decrease in BMR. Further evidence of this weight-defending process is a drop in body temperature, blood pressure, and pulse rate, as well as the growth of fine, downy hair (lanugo) on the torso; these changes represent serious medical consequences of starvation. Dietary restriction increases the risk of binge-eating episodes. Binge episodes introduce a large number of calories into the body. Self-induced vomiting and other methods of purging are ineffective means of compensating for binging because the majority of calories consumed during such episodes are retained. Finally, individuals who recover from AN *weigh more* after recovery but feel better about their bodies. Individuals who recover from BN *do not weigh significantly more* and feel better about their bodies. Armed with such information, a patient is better equipped to attempt to rid herself of an eating disorder.

Unfortunately, understanding what eating disorders are, what factors exacerbate them, what approaches decrease them, and the consequences of continued disordered eating may not provide patients with enough insight, motivation, support, or skills to alter their behaviors. Thus, psychotherapy is typically designed to provide some combination of these factors. The first psychotherapy reviewed, psychodynamic therapy, is focused on enhancing insight.

Psychodynamic Therapy

Psychodynamic therapy seeks to reveal the underlying causes of disorders and was among the first therapies regularly employed with patients suffering from eating disorders. As noted in Chapter 6, Hilde Bruch was a psychodynamically oriented psychotherapist who specialized in the treatment of eating disorders. As she was a pioneer in the field, her approach to eating disorders has had a significant impact on the way these disorders are understood and treated.

Psychodynamic therapies are nondirective. This means that the therapist does not choose the topics covered in sessions, and sessions are not organized around specific treatment goals. Instead, there is a more general goal: the patient will improve as a consequence of a therapy that helps her explore the meaning behind her symptoms. Eating disorder symptoms are viewed as expressions of intrapsychic distress, and the patient may not be consciously aware of the presence of the distress or its source. Patients often set the agenda for what is discussed in therapy. Early sessions may focus on concrete topics that are of interest to the patient—fear of weight gain, food, and calories. The psychodynamically oriented therapist listens to this information to learn more about the patient and build rapport. However, the meaning of symptoms is usually thought to reside beneath this surface level of calories, pounds, and food textures. Therefore, a psychodynamically oriented therapist will wait for the patient to turn to topics that seem to account for the high emotional importance given to food, eating, and weight. An example follows.

An adolescent girl reported that her parents routinely argued at the dinner table. Her symptoms began shortly after her father got up in the middle of a meal and walked out on the family, not returning for 15 months. The father is now back home, and the girl finds that she can tolerate eating only when he is there. From a psychodynamic perspective, the eating disorder could be interpreted as the patient's attempt to freeze the original dinner in time—refusing to allow the meal to continue until her father returned to the table. Hilde Bruch was a proponent of a fact-finding, noninterpretive style that encouraged patients to recognize their own feelings and motivations (Bruch, 1978). Importantly, this creates a collaborative approach to therapy. Although the patient may not be aware of why she engages in disordered eating behaviors at the initiation of therapy, she has an active role in uncovering and understanding these processes.

Psychodynamic interventions have received relatively little **empirical support** in the treatment literature. One reason for this is that insight-oriented or psychodynamic interventions are often combined with other intervention methods (most often antidepressant medications and behavioral techniques) (Brotman, Herzog, & Hamburg, 1988; Norring & Sohlberg, 1991; White & Boskind-White, 1981). This leads to confusion over what aspects of treatment contribute to change.

A further complication is the lack of a control group in studies assessing the treatment response among patients receiving psychodynamic therapy (Brotman et al., 1988; Norring & Sohlberg, 1991; White & Boskind-White, 1981). In order to assess whether a treatment produces recovery, the ideal study design randomly assigns participants to a treatment or control condition. This is called a *controlled study*. Change over time in the treatment condition is compared to change over time in the control condition, allowing conclusions regarding the impact of treatment on symptom change over time. In the absence of a control condition, it is not possible to rule out that patients may have improved over time without treatment (or with alternative treatment).

Finally, psychodynamic therapies are not amenable to standardization because the therapist does not direct the course of therapy. Directive treatments (discussed below) have been standardized through the creation of a treatment manual. In the absence of a treatment manual, it is difficult to ensure consistent application of therapy across participants in a given treatment condition.

Studies including nondirective or psychodynamic approaches within designs that employ (a) random assignment to different treatment conditions, (b) consistent application of an approach to each condition, and (c) distinct approaches across treatment conditions (Fairburn et al., 1986; Kirkley, Schneider, Agras, & Bachman, 1985; Walsh et al., 1997) have found that cognitive-behavioral interventions (discussion follows) are superior to nondirective therapy (Kirkley et al., 1985), short-term focal psychotherapy designed to reveal "underlying difficulties" (Fairburn et al., 1986), and psychodynamically oriented supportive psychotherapy (Garner et al., 1993; Walsh et al., 1997; Wilson et al., 1999). Thus, nondirective psychodynamic therapies are associated with less symptom improvement than cognitive-behavioral therapy.

Cognitive-Behavioral Treatments

Cognitive-behavioral therapies are directive therapies focused on the present (versus relational features of the rearing environment). These treatments view the eating disorder symptoms as a combination of irrational cognitions that need to be elicited, challenged, and replaced and behaviors that are reinforced (positively and negatively) by immediate consequences. For example, a cognitive-behavioral therapist may elicit from a patient a statement concerning the importance of being thin: "People will love me only if I'm thin." This belief can be challenged in several ways based on the patient's own observations. First, the patient can be asked to view couples in public settings and notice that many fat people appear to be in happy relationships. Second, the patient can be invited to question the value of love from an individual who places so much importance on physical appearance. Third, the patient can be asked whether there is anyone she loves who is not thin (e.g., a grandparent or mentor). In the end, the patient may come to adopt a belief that corresponds more closely to reality: "People who truly care about me as a person will love me no matter what I weigh." The accompanying figure presents a behavioral analysis in which the antecedents and consequences of disordered eating behavior are identified and an alternative behavioral response is substituted. For additional examples of irrational cognitions and how disordered eating behaviors are positively and negatively reinforced, see Chapter 7.

One widely used cognitive-behavioral intervention developed by Christopher Fairburn (1981) is divided into three stages. The first stage establishes control over eating with behavioral techniques. These techniques include:

1. self-monitoring of food intake, binge eating, and inappropriate compensatory behavior with a diary
2. prescription of a regular pattern of eating at least three meals and two or three snacks per day (going no more than 2 to 3 hours between periods of eating)
3. stimulus control (identifying triggers for binge-eating episodes and avoiding them)

Antecedents	Behavior	Consequences
Incredibly stressful day at work, trying to make last-minute changes to a program and fix mistakes to meet a deadline	Started eating as soon as I got home to unwind—became a binge episode	Thoughts about work obliterated while eating—completely zoned out while eating After episode, felt bloated, stomach hurt, felt disgusted and disgusting
	Alternative behaviors to deal with feeling stressed:	
	Call a friend to talk about day	Laugh about prospect of submitting program with all mistakes as if they were intentional; decide to get together for dinner
	Go for a walk outside	Thoughts about work dissipate; feel relaxed, a little tired, and hungry for dinner
	Take a long, hot shower or bath	Thoughts about work dissipate; feel warm, relaxed, and ready for dinner

Note: In each case, the alternative behavior is (a) incompatible with eating and (b) achieves the desired consequence of relieving stress from work.

FIGURE 9–1 Behavioral analysis of a binge eating episode.

Day _Monday_   Date _February 18_

Time	Food and Drink Consumed	Place	*	V/L	Context and Comments
7:45	1 bowl cereal w/ milk 1 cup decaf coffee	Home			Off to a good start. Determined to do well today.
8:50	1 cup decaf	Office			
10:35	1 apple	Office			
12:30	Strawberry yogurt 1 cup chicken soup	Cafeteria			
7:50	Macaroni & cheese Potato salad	Kitchen	*	V	Ate too much. Feel bad. Once again, I strayed from my diet.
8:10	Diet Sprite Large piece of cheesecake 10 Oreos Bag of Doritos (16 oz) 2 Twix bars Diet Sprite 5 scoops ice cream	Kitchen	 * * * * *	 V V	 Feel terrible. I lost control and couldn't stop. I am crying and I feel awful!!!!
10:05	Diet Sprite	Bedroom			Feel tired/calm. Determined to do better tomorrow.
10:40	Diet Sprite	Bedroom			

Column 2: All food and drink consumed should be recorded, including binges. Each item should be written down as soon as it is consumed. Episodes viewed as meals are identified with brackets.

Column 4: An asterisk is recorded when the individual feels that the food consumed was excessive.

Column 5: Record when self-induced vomiting (V), laxatives (L), or diuretics are used.

Adapted from Fairburn, C. (1995). Overcoming binge eating. New York: Guilford Press. Reprinted by permission of Guilford Press.

FIGURE 9–2 Food journal.

4. education on weight regulation, dieting, and risks of purging (as described in the section on "Psychoeducation" above)

The second stage reduces dieting and body image disturbance through a combination of behavioral and cognitive techniques and trains the patient to engage in problem solving. The steps of problem solving include:

1. identifying the problem as soon as possible
2. specifying the problem as accurately as possible

3. identifying alternative responses to the problem (as many as possible)
4. examining the consequences associated with each alternative response
5. choosing the best response (or combination of responses) available based upon anticipated consequences
6. acting on the selected response

The third stage works toward maintenance of progress and reduction of the risk of future relapse. For example, patients are encouraged to recognize and challenge dichotomous thinking in order to differentiate a lapse from relapse. Elimination of all-or-nothing thinking allows patients to have slips without having a full eating disorder return. Cognitive-behavioral therapy emphasizes work that patients complete outside of sessions because most of their lives occur outside of therapy. Therefore, homework assignments, such as maintaining a diary and writing out the stages of problem solving, are featured prominently in each stage of therapy.

Numerous studies support the efficacy of this and other forms of cognitive-behavioral therapy in the treatment of BN (Agras, Walsh, Fairburn, Wilson, & Kraemer, 2000; Fairburn et al., 1986, 1993; Kirkley et al., 1985; Mitchell et al., 1990; Safer, Telch, & Agras, 2001; Walsh et al., 1997) and BED (Agras, Telch, Arnow, Eldredge, & Marnell, 1994; Peterson & Mitchell, 1999; Wilfley, Agras, Telch, & Elise,1993; Wilfley et al., 2002). These studies have used manual-based treatments and random assignment to treatment or control conditions to ensure the validity of conclusions concerning the efficacy of cognitive-behavioral therapy. At this time, cognitive-behavioral therapy is considered the treatment of choice for BN and is recommended for BED (Keel & Haedt, in press; Shafran, Keel, Haedt, & Fairburn, in press). Similar results are lacking for AN (Keel & Haedt, in press; Peterson & Mitchell, 1999; Shafran et al., in press).

Interpersonal Therapy

Interpersonal therapy for BN originally developed as a control condition for cognitive-behavioral therapy (Fairburn et al., 1993). Although cognitive-behavioral therapy was superior to short-term focal psychotherapy (Fairburn et al., 1986), patients in the latter therapy did improve. In order to determine whether this was a consequence of self-monitoring and psychoeducation (therapeutic aspects shared between the interventions), a new control intervention was adapted from an existing interpersonal therapy for depression (Klerman, Weissman, Rounsaville, & Chevron, 1984). The rationale for interpersonal therapy was that patients with BN often report a number of different problems in interpersonal domains. These include being conflict avoidant, having conflicts between the need for independence and closeness, and having difficulties with role expectations and social problem solving (Apple, 1999). Interpersonal therapy comprises three phases:

1. *Identify interpersonal problems associated with the onset of BN.* This involves taking a personal history and examining significant life events, mood and self-esteem, and relationships. Patients are encouraged to associate bulimic symptoms with life experiences and to understand the role of interpersonal problems in the emergence of symptoms. The rationale of interpersonal therapy is covered in this phase, as well as common problem domains. Patients are encouraged to select specific problems on which to focus throughout treatment.
2. *Work on identified interpersonal problems.* Like psychodynamically oriented therapies, interpersonal therapy allows patients to introduce topics to therapy discussions as

they relate to the problem areas defined in phase 1. Techniques such as open-ended questioning, role plays, examining the consequences of change, and encouraging expression of feelings are used to assist patients (Apple, 1999).

3. *Discuss feelings about termination.* This phase involves reviewing gains and anticipating future problems and solutions.

Importantly, no mention of patients' eating problems or concerns about weight or shape occurs outside of their initial assessment. Similar to results from the initial study comparing cognitive-behavioral therapy with short-term focal psychotherapy (Fairburn et al., 1986), cognitive-behavioral therapy was superior to interpersonal therapy at treatment end (Agras et al., 2000; Fairburn et al., 1993). However, similar to results from another study comparing nondirective therapy to cognitive-behavioral therapy (Kirkley et al., 1985), these differences were not maintained at follow-up (Fairburn et al., 1993, 1995). Moreover, at 12-month follow-up, patients who had received interpersonal therapy for BN were doing as well as those who had received cognitive-behavioral therapy (Fairburn et al., 1993). Interpersonal therapy has also been found to be effective in the treatment of BED (Peterson & Mitchell, 1999; Wilfley et al., 2002). No such data have been reported for AN.

Because cognitive-behavioral therapy and interpersonal therapy appear to reduce eating disorder symptoms through different methods, some researchers have examined whether interpersonal therapy may help patients who do not respond to cognitive-behavioral therapy (Agras, Telch, Arnow, Eldredge, & Marnell, 1995; Mitchell et al., 2002). However, neither patients with BN (Mitchell et al., 2002) nor patients with BED (Agras et al., 1995) who failed to respond to cognitive-behavioral therapy demonstrated increased success following interpersonal therapy. A particular problem with this approach is the high dropout rate (Mitchell et al., 2002), suggesting that patients may become demoralized when initial treatment does not work. Thus, researchers have begun focusing on developing treatments that combine features of different effective interventions. For example, treatments that combine aspects of cognitive-behavioral therapy and interpersonal therapy are being examined for their efficacy in treating eating disorders. A type of cognitive-behavioral therapy that addresses problems in interpersonal function is dialectical behavior therapy.

Dialectical Behavior Therapy

Dialectical behavior therapy was originally designed to treat individuals with a personality disorder characterized by poor impulse control, self-destructive behavior, interpersonal difficulties, and significant mood fluctuations. Because many of these features are present in patients with eating disorders, researchers have begun to adapt this treatment for eating disorders.

Traditional dialectical behavior therapy is provided as a combination of individual cognitive-behavioral therapy focusing on symptoms in order of decreasing urgency (e.g., harmful purging behavior is addressed before the fear of never finding a romantic partner) and skills training groups that focus on building strength in four skills areas:

1. **Mindfulness**—the ability to be aware of internal feelings and external demands in a way that combines emotions with intellect in making wise choices.
2. **Distress tolerance**—the ability to develop safe ways of coping with painful emotions without resorting to impulsive (and often self-destructive) behaviors that ultimately increase emotional pain.

3. **Interpersonal effectiveness**—the ability to relate to people in a way that meets personal needs, the needs of the other person, and the need for self-respect.
4. **Emotional regulation**—the ability to experience emotions without having extreme fluctuations that interfere with life function.

Dialectical behavior therapy was successful in treating BN in one controlled study (Safer et al., 2001), and two uncontrolled studies suggest that it may be useful in the treatment of both BN and BED (Palmer et al., 2003; Telch, Agras, & Linehan, 2000). Wisniewski and Kelly (2003) have reported that this treatment can be applied to eating disorders with relatively modest revisions, including focusing on eating disorder behaviors in treatment goals and adding a nutrition skills module in the skills training groups (see the description of nutritional counseling below).

Many of the problems patients with eating disorders have in interpersonal function are thought to emerge within the context of poor family functioning (see Chapter 6 for a discussion of family factors in the development of eating disorders). Thus, interventions focused solely on the individual may fail to address a significant source of difficulties—the interpersonal context in which these problems emerge. Because AN is associated with a younger age of onset than BN or BED, this limitation is particularly relevant for these patients, who are often younger and still living at home. Family therapy seeks to address interpersonal function within the family as a system.

Family Therapy

Family therapy is more often used when patients are children or adolescents living at home. As described in Chapter 6, traditional family systems therapy involved evaluating the entire family as the patient (Minuchin et al., 1978). A newer approach to family-based therapy invites family members to be members of the treatment team rather than the patient (le Grange, 1999). Following a study indicating the superiority of a family treatment for younger eating disorder patients (Russell, Szmukler, Dare, & Eisler, 1987), the Maudsley model of family therapy has received increased attention and empirical support in the treatment of adolescents with AN. As with cognitive-behavioral therapy and interpersonal therapy, there are three phases to family therapy as developed by the Maudsley group:

1. *Refeeding the client.* Therapists support and reinforce parents' efforts to refeed their child and encourage parents to form a united front. Meanwhile, siblings are encouraged to be supportive of the patient; this reinforces appropriate boundaries between parental and sibling subsystems, as described in Chapter 6. Families are encouraged to devise their own plans for refeeding.
2. *Negotiations for a new pattern of relationships.* Once patients show willingness to participate in refeeding and achieve weight gain, weight gain with the least amount of conflict is allowed. Although symptoms remain central to this phase of treatment, other family issues are introduced to therapy. Of note, only issues that impact the parents' ability to ensure the patient's weight gain are covered, and only to the extent that they are relevant to the patient's symptoms.
3. *Termination.* After the patient has achieved a healthy weight, the focus shifts to encouraging a healthy relationship between patient and parents. This is particularly important because, up to this point, the patient's illness has formed the basis of family interactions. Reflecting the age of patients, themes of increased autonomy,

appropriate family boundaries, and preparation for children's departure from home are often covered in this phase (Dare, Eisler, Russell, & Szmukler, 1990).

Controlled studies have supported the efficacy of this intervention in patients with AN (le Grange, Eisler, Dare, & Russell, 1992; Robin et el., 1999), and sustained benefits of the intervention were supported in a 5-year follow-up study (Eisler et al., 1997) of the original study (Russell et al., 1987).

NONPSYCHOTHERAPY INTERVENTIONS

Many patients with eating disorders benefit from a combination of psychotherapy, nutritional counseling, medication, and medical management. This represents a multimodal team-based approach to the treatment of eating disorders. The following sections discuss the roles of nutritional counseling and medication in the treatment of eating disorders. Of note, nutritional counseling alone would not be recommended for the treatment of eating disorders. In contrast, evidence suggests that symptoms of BN may remit with medication treatment alone (Goldstein et al., 1995).

Nutritional Counseling

Despite the great attention paid to calories and food intake, many individuals suffering from eating disorders lack basic knowledge of what constitutes a well-balanced diet. This is somewhat understandable given that most people do not follow optimally nutritious diets (e.g., women consume approximately half of their recommended daily allowance of calcium) (Brunzell & Hendrickson-Nelson, 2001). Further, patients with eating disorders often have skewed understandings of daily caloric intake guidelines. Thus, nutritional counseling is an important aspect of treatment in eating disorders. The goals of nutritional counseling are to "attain medical stability, to normalize eating behaviors and weight, and to reestablish a healthy relationship with food" (Brunzell & Hendrickson-Nelson, 2001, p. 217).

In addition to providing basic nutritional information, nutritionists work with patients to reduce fears of forbidden foods, eliminate food myths, and help them recognize feelings of hunger and fullness. Nutritionists explain that calories in food come from carbohydrates, protein, and fats. Along with vitamins, minerals, and water, these sources of calories represent nutrients that are used to build the body, regulate its functions, and provide energy. Carbohydrates represent the primary source of energy for the body and should contribute 50% to 65% of the calories consumed in a day. Protein should constitute 10% to 20% of total caloric intake. Protein is important for building and maintaining organs, muscles, skin, hair, antibodies for fighting illnesses, enzymes, and hormones. It is also important for regulating water balance in the body. Finally, dietary fat provides essential fatty acids, carries fat-soluble vitamins, and contributes to the maintenance and function of body tissue. Fat should contribute 20% to 30% of the calories consumed in a day. Patients are gradually introduced to more varied diets that include recommended proportions of calories from carbohydrates, protein, and fats (Brunzell & Hendrickson-Nelson, 2001, p. 217).

The relationships among food intake, energy expenditure, and weight are often reviewed in some detail during nutritional counseling so that patients can act as informed consumers. Nutritionists can also employ behavioral techniques to plan for eating in social situations, as well as to plan responses to urges to binge or restrict.

Medication

Several different medications have been used to treat AN, BN, and BED. These include antidepressants, mood stabilizers, opioid antagonists, tetrahydrocannabinol (the primary component of marijuana), antipsychotics, and stimulants (Peterson & Mitchell, 1999). Of this impressive array of pharmacologic agents, antidepressants have emerged as the medications of choice in the treatment of BN (Mitchell, Raymond, & Specker, 1993; Peterson & Mitchell, 1999), and some data support their efficacy in the treatment of BED (Peterson & Mitchell, 1999). In particular, fluoxetine (commonly known by the trade name Prozac) is the only drug to have Food and Drug Administration approval for treating BN (APA, 2000). In contrast, another antidepressant, buproprion (trade name Wellbutrin), is not recommended for the treatment of eating disorders because of evidence that it may increase the likelihood of seizures in this population (Diamond, 2002). There is limited evidence that selective serotonin reuptake inhibitors may decrease the risk of relapse among women with AN who have achieved weight recovery (Kaye et al., 2001b; Kaye, Weltzin, Hsu, & Bulik, 1991b). As described in Jamie's case, several trials are underway for BED in the search for obesity medications.

Case Study

Jamie wasn't sure if he was receiving the active medication because no one he spoke to could tell him, including the physician who followed him for side effects and who adjusted the dosage. However, Jamie felt certain that he was taking the active medication. At first, it made him a little lightheaded and caused diarrhea. However, this phase quickly passed, and Jamie noticed that he felt more focused at work and that when he ate, he felt full much more quickly. As a study participant, he was not allowed to seek any additional treatment. However, this worked well for him because he was noticing a decrease in binge frequency, was losing weight, and wasn't spending hours a week in sessions or meetings or preparing special diet meals for himself. His only question was what would happen when the study was over. The physician who was meeting with him said that this would be up to Jamie. If he was in the medication condition, he could either remain on the medication or stop. If he was in the placebo condition, he could either ask to receive the medication or not. Because this was a new treatment, no information was available concerning the medication's long-term efficacy. So, there was no way of knowing whether the improvements achieved with the medication would be maintained.

For Jamie, and for many patients with BED, achieving weight loss is as important a treatment goal as achieving control over eating. Although it might seem that ending binge-eating episodes would lead to reduced weight, this is not necessarily the case. Many patients with BED overeat outside of their binge-eating episodes and do not get enough exercise. Thus, patients with BED have also been enrolled in behavioral weight loss programs.

Behavioral Weight Loss Programs and Binge Eating Disorder

As described in Chapter 1, BED is often associated with overweight and obesity. Thus, behavioral weight loss programs have been used for this diagnostic group. Before going any further in this section, it is important to note that this treatment approach is appropriate only for individuals who are overweight or obese. As described in earlier chapters, weight-loss dieting among normal-weight individuals appears to increase the risk of binge eating and BN, and weight-loss dieting among underweight individuals is dangerous.

Behavioral weight-loss programs provide patients with nutritional counseling, psychoeducation, a prescription to eat regular meals, and an explicit goal of reducing overall caloric intake and increasing energy expenditure to achieve weight loss. Triggers of overeating are identified, and alternative responses to those triggers are encouraged. In addition, various behavioral techniques for reducing overall food intake are offered. Thus, behavioral weight loss programs include techniques from behavioral and cognitive-behavioral therapy. However, the therapeutic goal is weight loss. There is no presumption of mental illness and no explicit goal of improving psychological function. Thus, behavioral weight loss programs are distinct from psychotherapeutic interventions despite using overlapping techniques.

Several studies have compared the efficacy of standard behavioral weight-loss programs to cognitive-behavioral therapy or programs with greater emphasis on cognitive-behavioral techniques for the treatment of BED (Agras et al., 1994; Marcus, Wing, & Fairburn, 1995; Marcus, Wing, & Hopkins, 1988; Porzelius, Houston, Smith, & Arfken, 1995). Results suggest that cognitive-behavioral therapy does not reduce binge eating or depression more than standard behavioral weight-loss treatments (Agras et al., 1994; Marcus et al., 1988, 1995; Porzelius et al., 1995). In addition, behavioral weight loss programs appear to produce greater weight loss than cognitive-behavioral therapy alone (Agras et al., 1994; Marcus et al., 1995). This pattern of results has led some researchers to conclude that behavioral weight-loss programs provide the psychological benefits of psychotherapy with the added benefit of weight loss for individuals who are overweight or obese (Gladis et al., 1998).

CONCLUSION

Several efficacious treatments have been identified for BN. These include cognitive-behavioral therapy, interpersonal therapy, and antidepressant medication. Several treatments that work for BN appear to be successful in treating BED. In addition, behavioral weight-loss treatments appear to lead to decreased weight and decreased eating disorder symptoms in BED. This is in direct contrast to the emphasis on eliminating dieting in cognitive-behavioral treatments of BN. However, it is important to recognize the weight differences between people suffering from BN versus BED. Discouraging weight-loss efforts among normal-weight individuals is a reasonable endeavor, as is promoting weight loss-efforts among those who are significantly overweight or obese. Moreover, recommended exercise and caloric intake for a patient with BN who stops dieting may not differ meaningfully from recommended exercise and caloric intake for a patient with BED who is trying to lose weight. In contrast to results for BN and BED, treatments with demonstrated efficacy for AN are limited, with the most support for a family-based intervention developed at the Maudsley Hospital in England.

Despite evidence for efficacious treatments, most individuals with eating disorders do not appear to receive these treatments. Individuals with eating disorders may be reluctant to seek treatment. Reluctance could be caused by fear of becoming fat, shame over disordered eating behaviors, or an inability to recognize the dangers of eating disorders. In addition, there have been reports of problems with insurance coverage for patients who do seek treatment for an eating disorder. Finally, even when individuals seek treatment with insurance coverage, they are often not offered treatments with demonstrated efficacy (Mussell et al., 2000). In a survey of randomly selected psychologists, the majority reported that they had never received training in the use of manual-based, empirically supported treatment approaches for eating disorders and that they used methods other than cognitive-behavioral therapy or interpersonal therapy when working with eating-disordered patients (Mussell et al., 2000). Thus, in addition to continued efforts to identify efficacious treatments for eating disorders, greater efforts are required in disseminating information and training for these interventions. At this time, multimodal team-based approaches are recommended for treating eating disorders. A treatment team would include a physician to monitor medical well-being, a nutritionist, a therapist, and, potentially, a psychiatrist for medication management.

KEY TERMS

Cognitive-behavioral therapy
Dialectical behavior therapy
Distress tolerance
Efficacy
Emotional regulation
Empirically supported treatment

Family therapy
Interpersonal effectiveness
Interpersonal therapy
Mindfulness
Psychodynamic therapy
Psychoeducation

CHAPTER 10

Prevention

As noted in Chapter 9, the number of individuals suffering from eating disorders far exceeds the availability of treatment. For this reason, several experts in the field have focused on prevention. Simply put, effective prevention would save time, money, and, most importantly, suffering.

This chapter starts by reviewing different theoretical models, or paradigms, of prevention. It then describes different levels of intervention and provides specific examples of eating disorder prevention programs within each level. Evidence of these programs' efficacy is reviewed for each level. The chapter ends with an examination of challenges to prevention research and future directions for this important work.

PREVENTION PARADIGMS

Just as there are different theoretical orientations contributing to the development of psychotherapies, there are different theoretical orientations contributing to the development of prevention programs. These paradigms of prevention reflect different ways of conceptualizing health and how it is maintained.

One common model is known as the **Disease-Specific Pathways Model** (Levine & Smolak, 2001) or *Disease Prevention Paradigm* (Rosenvinge & Borresen, 1999). This model seeks to identify and then modify the specific risk factors that contribute to the etiology of eating disorders. For example, in the Disease Prevention Paradigm, a girl would be encouraged to develop a positive body image in order to prevent her from developing an eating disorder. Thus, the success of a prevention program within this model is based on the accurate identification of specific risk factors and the ability to modify them.

A variation of the Disease Prevention Paradigm is the **Nonspecific Vulnerability-Stressor Model** (Levine & Smolak, 2001). Like the Disease Prevention Paradigm, it seeks to identify and modify risk factors that contribute to the etiology of eating disorders. However, rather than focusing on specific risk factors thought to relate uniquely to the onset of eating pathology, this model is interested in general risk factors that may also play a role in the etiology of many other problems (see Chapter 4 for a discussion of general versus specific risk factors). For example, in the Nonspecific Vulnerability-Stressor Model, a girl would be encouraged to develop a positive self-image in order to prevent her from developing problems such as depression and eating disorders. Because the Nonspecific Vulnerability-Stressor Model seeks to maximize overall health by reducing general risk factors and by promoting protective factors, it overlaps with the Health Promotion Paradigm (Rosenvinge & Borresen, 1999).

The **Health Promotion Paradigm** emphasizes protective factors rather than risk factors (Rosenvinge & Borresen, 1999). Whereas a *risk factor* promotes illness when present and does nothing when absent, a *protective factor* promotes wellness when present and does nothing when absent. Rosenvinge and Borresen have argued for using the Health Promotion Paradigm instead of the Disease Prevention Paradigm because the specific risk factors for eating disorders are not well understood and because focusing on information related specifically to eating disorders emphasizes the very things one is attempting to prevent. For example, a girl who never gave much thought to her weight or shape may become aware that she fails to match the ideal during a body image program. In addition to focusing on protective factors, the Health Promotion Paradigm advocates interventions designed for communities as well as individuals. Thus, the target for change is community action in addition to the behavior of a given individual in that community. For example, in the Health Promotion Paradigm, schools would be encouraged to promote valuing individual differences with regard to race, sex, and weight. This intervention would seek to reduce racism, sexism, and overvaluation of thinness/denigration of fatness (called *weightism*). The focus is on systemwide actions that influence health as well as on individual students' decisions about how to treat people who differ in race, sex, or weight. The goal of instilling the value of diversity among school children is not specifically related to the goal of preventing eating disorders. Still, promoting health in the general population has the consequence of reducing illness in individuals.

Another model of prevention that looks beyond the role of individual factors is the **Empowerment-Relational Model** (Levine & Smolak, 2001). This model is rooted in feminist theory and pursues change through empowerment of girls to transform their environments. Thus, the target for change is the environment, but the agent of change is the individual girl. For example, in the Empowerment-Relational Model, a girl would be encouraged to create her identity around a range of skills, rather than defining herself by her physical appearance, and to actively challenge social messages that objectify women and girls.

Reviewing the above examples, one can see variations in the methods used within each model to prevent eating disorders. However, these examples exaggerate the differences among the models. In practice, prevention programs tend to combine aspects of each model. There is no contradiction in having schools promote the value of diversity and encouraging girls to develop a positive self-image that includes what their bodies can do as an aspect of positive body image. The following section provides a brief overview of themes and content common to several prevention programs and relates them to the models described above.

PREVENTION THEMES AND CONTENT

Across different types of prevention programs, certain themes are commonly emphasized and reflected in program content. Consistent with the Disease Prevention Paradigm, these themes tend to reflect attempts to directly address specific risk factors that emerge from the current sociocultural context (see Chapters 4 and 5). For example, many programs attempt to prevent or reduce body dissatisfaction and dieting because these are considered risk factors for the development of eating disorders. To achieve these ends, programs educate participants on the arbitrary nature of the thin ideal, determinants of body size, nutritional needs, consequences of dieting, and consequences of disordered eating.

In addition to focusing on specific risk factors for eating disorders, several programs also seek to promote resilience by addressing more general factors related to mental health. Consistent with the Nonspecific Vulnerability-Stressor Model, programs address methods for improving self-esteem, stress management, assertiveness, and problem-solving skills. As described in Chapters 4 and 7, Vohs et al. (1999) found that weight dissatisfaction and perfectionism predicted increased bulimic symptoms only in women who reported low self-esteem. Thus, interventions designed to improve self-esteem should protect participants from the development of eating disorders as well as other problems related to self-image.

Consistent with the Health Promotion Paradigm, several programs offer guidance on healthy eating and exercise habits. This is intended to provide students with healthy options for weight control. Although weight control for the purpose of achieving an unrealistic and unhealthy thin ideal is *not* endorsed by any prevention program, many programs realize the importance of giving adolescents accurate information about nutrition and exercise so that they are protected both from developing an eating disorder and from becoming obese.

Finally, many prevention advocates seek to address change at a broader sociocultural level. Programs have attempted to increase students' awareness of discrimination against the overweight and obese so that they will challenge weightism as readily as they would challenge racism (Steiner-Adair et al., 2002). They also have sought to improve students' awareness of how peer pressure and teasing increase body dissatisfaction and unhealthy weight loss behaviors. In addition to helping girls recognize, challenge, and reject social messages of the importance of being thin, these programs advocate changing the messages presented in popular culture. They have initiated dialogues with magazine editors, advertising agencies, companies that market products to women, and government representatives. Consistent with the Empowerment-Relational Model, the goal is to get students actively involved in changing the social environmental factors that may contribute to eating disorders.

IMPLEMENTING PREVENTION AND LEVELS OF INTERVENTION

After determining the goal of, audience for, and content of prevention, one must decide how and when to deliver the program. In general, prevention means stopping an event before it occurs. Prevention programs can be divided into three categories based on the timing of intervention: universal, selective, and targeted. **Universal prevention programs** work toward the goal of primary prevention—preventing problems before they begin. Thus, universal prevention programs are used with a general population like students in a school system. **Selective prevention programs** are also aimed at preventing problems before they begin. However, rather than involving all members of a population, they focus on individuals who are at increased risk for problems (for example, only girls instead of all students in a school). Because the girls have evinced no problems thus far, this is still a form of primary prevention. **Targeted prevention programs** work toward the goal of secondary prevention—once problems emerge, preventing them from developing into more serious problems. Therefore, targeted prevention programs are aimed at individuals who are already reporting some problems with their eating attitudes and behaviors.

The following section provides an example of a specific prevention program designed for each level of intervention (universal, selective, and targeted) and reviews evidence of the success of different programs within each level in altering knowledge, attitudes, and behaviors related to disordered eating.

Universal Prevention Programs

Wade, Davidson, and O'Dea (2003) examined two universal prevention programs by adapting two existing programs, a media literacy program originally developed by the Eating Disorders and Awareness Program (EDAP) and a program to enhance self-esteem originally developed by O'Dea and Abraham (2000). Each program was reduced from its original length (16 and 9 sessions, respectively) to five 50-minute sessions. Participants in this study were boys and girls with a mean age of 13 years. They were randomly assigned to the media literacy program, the self-esteem program, or a control condition (religious education). The topics covered in each session for the two prevention programs and related materials and activities are as follows:

GO GIRLS! (media literacy program)

1. Consequences of a negative body image and the media's impact (both negative and positive) on our body image
   - Definition of body image
   - Outcomes of negative body image using "Full Monty"/"Center Stage"
   - List 3 things that influence the way I think I should look
2. Stories that advertisements tell us (both good and bad) and how advertisements can be altered to make up stories
   - Small group work: selection of advertisements and stories they are trying to tell—are they realistic?
   - "The Famine Within"—benefits of encouraging consumers to be dissatisfied with their appearance
   - Before and after ads: competition to guess the alterations
3. Becoming a critical media viewer: consumer activism using e-mails and letters to communicate with companies about their advertising
   - Defining activism and becoming a critical media reviewer
   - Brainstorm different ways in which we can engage in activism
   - Select companies from ads & e-mail one praise and one protest letter
4. & 5. Preparation of a media awareness presentation addressing the question "Is advertising harmful?" using either a poster, short play, or debate
   - Small group work on project, format decided by each group
   - Presentation of work in class followed by feedback and discussion
   - Feedback from e-mail replies
   - Tasks for the future?

Everybody's Different (self-esteem program)

1. Coping with stress and learning relaxation
   - Class brainstorm—what is stress?
   - What makes people feel stressed?
   - Small groups—what can we do to feel better?
   - Relaxation exercise with tape

2. "What makes up a person?"
   - Class exercise: define self-image
   - What makes up a person?
   - Advertising self as a good friend
3. Learning to observe positive aspects in others and communicating it
   - How can self-image be destroyed?
   - How to give positive messages
   - Small groups: write one positive thing about each person
4. Challenging stereotypes in society
   - Defining stereotypes
   - Small group: stereotypes of men & women
   - Sending up the stereotype using magazine ads
   - Collages of stereotypical messages about people
5. How do others affect our self-concept?
   - Role play of vignettes of difficult situations
   - Discussion of feelings and how to change the situation
   - Alternative role play based on discussion

(Source: Wade, Davidson, & O'Dea. A preliminary controlled evaluation of a school-based media literacy program and self-esteem program for reducing eating disorder risk factors. Copyright © 2003 by Wiley Periodicals, Inc. *Reprinted with permission of John Wiley & Sons. Inc.)*

Wade et al. (2003) examined the effects of both programs on specific and general risk factors for the development of eating disorders, including body dissatisfaction, weight/shape concern, dieting, and self-esteem. They hypothesized that both programs would reduce eating disorder risk factors and improve self-esteem relative to the control condition. Inclusion of boys provided an opportunity to help boys reduce their own risk of disordered eating. It was also intended to increase boys' awareness of their role in creating a social environment conducive to eating disorders so that they could help change the environment. Indeed, all participants were encouraged to become socially active in challenging cultural messages (e.g., commercials or magazine advertisements) that contribute to body dissatisfaction.

Results of this study suggested that the media literacy program significantly reduced weight concern compared to both the self-esteem program and the control condition immediately following intervention. By contrast, no differences were found for shape concern or dietary restraint. At the 3-month follow-up, the three groups were reporting equivalent levels of weight concern, shape concern, and dietary restraint, suggesting no lasting effect of interventions on specific risk factors. For general risk factors, no group differences were found for measures of self-esteem immediately following intervention. At the 3-month follow-up, group differences were found on measures of self-esteem. However, *none* of the differences reflected greater self-esteem among participants in the self-esteem program (Wade et al., 2003). Thus, this study provided very limited support for the efficacy of either program in reducing the risk of eating disorders.

Like the Wade et al. (2003) study, most universal prevention programs have been initiated in schools because they provide an ideal audience for primary prevention. Given their educational setting, these programs often emphasize psychoeducation. Not surprisingly, they often find improved knowledge among participants (Grave, De Luca, & Campello, 2001; Kater, Rohwer, & Levine, 2000; Levine, Smolak, & Schermer, 1996) and some have reported improved attitudes regarding body image (Grave et al., 2001; Kater et al., 2000; Varnado-Sullivan et al., 2001; Wade et al., 2003). However, most find no improvement in behaviors (Austin, 2000; Levine & Smolak, 2001; Littleton & Ollendick, 2003).

Reasons for the limited influence of universal prevention programs include the short duration of intervention. Interventions have ranged from 3 sessions (Buddeberg-

Fischer & Reed, 2001) to 10 sessions (Kater et al., 2000; Levine et al., 1996). Given the multiple factors contributing to the development of eating disorders (see Chapters 5–8), it would be miraculous if a 10-session intervention could prevent them. The limited duration of interventions reflects constraints on new curriculum that can be added in schools already feeling pressured to meet ever-increasing demands with ever-decreasing resources. For example, several prevention programs rely on teachers to conduct sessions (Smolak, Harris, Levine, & Shisslak, 2001). Although health-related school staff support inclusion of prevention material in school curricula (Neumark-Sztainer, Story, & Coller, 1999a), this does not necessarily translate into full adherence by teachers in implementing the program. For example, in Levine et al.'s (1996) universal prevention program, 31% of teachers skipped a 1-hour lesson on media analysis, and 50% devoted 5 minutes or less to explaining a key point in the lesson. Thus, time constraints in school settings likely contribute to both a small number of sessions and incomplete delivery of information. Such time constraints limit the use of interactive techniques that are more effective than traditional teaching methods (Stice and Shaw, 2004).

Another challenge to universal prevention programs is that researchers are trying to demonstrate the absence of a change. By definition, if one starts with young students who do not have problems with their body image or eating, there are only two possible outcomes. Students can either stay the same (reflecting successful prevention) or they can get worse. Most research methods (including statistical analyses used in research) are designed to detect a change in response to an intervention, not the absence of change.

Selective Prevention Programs

Steiner-Adair et al. (2002) designed a prevention program, Full of Ourselves, for girls between the ages of 12 and 14 years that could be delivered in school or in community organizations. It consists of eight units and includes more than 70 activities for participants, including group discussions, art activities, and role plays. The topic of each unit and related activities are as follows:

Full of Ourselves: Advancing Girl Power, Health, and Leadership
Unit 1: Full of Ourselves

- Icebreaker
- Establish ground rules
- "Full of Ourselves" brainstorm
- Freewriting on key program topics
- Bioenergetic punching (physical exercise to give girls embodied experience of throwing their weight into a punch)
- Body scan (awareness activity to detect and release signs of stress)
- "Dear Body" journal entry

Unit 2: Body Politics

- Discussion about changing body during puberty
- Weightism activity
- Debunking myths about body and dietary fat
- One-minute body scan
- Role plays to build assertiveness
- Group pledge (declaration of positive intentions towards self and others)

Unit 3: Claiming Our Strengths

- Ethnography assignment to detect weightism in the world
- "Tree of Strength" art activity to identify admirable women
- A positive self-assessment
- Body appreciation guided relaxation

Unit 4: Combating Weightism

- Ethnography incident reports on weightism
- Role plays to combat weightism
- Interviews as a way of countering prejudice (interview relating experiences of weightism)
- "Hi Body" guided meditation
- Affirmations

Unit 5: Media Literacy

- "10 Things I Find Beautiful": a freewrite
- Defining personal values vs. media values
- Group collage art activity
- Three-minute body scan
- Design your own magazine
- Letter-writing campaign to magazine editors and advertisers
- Body-outline drawing

Unit 6: The Dieting Dilemma

- Quiz to dispel myths about fad diets, define emotional hungers, etc.
- "Get Savvy" role plays
- Athletic game or outdoor activity

Unit 7: Nutrition Basics

- A questionnaire about eating
- Conscious eating activity
- "Mommy, May I?": How to feed your healthy "daughter?" (activity in which girls take hypothetical role of mother to daughter and consider healthy food choices from this perspective)
- Picnic in the park

Unit 8: The Power of Positive Action

- Body statues theater activity
- Coping skills
- The role of emotional hunger
- Menu of other hungers (spiritual, intellectual, friendship, creative, etc.)
- How to help a friend?
- Personal contracts

Source: Steiner-Adair, Sjostrom, Franko, Pai, Tucker, Becker & Herzog. Primary prevention of risk factors for eating disorders in adolescent girls: Learning from practice. Copyright © 2002 by Wiley Periodicals, Inc. Reprinted with permission of John Wiley & Sons, Inc.

The Full of Ourselves program emphasized "a strong feminist, sociopolitical perspective" and "translating knowledge and awareness into personal and public action" (Steiner-Adair et al., 2002, pp. 402–403). Thus, it focused on girls and was led by women.

In addition, the program sought to develop leadership skills among girls by having participants serve as role models in a second program for girls between the ages of 9 and 11 years, Throw Your Weight Around: A Guide for Girl Leaders. The authors hypothesized that the prevention program would lead to improved knowledge about healthy eating, improved body image, and improved eating behaviors. In addition, they predicted that participants would report greater self-esteem following intervention compared to controls. Unlike the Wade et al. (2003) study, not all participants were randomized to the intervention versus control groups.

Results indicated that participants in the Full of Ourselves program reported increased knowledge and better body image following the intervention compared to controls. These improvements were maintained at the 6-month follow-up assessment. Still, the program had no apparent effect on awareness or internalization of the thin ideal, dieting, or self-esteem.

Like the Steiner-Adair et al. (2002) program, selective prevention programs focus on girls because they are at greater risk than boys for developing eating disorders. In further contrast to universal programs, selective prevention programs have included older girls and young women, with participants ranging from 10 years (Piran, 1999) to 25 years of age (Phelps, Sapia, Nathanson, & Nelson, 2000). Several selective prevention programs have included girls past the age of risk for onset of eating disorders, so it is not entirely accurate to depict them as working with students before any problems have emerged. Nevertheless, participants are not specifically targeted on the basis of having problems with body image or disordered eating attitudes or behaviors. Thus, this is still considered a form of primary prevention.

Several controlled selective prevention studies have reported improvements in knowledge and attitudes associated with intervention compared to a control condition (Moreno & Thelen, 1993; Steiner-Adair et al., 2002; Stewart, Carter, Drinkwater, Hainsworth, & Fairburn, 2001; Withers, Twigg, Wertheim, & Paxton, 2002). In some cases, these improvements were maintained at follow-up (Moreno & Thelen, 1993; Steiner-Adair et al., 2002). Like universal prevention programs, few selective prevention programs produced improvements in behavior (Austin, 2000; Levine & Smolak, 2001; Littleton & Ollendick, 2003), and several programs failed to find improvements in the intervention group compared to controls (Baranowski, & Hetherington, 2001; Martz & Bazzini, 1999; Martz, Graves, & Sturgis, 1997; McEvey & Davis, 2002). Frequently, this occurred because improvements were demonstrated in both the intervention and control groups over time (Baranowski, & Hetherington, 2001; McEvey & Davis, 2002). Finally, one controlled study (Mann, Nolen-Hoeltsema, & Huang, 1997) of college freshmen found that individuals in the prevention program actually developed more eating disorder symptoms over time compared to individuals in the control condition. This has raised concern that prevention programs introduce the risk of doing more harm than good when they inadvertently instruct students in the use of disordered eating behaviors, or normalize or even glamorize eating disorders.

Of interest, selective programs that produced improvements tended to focus on younger adolescents (Moreno & Thelen, 1993; Steiner-Adair et al., 2002; Stewart et al., 2001; Withers et al., 2002), and those studies failing to find an effect (or finding a harmful effect of intervention) tended to focus on college-age students Mann et al., 1997; (Martz & Bazzini, 1999; Martz et al., 1997). This may be due to higher levels of disordered eating in older participants (see Chapter 4 for a discussion of developmental increases in eating disorder risk). Santonastaso et al. (1999) found that their selective prevention program produced no improvement relative to the control condition in girls with higher levels of disordered eating; by contrast, girls with lower levels of disordered eating improved significantly. The authors suggested that once problems become entrenched, more extensive interventions may be needed. Such interventions are offered by targeted prevention programs.

Targeted Prevention Programs

Celio and colleagues (2000) compared two targeted prevention programs, Student Bodies and Body Traps, and a wait list control condition in college women who reported high levels of body dissatisfaction. Thus, this prevention targeted women on the basis of body image disturbance. However, women with AN or BN were excluded from the study. Student Bodies is an Internet program that combines psychoeducation with cognitive-behavioral therapy exercises. Body Traps is a classroom intervention with a focus on psychoeducation. The basic designs of the two programs are as follows:

Student Bodies

Three face-to-face sessions (over an 8-week period)
> Weeks 1 and 2: Orientation to program
> Week 6: Group discussion of body image dissatisfaction

Academic readings (one or two articles per week)
Written reflections in response to academic readings (1–2 pages)
On-line readings on body image, exercise, nutrition, and eating disorders; cognitive-behavioral exercises
On-line body image journal (at least one entry per week [suggested])
Discussion group messages (at least two messages per week, one in response to a group member)

Body Traps

Eight 2-hour class meetings (over an 8-week period)
> Lecture or guest speaker
> Group discussion

Academic readings (one or two articles per week)
Written reflections in response to academic readings (1–2 pages)

For both interventions, participants were asked to complete weekly readings, and a weekly reflection paper and take part in group discussions (which occurred on-line for Student Bodies). Both programs covered four topics: eating disorders, healthy weight regulation, nutrition, and exercise, divided into eight weekly programs: Body image, Eating disorders, Weight regulation, Diet check, General nutrition, Food item analysis, Exercise, and Diary.

The primary differences between the programs were that Student Bodies occurred on-line and Body Traps occurred in a classroom, and Student Bodies included weekly cognitive-behavioral exercises (e.g., observing real women in public places and comparing them to magazine models), while Body Traps remained psychoeducational. In addition, Student Bodies encouraged communication among participants between on-line group discussions. The authors hypothesized that both programs would reduce body dissatisfaction and disordered eating compared to the control condition and that these improvements would be maintained at follow-up.

Participants in Student Bodies reported lower weight/shape concerns compared to controls, but no differences were found between controls and participants in Body Traps. At the 6-month follow-up, participants in Student Bodies continued to report fewer weight/shape concerns, fewer eating concerns, and less dietary restraint compared to controls. Again, no differences were found between controls and participants in Body

Traps (Celio et al., 2000). These results are particularly notable because differences attributable to the prevention program were maintained at the 6-month follow-up and included at least one measure of behavior—dietary restraint. Unfortunately, no differences were found across groups on a measure of bulimic symptoms (Celio et al., 2000).

Like the program in Celio et al.'s (2000) study, targeted prevention programs are specifically designed for people who already have problems with body image or eating. Participants are often college-age women who report significant body image disturbance. These programs often exclude individuals with AN or BN (because one can not prevent an event after its onset); however, many of the participants may be diagnosable with an EDNOS (see Chapter 1 for a description of different diagnostic categories). Therefore, targeted prevention programs bear the greatest resemblance to treatment, and several of these programs include techniques originally developed in treatment studies, such as cognitive-behavioral techniques.

Results of studies have been somewhat promising. In general, participants in targeted prevention programs have reported improvements in knowledge and attitudes following intervention (Celio et al., 2000; Franko, 1998; Stice et al., 2001; Stice, Trost, & Chase, 2003; Winzelberg et al., 1998; Zabinski et al., 2001), and in all but three studies (Stice et al., 2001, 2003; Zabinski et al., 2001), these improvements were greater than those reported by controls and were maintained at follow-up. In addition, there is some evidence of improved behavior compared to controls at follow-up (Celio et al., 2000).

CONCLUSION

Prevention programs have demonstrated limited success (Carter, Stewart, Dunn, & Fairburn, 1997; Kater et al., 2000; Paxton, 1993; Rocco, Ciano, & Balestrieri, 2001; Santonastaso et al., 1999; Smolak, Levine, & Schermer, 1998; Varnado-Sullivan et al., 2001). Most often, improvements have been shown for knowledge and attitudes but not behaviors (Pearson, Goldklang, & Striegel-Moore, 2002; Steiner-Adair et al., 2002). For example, participants may report greater acceptance of heavier body types, but they do not report reduced dieting. Results that come closest to altering behavior come from targeted prevention studies in which eating disorder symptoms are reduced in a high-risk group following intervention. Across outcomes, targeted programs produce greater effects than universal programs (Stice & Shaw, 2004). Still, this may reflect treatment efficacy rather than prevention efficacy. Thus, prevention studies have yet to demonstrate powerful influences on preventing eating-disordered behavior. Rosenvinge and Borresen (1999) have argued that limited results reflect the limited understanding of factors that increase the risk of eating disorders. This calls for more research to reveal risk factors for eating disorders and programs that do not rely on altering specific risk factors to have an influence.

A second challenge in prevention is that improvements demonstrated immediately after intervention dissipate over the course of follow-up (Pearson et al., 2002; Stewart et al., 2001; Stice et al., 2003; Withers et al., 2002). As described above, the duration of programs is limited, with many programs providing as few as three (Buddeberg-Fischer & Reed, 2001; Rocco et al., 2001) or five sessions (Baranowski & Hetherington, 2001; Paxton, 1993; Wade et al., 2003). Indeed, two prevention studies used a videotape as the intervention (Moreno & Thelen, 1993; Withers et al., 2002). Given that girls reported watching 3.2 hours of television per day in one study (Tiggemann & Pickering, 1996), it is unclear how one 22-minute video could produce a lasting influence on attitudes after

1 month (Withers et al., 2002), much less throughout the period of risk for developing an eating disorder. Across programs, number of sessions is associated with program effectiveness (Stice & Shaw, 2004). Thus, modest interventions of limited duration may produce modest changes of limited duration. The solution is to increase the resources for implementing prevention programs. The greatest constraint on the scope of prevention is limited time available to work with children.

A third challenge in prevention has come from finding similar improvements in experimental and control groups (Baranowski & Hetherington, 2001; Stice et al., 2003). Although it is good to find improvement, it is difficult to interpret its meaning when no group differences are found. Improvement could reflect nonspecific benefits of encouraging healthy eating. It could reflect a phenomenon known as *regression to the mean*, in which individuals with more extreme scores on a measure of disordered eating would be expected to score closer to the mean when retested. It could reflect that individuals with problems improve as a function of "time healing all wounds." Alternatively, it may reveal important self-selection biases in who chooses to participate in prevention studies. In the case of targeted prevention programs, only individuals who are motivated to improve would likely volunteer, and this motivation may account for improvements over time independent of being included in the intervention versus the control group.

In thinking about the content of the prevention programs discussed above and even the paradigms in which prevention programs are conceived, it is clear that these programs have focused primarily on sociocultural factors described in Chapter 5 (media images, body image, and dieting), and, to a lesser extent, on some of the general risk factors described in Chapter 4. Although researchers have called for designs that would include families (see Chapter 6 for a discussion of family factors), this has yet to be successfully implemented (Littleton & Ollendick, 2003; Varnado-Sullivan et al., 2001). Thus, one way of thinking about prevention versus treatment is that prevention tends to focus on social factors, and to a lesser extent on some psychological factors, while treatment spans the full range of social, psychological, and biological factors. The emphasis on social factors in prevention programs reflects the public health focus of prevention as a discipline. However, this emphasis has two implicit premises. First, social factors have the greatest influence on the development of eating disorders. Second, social factors are the easiest to change. Perhaps another reason for the limited success of prevention programs thus far is an unmet need to critically evaluate these premises.

Future Directions for Prevention Programs

In order to improve future prevention programs, the following recommendations were provided after a roundtable discussion of experts convened by the National Institute of Mental Health:

1. Develop common definitions of symptoms, syndromes, risk factors, and outcomes to better assess progress in epidemiology and prevention trials.
2. Encourage the integration of basic social science research in prevention approaches.
3. Encourage research on neural mechanisms of eating disorders at the animal level. Foster cross-discipline interactions among animal experimentalists, clinicians, and other researchers in the field.
4. Develop guidelines for assessing the scientific merit of eating disorders prevention trials.
5. Develop approaches to assess and minimize iatrogenic effects (for example, producing the disordered behaviors the program attempts to prevent).

6. Encourage research in biology, personality traits, family and social groups, and societal norms and values, all of which influence the development of eating disorders.
7. Increase awareness that eating disorders are a public health problem and that prevention efforts are warranted.
8. Adopt an approach that considers the public health impact of these disorders.
(*Source:* Pearson, Goldklang, & Strigel-Moore. Prevention of eating disorders: Challenges and opportunities. Copyright © 2002 by Wiley Periodicals, Inc. *Reprinted with permission of John Wiley & Sons, Inc.*)

These recommendations reflect an expansion of prevention paradigms to examine the full range of etiological risk factors in eating disorders, from neuronal communication to cultural constructions of gender. They also reflect some of the impediments to developing efficacious prevention programs, which range from deficits in understanding the exact causes of eating disorders to societal stigmatization of eating disorders as problems that people choose to have (Crisp, Gelder, Rix, Meltzer, & Rowlands, 2000). Such ill-informed beliefs reduce support for prevention, limiting the success of this important endeavor.

KEY TERMS

Disease-Specific Pathways Model/Disease
   Prevention Paradigm
Empowerment-Relational Model
Health Promotion Paradigm

Nonspecific Vulnerability-Stressor Model
Selective prevention program
Targeted prevention program
Universal prevention program

CHAPTER 11

Long-Term Course and Outcome

This chapter examines the long-term **course** and **outcome** associated with eating disorders. *Outcome* refers to how well patients are doing at some point in time after they have been initially encountered (e.g., what percentage of patients have recovered from their eating disorder). *Course* refers to the path patients have taken between the time when they were first encountered and the time when the outcome is assessed. For example, two patients could have the same outcome (recovery) but could have taken very different pathways (or courses) to that outcome.

Although research on long-term course and outcome is largely descriptive, it has the potential to improve the diagnosis, understanding, and treatment of eating disorders. Differences in course and outcome across eating disorders can reveal valid distinctions among disorders (Kendell, 1989). Accurate distinctions among disorders will ultimately help to reveal their etiology. For example, valid definitions are required to identify the specific genes that increase the risk of eating disorders (see Chapter 8). Finally, it is essential to understand both the natural course of the illness and its course following intervention to evaluate whether a treatment works. This chapter reviews and then compares data on the long-term course and outcome of AN, BN, and BED. The following outcome domains are covered: mortality, recovery, **relapse, crossover,** and **prognostic** variables (variables that predict outcome). Because of differences in time when specific eating disorders were first identified (ranging from 1873 for AN to 1994 for BED), the availability of information on their outcome differs significantly.

ANOREXIA NERVOSA

Mortality

AN has been associated with one of the highest risks of premature death compared to other psychiatric disorders (Harris & Barraclough, 1998). Approximately 5% of patients diagnosed with AN have died by follow-up across outcome studies (Steinhausen, 2002; Sullivan, 1995). In order to understand how much the risk of death is increased in AN, studies use a **standardized mortality ratio.** This is a ratio of the observed number of deaths in a specific group (e.g., patients with AN) to the expected number of deaths in a matched population. Values significantly greater than 1.0 reflect an elevated risk of death. Standardized mortality ratios have ranged from 1.32 (Crisp, Callender, Halek, & Hsu, 1992) to 12.82 (Eckert, Malmi, Marchi, Grove, & Crosby, 1995) across studies. Several recent studies have reported standardized mortality ratios of around 10.0, suggesting that the risk of death increases 10 times when a person suffers from AN (Keel et al., 2003; Møller-Madsen, Nystrup, & Nielsen, 1996; Zipfel, Lowe, Reas, Deter, & Herzog, 2000).

Earlier studies tended to report starvation as a primary cause of death in AN; conversely, more recent studies have reported suicide as a leading cause of death (Nielsen et al., 1998). This shift may reflect several trends over time. For example, the diagnostic criteria for AN shifted from requiring a "loss of 25% of prior body weight" to "weight 15% below that expected for age and height." Reflecting this change, epidemiological data have demonstrated that the weights of patients seeking treatment for AN have increased over time (Eagles, Johnston, Hunter, Lobban, & Millar, 1995). Thus, fewer patients may be at risk for death by starvation. This pattern also may reflect the fact that many patients receive treatment earlier in the course of their illness. Finally, there may have been improvements in techniques employed to refeed undernourished patients over time.

Few predictors of a fatal outcome have been revealed. These include low weight (Herzog, Deter, Fiehn, & Petzold, 1997; Patton, 1988), poor psychosocial functioning (Engel, Wittern, Hentze, & Meyer, 1989; Keel et al., 2003), longer duration of follow-up (Keel et al., 2003; Steinhausen, 2002), and severity of alcohol use disorders (Keel et al., 2003). Low weight likely contributes to mortality because of the severe medical consequences of starvation (see Chapter 8). Poor psychosocial functioning may contribute to the risk of death by suicide. Longer duration of follow-up likely reflects the cumulative deleterious effects of starvation on physical health. Finally, alcohol use disorders may contribute to the suicide risk, and the risk of death by alcohol poisoning may be elevated in individuals with low weight and excessive alcohol consumption (Keel et al., 2003).

Recovery

Although a longer duration of follow-up has been associated with an increased risk of death, it is also associated with higher rates of recovery (Herzog et al., 1999; Steinhausen, 2002). Recovery rates increase slowly and steadily over time; patients with AN continue to recover many years after intake (Herzog et al., 1999) or treatment (Strober, Freeman, & Morrell, 1997b). Collapsing recovery rates across studies, Steinhausen (2002) reported that approximately 46% of patients recover, 33% improve (but remain symptomatic), and 20% remain chronically ill.

Relapse

Relapse occurs when a person has achieved remission from a disorder and then the disorder returns. Morgan and Russell (1975) reported that 51% of patients hospitalized for AN required readmission over the course of follow-up. Herzog and colleagues (1999) reported that 40% of women with AN who achieved full recovery later relapsed. Finally, Strober et al. (1997b) reported that approximately 30% of women who had achieved weight recovery during hospitalization relapsed after discharge. This study found lower rates of relapse among women considered partially recovered (9.8%) or fully recovered (0%) over follow-up. These latter data indicate that a more stringent definition of recovery (or remission) leads to a decreased risk of relapse. Overall, over a third of women who achieve weight recovery will lose weight, relapsing into AN. A common pattern among patients with AN is to experience improvement in weight (a sign of recovery) as a consequence of the development of binge-eating episodes (a sign of cross-over).

Crossover

Crossover is the transition from having one eating disorder to having another eating disorder. Thus, as an outcome, it is distinct from both recovery and relapse. Most women with ANR develop symptoms of binge eating and purging over time (Eddy et al., 2002). This finding is consistent with the hypothesis that dietary restriction increases the susceptibility to binge eat (Polivy & Herman, 1985). If binge eating and purging continue at low weight, then the person suffers from ANBP. If binge eating results in weight gain and the binge-purge behaviors continue at normal weight, then the person has crossed over from AN to BN. Across follow-up studies, approximately 10% to 50% of individuals with AN cross over to BN (Herzog, Keller, & Lavori, 1988).

Prognostic Factors

Prognostic factors are features that predict disorder course or outcome (also referred to as *prognosis*). Figure 11–1 presents prognostic factors adapted from a recent review of

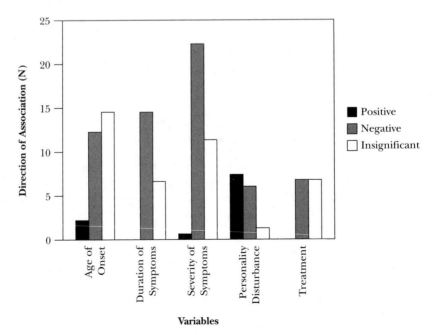

FIGURE 11–1 Prognostic indicators of a favorable course or outcome in AN.

outcome in AN (Steinhausen, 2002). No prognostic factor has been unambiguously associated with outcome. However, some tentative conclusions can be drawn from the pattern of contradictory findings. For example, 13 studies suggest that an older age of onset is associated with a worse prognosis in AN, and 14 studies suggest no significant association. Conversely, only two studies suggest that an older age of onset is associated with a favorable prognosis in AN. Similarly, 14 studies suggest that a longer duration of symptoms prior to presentation is associated with a poor prognosis in AN, and 7 studies suggest no significant association. Conversely, no studies suggest that a longer duration of symptoms is associated with a favorable prognosis in AN. Thus, the weight of evidence suggests that an older age of onset and a longer duration of illness are associated with lower recovery rates. These findings may demonstrate that an early age of onset is predictive of a better course and outcome only if there is a short delay before seeking treatment.

BULIMIA NERVOSA

Mortality

Across outcome studies, approximately 0.3% of patients with BN have died (Keel & Mitchell, 1997). Standardized mortality ratios for BN have ranged from 1.3 (Keel et al., 2003) to 9.38 (Patton, 1988). However, neither of these ratios differed significantly from 1.0.

The true risk of death in BN may be underestimated because of limited follow-up duration across studies. In addition, several BN outcome studies have been unable to locate patients at follow-up. If some of these missing patients died, then studies would underestimate mortality. Nielsen (2001) reported a significantly elevated standardized mortality ratio for BN after combining results across several studies. However, Nielsen included patients with the binge-purge subtype of AN, potentially increasing the rate of death. Keel et al. (2003) found that mortality was similarly elevated in both subtypes of AN but not in BN. Moreover, no original report found a significantly elevated standardized mortality ratio in BN. Thus, patients with BN do not appear to be at increased risk for death.

Primary causes of death have included suicide and automobile accidents (Keel & Mitchell, 1997). However, these are similar to the causes of death reported for adolescent and young adult women. No predictors of mortality have been found for BN.

Recovery

Prospective longitudinal studies of the course of BN suggest that the majority of patients recover, like Jean, from their eating disorder at some point during follow-up (Herzog et al., 1999; Miller, Keel, Mitchell, Thuras, & Crow, 2004). Combining results across outcome studies, Keel and Mitchell (1997) reported that approximately 50% of individuals with BN recover and maintain their recovery, 30% are improved but maintain partial syndromes, and 20% continue to meet full criteria for BN. Longer follow-up studies suggest that the rate of full BN drops to 10% at 10-year follow-up (Collings & King, 1994; Keel et al., 1999).

Case Study

Jean responded well to treatment and was free from symptoms within 4 months of starting therapy. She was particularly concerned about relapsing because she knew how easily this could happen. Her therapist encouraged her to join a support group for patients who had recovered from eating disorders. The therapist felt that this might help Jean appreciate how far she had come and support Jean when she felt pressure to diet or lose weight. One of the most important achievements of therapy was helping Jean recognize that she was at a healthy weight without dieting. In addition, Jean's therapist encouraged her to reveal her eating problems to her boyfriend so that he could provide support. Jean stayed in the support group for approximately 8 months. She formed two close friendships there and continued to socialize with the members. In fact, one of the group members was a bridesmaid at Jean's wedding. Jean found that the older she became, the less she cared about her weight and shape. This was particularly true after she had her first child. She was concerned that she would lose control over the weight gain associated with pregnancy, but she didn't. She actually liked the way her body looked during pregnancy, and afterward she was too busy with her baby daughter to worry about her weight. In addition, Jean was committed to setting a good example for her daughter, Eva. She wanted Eva to have high self-esteem and accept her body exactly as it was. Toward this goal, Jean finally confronted her mother when she commented that Eva was eating too much. Jean told her that Eva's appetite and weight were perfectly healthy and normal for a girl of her age, and that such critical comments were neither helpful nor welcome. Ten years after treatment, Jean remained happily married with two children and was working as an office manager. She occasionally ate too much and felt fat when she was under stress. However, her eating disorder never returned.

———— •◆• ————

Relapse

Rates of relapse have ranged from 26% to 50% across follow-up studies of BN (Fairburn, et al., 2000; Fichter & Quadflieg, 1997; Keel & Mitchell, 1997). Similar to the patterns observed with AN, more stringent definitions of recovery are associated with lower relapse rates (Field et al., 1997; Olmsted, Kaplan, & Rockert, 1994). This pattern raises the question of whether studies are assessing relapse or simple symptom fluctuation. That is, are patients truly remitting and relapsing or are their symptom levels simply fluctuating around diagnostic thresholds? Despite considerable differences in definitions of remission/recovery across studies (Keel, Mitchell, Davis, Fieselman, & Crow, 2000a), relapse rates converge around 30% across most studies (Keel & Mitchell, 1997).

Crossover

Across follow-up studies, between 0% and 7% of patients appear to cross over from BN to AN (Fichter & Quadflieg, 1997; Keel & Mitchell, 1997). Rates this low raise the question of whether those individuals who cross over from BN to AN may have had a history of AN before developing BN. In such cases, the return of AN would represent relapse rather than true crossover. Crossover to BED also seems low, ranging from 0% to 1.1% (Fichter & Quadflieg, 1997; Keel & Mitchell, 1997; Keel et al., 1999).

Keel and colleagues (2000b) reported that, over time, women with BN were more likely to continue to suffer from BN than cross over to either AN or BED. Conversely, at long-term follow-up, approximately 10% of women were found to have a purging disorder—characterized by recurrent purging in the absence of binge episodes at normal weight. The likelihood of suffering from a purging disorder did not differ significantly from the likelihood of suffering from BN at long-term follow-up. Further, women were significantly more likely to suffer from purging disorder than from BED (Keel et al., 2000b). Thus, when crossover occurs in BN, it most often involves crossing over to a purging disorder.

Prognostic Factors

Figure 11–2 presents prognostic factors updated from a recent review of outcome in BN (Keel & Mitchell, 1997). Few prognostic factors have been replicated across studies. Similar to the pattern observed for AN, six studies reported that a longer duration of symptoms was associated with a poor prognosis in BN, and three studies found no significant association. However, no studies reported that a longer duration of symptoms was associated with a favorable prognosis in BN. Similarly, six studies suggested that personality disturbance was associated with a poor prognosis, and four studies found no significant association. No studies reported that personality disturbance was associated with a favorable outcome. Both longer duration of illness and personality disturbance may decrease the likelihood of a response to treatment.

Overall, treatment seems to either improve or have no impact on BN outcome. Keel and Mitchell (1997) found that studies with a shorter duration of follow-up tended to find a favorable effect of treatment on outcome. Studies with a longer duration of follow-up tended to find no significant association between treatment and outcome. Notably, few studies have evaluated the long-term impact of treatment on recovery in BN. At 5- to 9-year follow-up, Fairburn et al. (1995) found that both cognitive-behavioral therapy and interpersonal therapy were associated with a better outcome than behavioral therapy. However, most other authors have failed to find an impact of treatment on long-term outcome in BN (Collings & King, 1994; Fallon, Walsh, Sadik, Saoud, & Lukasik, 1991; Keel et al., 1999).

How can we reconcile the short-term treatment efficacy of cognitive-behavioral therapy and antidepressant medications (Peterson & Mitchell, 1999) with the rather bleak picture of their long-term impact (Keel et al., 1999)? The key may be in evaluating the long-term *course* rather than the long-term *outcome* of BN. If the outcome represents the

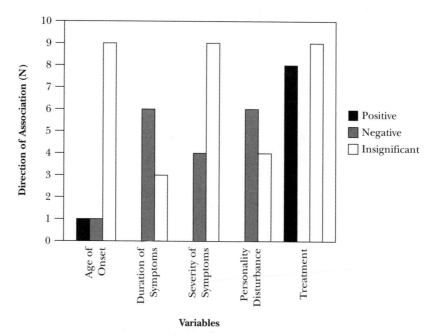

FIGURE 11–2 Prognostic indicators of a favorable course or outcome in BN.

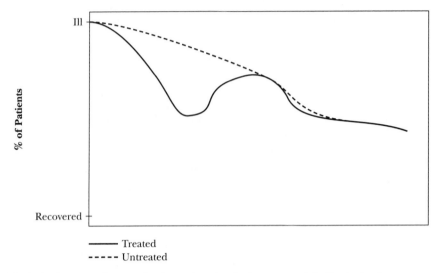

FIGURE 11–3   Increased rates of relapse in a treated group explain the lack of treatment effect at long-term follow-up.

final destination, then the course represents the path taken to that destination. Two course patterns could account for the distinct pictures of treatment impact provided by short-term versus long-term outcome studies. First, increased relapse rates in women who responded to treatment could reduce the long-term efficacy of initially successful interventions (see Figure 11–3). Second, eventual recovery among women who did not receive treatment would obscure the initial benefits of treatment (see Figure 11–4). Thus, treatment could

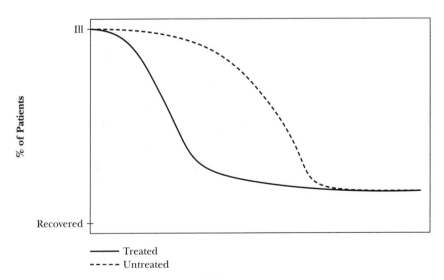

FIGURE 11–4   Eventual recovery in an untreated group explains the lack of treatment effect at long-term follow-up.

speed recovery without showing an impact on long-term outcome (Keel, Mitchell, Davis, & Crow, 2002b). Data support the latter explanation. Miller et al. (2004) reported that women who received cognitive-behavioral therapy achieved recovery sooner and maintained it longer than women who did not receive this therapy. Furthermore, relapse rates did not differ across treatment conditions.

BINGE-EATING DISORDER

Since the introduction of BED in the *DSM-IV* (APA, 1994), a number of treatment studies have been published, and several have provided short-term and intermediate follow-up data (Agras, Telch, Arnow, Eldredge, & Marnell, 1997; Cachelin et al., 1999; Ciano, Rocco, Angarano, Biasin, & Balestrieri, 2002; Devlin, Goldfein, Carino, & Wolk, 2000; Peterson et al., 2001; Ricca et al., 2001). Nevertheless, relatively little is known about the long-term course and outcome of BED. At this point, two studies (Fairburn et al., 2000; Fichter et al., 1998) have characterized the course and outcome for this disorder at 5 or more years following presentation. Because of the limited number of long-term follow-up studies, the results of these two studies are reviewed individually below.

Fichter et al. (1998) reported one death among 68 patients treated for BED at 6-year follow-up, resulting in a crude mortality rate of 1.5%. Fairburn et al. (2000) reported no deaths in their cohort of 48 individuals with BED recruited from the community. Rates of full BED at follow-up were 4% (Fairburn et al., 2000) and 5.9% (Fichter et al., 1998), with 57.4% (Fichter et al., 1998) to 82% (Fairburn et al., 2000) of patients reported as improved or recovered. Fairburn et al. (2000) reported that relapse occurred in 4–10% of recovered individuals across various points of follow-up. Crossover to AN did not occur and crossover to BN was rare, ranging from 3% (Fairburn et al., 2000) to 7.4% (Fichter et al., 1998). Neither study reported on predictors of the long-term course or outcome of BED.

COMPARISON OF EATING DISORDERS

Anorexia Nervosa and Bulimia Nervosa

Both within studies (Fichter & Quadflieg, 1999; Keel et al., 2003) and across studies (Keel & Mitchell, 1997; Steinhausen, 2002), AN appears to be associated with a significantly increased risk of premature death and BN does not. Suicide attempts are more common in AN than BN (Franko et al., in press), and starvation likely compromises the health of individuals with AN, leaving them less likely to survive a suicide attempt.

Within studies (Fichter & Quadflieg, 1999; Herzog et al., 1999), AN has been associated with lower rates of recovery compared to BN. Collapsing results across studies suggests a similar distribution of recovery, improvement, and chronicity across syndromes (Keel & Mitchell, 1997; Steinhausen, 2002). However, this latter comparison is flawed because of differences in the duration of follow-up between the disorders. As noted above, longer duration of follow-up is associated with higher rates of recovery for both disorders (Keel et al., 1999; Steinhausen, 2002), and the duration of follow-up has been longer for AN than BN.

AN and BN have similar relapse rates (Herzog et al., 1999), but the relationship between relapse and chronicity likely differs between the disorders. Because a high percentage of women with BN recover at some point during follow-up, the chronic course appears to be characterized by a pattern of remission and relapse. Because a smaller percentage of women recover from AN, the chronic course of AN is marked by a more steady presence of symptoms. This difference also may be reflected in the nature of the core features of these syndromes. For AN, the core symptom is the absence of a behavior—eating. For BN, the core symptoms are the presence of two behaviors—binge eating and purging. Thus, in order to develop AN, an individual must avoid eating consistently. In contrast, a woman can develop BN by having relatively normal eating behaviors interrupted by episodes of abnormal eating behaviors.

Patterns of crossover also differ markedly between AN and BN. Approximately 10% to 50% of women with AN cross over and develop BN, and approximately 30% of women with BN report a prior history of AN. Conversely, only 0% to 7% of women with BN have been reported to cross over and develop AN. This pattern likely reflects the consequences of the core features of each disorder. Specifically, intense dietary restriction and weight loss likely increase the risk of developing binge-eating episodes. Conversely, large binge-eating episodes likely protect against low weight. Indeed, comparisons of the subtypes of AN suggest that binge eating and purging are associated with higher weight.

AN and BN appear to have different prognostic indicators. However, this is likely a function of the difference in the number and size of outcome studies for the two disorders. An early age of onset was associated with an improved prognosis in AN but was unassociated with the prognosis in BN. Currently, the most effective treatments for AN involve family interventions (see Chapter 9). These are likely to be more useful for young adolescent patients who live with their parents. Thus, little is known about the effective treatment of older patients with AN. In contrast, BN develops during young adulthood. Successful treatments include cognitive-behavioral therapy and antidepressant medications. These are likely to work well across the developmental range of late adolescence to middle age.

Longer duration of symptoms at intake predicts a worse outcome for both AN and BN. Severity of symptoms appears to be associated with the prognosis of AN but not BN. This result may reflect the fact that chronicity in AN is associated with a steady course whereas chronicity in BN is associated with considerable symptom fluctuation. If this is true, then a single measure of symptom severity in BN would be an unreliable indicator, limiting its ability to predict BN outcome. By contrast, the overall duration of illness would capture the length of time a patient struggled with an eating disorder, regardless of course fluctuations.

Personality disturbances have been associated with a worse prognosis for both AN and BN. However, the nature of personality disturbances has differed. Obsessive-compulsive personality features have been associated with a worse prognosis in AN (Steinhausen, 2002). Conversely, borderline personality features and marked impulsiveness have been associated with a worse prognosis in BN (Keel & Mitchell, 1997). These findings likely reflect differences in the core symptoms of these disorders. AN is marked by rigid adherence to dietary restriction, BN by recurrent loss of control over eating. As described above, these differences are also reflected in the disease course among those who remain chronically ill.

The impact of treatment on disorder outcome differs between AN and BN. Although treatment has not been significantly associated with the long-term outcome in BN (Keel et al., 1999), it has been associated with a differential course (Miller et al., 2004). Thus, treatments that have demonstrated efficacy for BN appear to speed recovery. In contrast, few treatments are associated with a long-term outcome in AN. There is evidence that a longer duration of inpatient treatment is associated with a worse outcome in AN (Steinhausen, 2002 see the figure on page 157). This likely reflects the effect of increased disorder severity increasing treatment use (Keel et al., 2002). One study found that family-based treatment was superior to individual treatment at 5-year follow-up (see Chapter 9). New controlled treatment studies have been initiated for AN, but more time is needed to evaluate the long-term impact of these treatments on AN course or outcome.

Bulimia Nervosa and Binge-Eating Disorder

As in BN, the risk of a fatal outcome may not be elevated in BED. However, obesity in BED may contribute to increased mortality when the duration of follow-up increases across studies. The comparison of recovery in BN and BED has produced inconsistent results. Fairburn and colleagues (2000) found that rates of recovery were higher for BED compared to BN, but Fichter and colleagues (1998) failed to find any differences in outcome. Fichter et al. (1998) recruited participants from an inpatient treatment program, and Fairburn et al. studied women recruited from the community. Arguably, women receiving inpatient treatment for BED may have a more severe illness compared to women with BED in the community. Thus, selection factors that lead patients to seek inpatient treatment may explain the increased similarity of outcomes between BN and BED in Fichter et al.'s study.

CONCLUSION

As noted at the beginning of the chapter, data on long-term course and outcome could improve the diagnosis, understanding, and treatment of eating disorders. Such data support the predictive validity of distinguishing between AN and BN. These disorders appear to be associated with different rates of mortality, recovery, and crossover, as well as distinct sets of prognostic indicators (including different treatment responses).

Few studies have assessed the long-term outcome of BN and BED, and even fewer have examined the natural history of these disorders at long-term follow-up. Indeed, almost all longitudinal studies of eating disorders are based on treatment-seeking samples even though the majority of women with eating disorders may not seek treatment (Fairburn et al., 1996, 2000). Using treatment-seeking samples introduces certain biases in study results. For example, follow-up studies based on treatment-seeking samples may present a more dire description of outcome. Alternatively, treatment may increase the rate of recovery (Fairburn et al., 1995) or reduce the time to recovery (Keel, Mitchell, Davis, & Crow, 2002; Miller et al., 2003). Thus, more data are needed to evaluate the validity of distinguishing between BN and BED.

Features that are associated with the maintenance of eating disorder symptoms may play a role in the initiation of eating disorders. Evidence that obsessive-compulsive features are associated with the prognosis in AN, while impulsive-borderline features are associated with the prognosis in BN, offers the opportunity to reveal risk factors that may be specific to each eating disorder. Improved understanding of the etiology of eating disorders holds the promise of their prevention.

KEY TERMS

Course	Prognostic
Crossover	Relapse
Outcome	Standardized mortality ratio

CHAPTER 12

Conclusion

Eating disorders represent a serious form of psychopathology. They are associated with great distress, impairment in life functioning, and significant medical risk. Among the different forms of mental disorders presented in the *DSM-IV* and *ICD-10,* few demonstrate such a clear influence of culture in the prevalence and presentation of symptoms. Yet, eating disorders are not restricted to modern Western culture. Similarly, few disorders show the imbalanced gender ratio presented by eating disorders. Yet, eating disorders are not restricted to women. Epidemiological patterns provide some hints to the etiology of these disorders without fully explaining why one individual develops an eating disorder and another does not. Moreover, eating disorders represent a fascinating example of social, psychological, and biological factors conspiring to produce a specific kind of mental illness. This chapter summarizes information presented in this book in the context of information originally presented for the case studies and briefly examines current debates within the field. This chapter ends with a consideration of potential directions for future research endeavors.

CASE STUDIES REVISITED

Case of Anorexia Nervosa

Emily described herself as being "forced into treatment" by her school. She was a sophomore at a prestigious university. Emily made it clear that she thoroughly resented the university's interference in her private life since she had top grades in all of her classes and was clearly fine. She saw no reason to be in therapy or any sort of treatment. Emily was 5 feet 10 inches and weighed 109 pounds. This placed her weight at approximately 76% of that expected for her height and age. Her college roommates were extremely worried about her because she had to be taken to the emergency room after fainting in the dining hall. When asked about the incident, Emily said that she had lost track of the time, hadn't eaten all day, and became lightheaded after her afternoon run. However, she asserted that this was very unusual for her and that she always had a high-energy snack before exercising. In fact, she said that she always carried food with her because she had a tendency to be hypoglycemic and that, in contrast to what people thought, she was eating all the time. When asked to describe what she would eat during a given day, Emily said that she had cereal for breakfast, snacked throughout the day, had a salad for lunch, snacked throughout the afternoon, and then ate a full dinner. Upon further questioning, she stated that she ate one packet of instant oatmeal made with spring water for breakfast in her room. Her snacks consisted of celery sticks, carrot sticks, or sugar-free gum. For lunch, she ate a "huge" plate of salad greens without dressing from the dining hall's salad bar. Dinner was the only meal that varied from one day to the next. She might eat skinless chicken breast with half of a baked potato and a green vegetable. Occasionally, she ate half a cup of pasta with tomato sauce and vegetables added from the salad bar. On days when the dining hall served nothing she liked, she ate two slices of bread with cottage cheese spread over each slice and tomatoes on top—she likened this to pizza—with a large salad. She stated that she didn't eat red meat because she didn't like the idea of eating cute, furry animals. In fact, she didn't care for meat as a food group but made sure that her diet always included protein because she knew it was important for muscle development. Emily considered muscle development to be important because she felt that she was constantly struggling with a "lop-sided" body. She felt that her shoulders and arms were too thin and sticklike, while her hips, thighs, and buttocks were rotund. She described herself as having a "classic pear shape." To improve her muscle definition, Emily exercised rigorously. She ran every afternoon after classes and before dinner. On weekends, she added weight training to her routine. She had read that metabolism increased both during and after exercise and felt that this pattern increased the probability that the dinner she ate would be used to fuel her body rather than being stored as fat. She was terrified of becoming fat. When asked about her menstrual cycle, Emily stated that it had "always been irregular." She started menstruating later than most girls, around 14 years of age, and had a period only every 3 months. When she was 16, her doctor prescribed birth control pills to increase the regularity of her menstrual cycle. This had caused her to gain weight, and this was when she first began to diet and lose weight. Her mother attributed her weight change to Emily's loss of "baby fat," and her friends expressed admiration of her self-control. Emily once was approached in the shopping mall, asked if she had ever considered becoming a model, and given the card of a modeling agency. Although flattered, she did not pursue this opportunity because she planned to go to a good college, then go to law school, and eventually become a judge. She felt that a career in modeling would be a waste of her intellect and that it required people to focus on superficial things like appearance.

―――――――― • ◆ • ――――――――

Case of Bulimia Nervosa ―――――― • ◆ • ―――――――――――――――

Jean was a 27-year-old secretary who lived with her boyfriend of 2 years. She was 5 feet 4 inches tall and weighed 138 pounds. She came in for treatment because of a return of eating problems that she thought had ended in college. In college, she had binge-eating episodes and had engaged in self-induced vomiting. She spent a great deal of time trying to hide these behaviors from her roommates and from her family when she went home during breaks. However, her roommates confronted her after a particularly bad episode in which she had gone to the bathroom to self-induce vomiting four times within a 2-hour period. She had received treatment that allowed her to stop binge eating and purging on a regular basis. She continued to have occasional slips—times when she felt she had eaten too much and purged to avoid weight gain. However, these had occurred rarely, and there were times when she prevented herself from vomiting when she felt she had eaten too much. About a year and a half ago, she noticed that she was gaining weight and could no longer fit into the same size jeans she had worn since high school. Jean said that she couldn't bring herself to buy larger jeans because she couldn't feel good about herself unless she fit into that specific size. She decided to diet and go to the gym more regularly. At first, her new fitness routine worked, and she lost approximately 7 pounds. At 125 pounds, Jean felt great about herself and found that she was more likely to want to go out with friends and to flirt with and get attention from men. However, when she and her boyfriend started living together, she had a hard time resisting the tempting foods he kept in the kitchen. When she lived alone, she had never had cookies, ice cream, or potato chips in the house because these had been common triggers for binge-eating episodes. Now these foods were always around. At first, she simply resisted eating them because they were not part of her diet. However, one night while her boyfriend was out with his friends, Jean ate an entire bag of potato chips and finished off a package of cookies and three fourths of a gallon of ice cream. Disgusted with herself and in pain from the amount of food she had consumed, she made herself throw up. Afterward, she went to the store to replace what she had eaten. She ended up throwing out some of the new ice cream and cookies in order to hide all evidence of her binge. Jean vowed that she would not eat any more of these "dangerous foods" and told herself that this was just a slip. However, the next week, when she was alone in the apartment, the same cycle happened again. She would binge and purge only when she was alone, but whenever this happened, she could not resist. Binging and purging were now happening several times per week. She regained the weight she had lost and found that it was creeping up above her prediet weight. She then redoubled her efforts at dieting to counteract the effects of her binge episodes in addition to using self-induced vomiting. She even began vomiting when she ate normal amounts of food because she believed that it was necessary to eat as little as possible in order to get rid of the unwanted weight. She felt disgusted with herself. As her weight increased, she felt worthless and revolting.

Case of Binge Eating Disorder

Jamie's problem was simply stated as follows: "I eat too much. For some people, it's alcohol, for some it's cocaine; for me it's food." Jamie said that this had always been true; even as a small child, a whole box of Twinkies was a single serving. For a junior high school bake sale, Jamie's mother had baked a cherry pie. The pie, Jamie's favorite dessert, was gone before the start of school that day. When asked for the dessert, Jamie lied to conceal the gluttony. There had been many times like this throughout childhood, episodes of eating all of something rather than just one serving. However, because Jamie was tall and athletic, the big appetite was often a source of pride rather than embarrassment. In fact, everyone on the athletic teams ate large amounts of food, so Jamie didn't feel unusual most of the time. The realization that there was an eating problem did not emerge until the end of college, when Jamie started interviewing for jobs. It was the first time Jamie needed to buy a suit but couldn't fit into any of the sizes offered in the normal department store. Jamie was embarrassed by having to go to a special store that stocked larger sizes. Currently, Jamie weighed 360 pounds despite several diets and several different weight loss programs. Jamie was frequently able to lose some weight on these programs; the greatest weight loss was 50 pounds, down from 280 to 230 pounds. However, as at all other times, the weight came back—and more. Jamie denied eating when not hungry but acknowledged eating to the point of being uncomfortably full. Jamie felt that this was because, when hungry, eating occurred at one rate: "as much and as quickly as possible." This was true for all favorite foods. Jamie said it was like being a "food addict"; there was no way to stop until all of the food was gone. For example, Jamie would consume three supersize value meals from the local fast food restaurant in the car on the way home from work. Eating alone in the car was "the best" because "I can just zone out." However, terrible guilt followed these episodes because Jamie knew that eating so much junk food contributed to the weight problem—and could lead to heart problems. However, Jamie didn't like salads, vegetables, or fruit because they were bland and boring. Jamie said, "I wish I felt about fast food the way that I feel about salads because then I would be thin as a rail." Jamie wanted to know if there was any medication that would cause weight loss or make it easier not to eat. Based on all of the TV advertisements, Jamie felt like a good candidate for medication because there was definitely an eating problem occurring every day—often throughout the day.

In the *DSM-IV-TR* and *ICD-10*, two eating disorders are formally recognized, AN (exemplified by Emily) and BN (exemplified by Jean). The *DSM-IV-TR* also provides a provisional diagnostic category of BED (exemplified by Jamie). However, most individuals who suffer from eating disorders do not fit into one of these three categories. These individuals would be diagnosed with an EDNOS or an atypical eating disorder. Studies often exclude individuals with EDNOS because there are no standard definitions for most of these disorders, and absence of standard definitions decreases the likelihood of replicating study results. To the extent that EDNOS represent subthreshold diagnoses that exist on a continuum with AN and BN, the causes, consequences, and effective treatment of EDNOS may be adequately addressed by research on defined eating disorders. Thus, one debate within the field is whether eating disorders exist on a continuum or represent distinct categorical entities.

Proponents of the continuum view point to similarities in who is vulnerable to developing eating disorders, the symptom overlap among disorders, and the high longitudinal crossover between AN and BN. Emily and Jean both fear weight gain and engage in dietary restriction, and Jean and Jamie both experience uncontrollable urges to binge eat. Emily is underweight, Jean is normal weight, and Jamie is overweight. In several ways, these cases do appear to exist on a continuum of disordered eating attitudes and behaviors. However, evidence of discontinuity between AN and BN exists as well, and this evidence indicates the need for caution in assuming continuity between these disorders and EDNOS. For example, although BN appears to be a culturally bound syndrome, AN does not, suggesting that the disorders likely have distinct etiological features. Further, initial molecular genetic research suggests that specific genes may be related to specific eating disorder subtypes and not to eating disorders in general. To the extent that AN and BN are caused by different factors, this suggests that they do not exist on a continuum. In addition, BN responds to treatment with cognitive-behavioral therapy, interpersonal therapy, and antidepressant medication, whereas AN does not. This again suggests that AN and BN may represent distinct categories. Finally, AN and BN are associated with distinct courses and outcomes. The implications of this debate are far-reaching. Much of the research on risk factors and prevention, as well as experimental analogue studies, examine disordered eating attitudes and behaviors rather than specific eating disorders. The extent to which relevant data come from studies comparing high versus low scorers on continuous measures of dietary restraint or bulimic symptoms for understanding AN and BN may be limited by the extent to which the continuum model of eating disorders is valid.

Chapter 2 reviewed evidence that BN appears to represent a culture-bound syndrome, consistent with evidence that this disorder is caused by an overemphasis on the importance of weight in modern Western culture. In contrast, AN appears to have emerged as a distinct syndrome long before the modern idealization of thinness and seems to be present in non-Western cultures among individuals who have not been exposed to Western ideals. These findings suggest that body image disturbance may represent a more central feature in BN than in AN. However, these differences are not apparent in the case histories of Emily and Jean. In both cases, body image disturbance appears to be the motivation for their disordered eating. The difference may exist in the extent to which body image concerns represent a *cause* versus an *interpretation* of disordered eating. Thus, another significant debate within the field is whether weight concerns represent a central feature of AN or not.

Proponents of the view that weight concerns are a central feature of AN point to the increasing incidence of AN coinciding with increased idealization of thinness and the role weight concerns play in many patients' initial food restriction and continued refusal to eat. In addition, studies in the United States and Canada suggest that individuals with atypical AN (that is, AN without an intense fear of fat) simply look like individuals with a less severe version of AN at presentation and follow-up. This would suggest that weight concerns are important in defining AN because the symptom is associated with the outcome in clinically meaningful ways. This debate is almost impossible to resolve by assessing individuals in modern Western cultures. In a Western culture, weight concerns represent a meaningful symptom of AN. That is, a patient's expression of terror over gaining weight reflects the intensity of her disorder—even if weight concerns represent an interpretation of self-starvation rather than the true cause. Thus, varying levels of weight concerns are analogous to varying levels of underweight; both represent differing levels of symptom severity. Because outcome studies suggest that symptom severity is associated with the outcome in AN, it would be surprising if women with more severe weight concerns did not experience worse outcomes compared to women with less severe weight concerns. A more valid comparison can be made in non-Western cultures, where there would be alternative explanations for self-starvation. What might be explained as terror over gaining weight in one context can be expressed as terror over feeling sick in another. The intensity of the expression, terror versus discomfort, could be similar even though the focus differed by cultural context. In non-Western cultures, differences in severity have not been found between AN patients with and without weight concerns, suggesting that weight concerns may not be a central feature of AN. Importantly, in a culture with ubiquitous idealization of thinness and denigration of fatness, there are individuals who do develop AN because of these messages. A question remains: how many of them might have developed AN without these messages?

Chapter 3 examined the stereotype that eating disorders predominantly affect White girls. This chapter revealed that eating disorders appear to be underrepresented among Black individuals but that rates of eating pathology appear to be similar among White, Asian, Hispanic, and Native American groups in the United States. Jean is a Korean American woman, and strong pressure to lose weight comes from her mother, who was born in Korea. Thus, eating disorders are not restricted to White individuals any more than they are restricted to Western cultures. Eating disorders are more common in women than men. Nevertheless, these disorders may go undetected in men when they do not conform to the typology presented by women. Notably, Jamie does not have body image disturbance because the concern he feels over his weight seems appropriate given the health risks associated with his obesity. A diagnosis of BED does not require body image disturbance, and this may explain why this disorder has a less skewed gender distribution. If one decides that body image disturbance is a central feature of all eating disorders, this might decrease the number of individuals diagnosed with BED, particularly men. Within the field, there is debate about whether diagnostic criteria should be expanded so that they become more inclusive and more representative of the population with eating problems.

Proponents of expanded criteria note that we tend to treat what we define. Thus, definitions that exclude certain portions of the population from diagnosis also exclude them from treatment. In defining eating disorders, others have called for a more parsimonious approach that defines the least possible number of categories. These individuals note that there are risks inherent in pathologizing behaviors that do not represent an actual disorder. For example, they have raised the question of whether BED is an eating disorder or is better conceptualized as the convergence of major depressive disorder and obesity. These individuals point to the symptom overlap between depression and BED, the high levels of depression in patients with BED, the similar gender distributions between depression and BED, and the fact that BED responds to many of the treatments with demonstrated efficacy in treating depression. They question whether it is ultimately more helpful or more harmful to add a diagnosis of BED in an obese person already diagnosed with depression. However, one consequence of deciding that BED is not an eating disorder would be a dramatic reduction in the representation of men and Black women among those diagnosed with an eating disorder. This raises the specter that criteria do not simply reflect who suffers from eating disorders but actively creates gender and ethnic differences in the distribution of these disorders.

Chapter 4 reviewed different methods for examining risk factors for eating disorders. These include studies of correlates, longitudinal studies, experimental studies, and studies of natural phenomena. The limitations of each method were revealed. For example, dieting appears to be a common correlate of eating disorders in the case studies of Emily, Jean, and Jamie. This pattern suggests that dieting may serve as a risk factor for eating disorders. However, dieting seems to be a response to obesity in Jamie's case, revealing why correlations do not prove causation. Probably one of the more heated debates in the field at this time is whether dieting represents a risk factor for eating disorders or an important and safe intervention in the prevention of obesity.

Proponents of dieting note that obesity is increasing in the United States. As a consequence, certain weight-related diseases are increasing as well. For example, type II diabetes is increasing among adolescents as a consequence of increasing obesity rates. Thus, from a public health perspective, weight loss appears to be an important goal for many adolescents. However, several individuals in the field of eating disorders feel that the emphasis should be placed not on weight loss dieting but on healthy eating and physical activity. These individuals feel that focusing on a number, such as BMI (weight in kilograms divided by the square of height in meters) encourages attitudes that lead to eating disorders. They argue that the emphasis on weight reflects societal biases against overweight individuals. They point to the limited long-term efficacy of weight-loss dieting and the extent to which this sets people up for failure, decreases self-worth, and may contribute to the onset of binge eating. However, data on the relationship between dieting and eating disorders are based largely on normal-weight populations. So, conclusions about the risks of dieting in the development of eating disorders may not generalize to people who are significantly overweight. This possibility seems to be supported by the efficacy of behavioral weight-loss programs in the treatment of BED. These programs appear to be able to produce weight loss *and* decrease binge eating. However, this does not answer the question of what message health professionals should give to healthy, normal-weight children when the goal is to prevent both eating disorders and obesity.

Chapters 5 and 6 examined two forms of social influence that may contribute to the development of eating disorders. At a societal level, media messages reinforce the importance of thinness and the denigration of fatness. A common thread in all three case studies is the importance of not being fat. This appears to contribute to self-starvation in Emily's case, self-induced vomiting in Jean's case, and significant distress over binge eating in Jamie's case. Families may contribute to the development of eating pathology by serving as a conduit of such messages. Notably, even psychodynamic and systems-oriented theories include the presence of disturbed parental eating patterns, suggesting that parents may directly model behaviors that reinforce the thin ideal. Disturbed parental eating patterns also may reflect the influence of genetic factors on the environments parents create for their children. Thus, genetic and environmental factors may be correlated and enhance the influence of familial factors on eating disorders. Although genetic and environmental factors likely work in concert to increase the risk of eating disorders, nature-versus-nurture debates still occur in the field.

Despite the general consensus that a biopsychosocial model is necessary to understand the causes, treatment, and prevention of eating disorders, experts disagree on what focus will provide the "next big break" in the field. Proponents of biological research feel that molecular genetic and neuroimaging studies represent the future of the field and note the limited impact of psychosocial investigations. Proponents of psychosocial research feel that biological approaches have limited relevance for understanding disorders that appear to be dramatically influenced by psychosocial factors. Both sides point to examples of shoddy methodology and poorly supported conclusions in the other's area. Indeed, for any area of inquiry, one can find examples of poorly conducted research. Still, it would be an error in logic to conclude from specific examples of poor research that an entire area of inquiry has little value.

Chapter 7 described psychological factors that appear to contribute to the onset and maintenance of eating disorders. Individuals with AN and BN appear to share cognitive distortions such as dichotomous thinking, selective abstraction, and overemphasis on the importance of weight and shape. For example, both Emily and Jean believe that some foods are good (e.g., salad) and other foods are bad (e.g., ice cream). In addition, the symptoms of eating disorders appear to represent a vicious cycle in which disturbed patterns are maintained through processes of positive and negative reinforcement. For example, Emily's dietary restriction and Jean's self-induced vomiting are negatively reinforced by their fear of gaining weight, and both Jean and Jamie find themselves irresistibly drawn to the rewarding effects of forbidden foods. Personality may provide the predisposition for thinking and behaving in ways that contribute to the development of eating disorders. Like Emily, individuals who develop ANR have been characterized as perfectionistic, rigid, and reserved. Individuals with bulimic symptoms have been characterized as impulsive and emotionally labile. Interestingly, perfectionism also has been used to characterize individuals who develop BN. Thus, it is possible for Jean to have perfectionist strivings to maintain a certain body type but to fail to meet these rigid standards because of problems with impulse control. Within the field, an interesting question has been raised concerning the role of personality as a predisposition to eating pathology versus a defining aspect of this pathology.

Some researchers have argued that personality is so closely involved in the development of eating disorder subtypes that personality features should be included in defining the subtypes. For example, extreme perfectionism and rigidity would be symptoms on par with self-starvation in defining ANR. These researchers have argued that identifying stable personality traits that exist before and after the eating disorder holds promise for understanding the true causes of eating pathology by identifying a stable phenotype. Others have noted the significant instability and inconsistency of personality findings for most other eating disorders. For example, problems with impulse control appear to remit with the remission of bulimic symptoms, suggesting that these problems may not reflect personality traits at all. Thus, personality disturbance may play a more central role in understanding the pathology of ANR compared to the other eating disorders.

Chapter 8 introduced biological factors thought to contribute to the risk of eating disorders, as well as biological correlates and consequences of these disorders. Serotonin dysregulation has been described as a correlate of eating disorders, particularly BN. Neuropeptides that regulate weight and feeding have also been implicated in the etiology of eating disorders. Genes appear to play an important role in the etiology of these disorders, and genes related to serotonin function have received the most attention and support in molecular genetic studies. Taken together, these factors may influence the body's response to food restriction and its defense against starvation. Differences between Emily's and Jean's reactions to dietary restriction may represent the absence of a biological weight-defending mechanism in Emily, leading to Emily's emaciation and explaining Jean's binge eating. However, interpretation of biological correlates is complicated by the possibility that they may represent biological consequences of an eating disorder. Because eating is central to life, disruptions in food intake and extreme methods of weight control lead to serious medical consequences. Thus, one debate in the field has centered on the validity of examining biological differences between controls and patients recovered from an eating disorder.

Some have argued that differences found between recovered patients and controls reflect stable predisposing factors that contributed to the onset of the disorder. Others have argued that these differences may reflect a consequence of the eating disorder that remains, like a scar, after the disorder remits. Moreover, comparisons of brain function between controls and recovered patients raise an interesting logical paradox. If a factor is related to the onset of an eating disorder, why would the disorder remit when the factor is still present? In contrast, if the factor is present only when the disorder is present, it could mean that the factor was caused by the disorder. The best answers to these questions come from prospective longitudinal studies. However, the current technologies for evaluating brain function are too invasive and too expensive to be included in large prospective longitudinal studies.

Chapter 9 provided information concerning the treatment of AN, BN, and BED. Several efficacious treatments have been identified for BN and BED. Reflecting this, Jean has a history of successful treatment response and ultimately achieves lasting recovery following treatment. Efficacious treatments for BN and BED include cognitive-behavioral therapy, antidepressant medication, and interpersonal therapy. These interventions have efficacy in treating depression and anxiety disorders as well. In contrast, the most efficacious treatment identified for AN thus far is a family-based intervention. Several factors may explain why one treatment does not seem to work for all eating disorders. These include age differences across the eating disorder categories and differences in the extent to which the disorders are ego-syntonic (as in Emily's case) versus ego-dystonic (as in Jean's and Jamie's cases). However, beyond the issue of treatment efficacy is that of treatment effectiveness—that is, how well treatments work in the real world. Debates surround the reasons why most clinicians do not use empirically supported, manual-based treatments in working with patients with eating disorders.

From the researcher's perspective, failure to use empirically supported, manual-based treatments reflects clinicians' lack of knowledge and training. The answer is to work harder to disseminate information from treatment research. From the clinician's perspective, treatment studies lack ecological validity because patients in those studies are not representative of the larger population of patients seen by clinicians. Quite often, controlled treatment studies restrict inclusion to patients who meet full criteria for AN, BN, or BED, have no current problems with substance use, and do not report suicidal intentions. Clinicians rarely encounter such uncomplicated cases. A second concern of clinicians is the perceived rigidity of using a manual-based treatment. They fear that this will reduce their ability to establish rapport with patients, which may result in an ambivalent patient's decision to leave treatment prematurely. Clearly, there are valid concerns on both sides of the debate. Patients have the right to expect that a clinician will provide them with the treatment most likely to promote recovery. Clinicians have the right to expect that researchers will conduct research on treatments that can be successfully implemented in the real world.

Chapter 10 reviewed efforts to design efficacious programs to prevent eating disorders. At this early stage of development, prevention programs have demonstrated some limited success, particularly at the level of targeted interventions. More information on the causes of eating disorders would facilitate prevention efforts; however, the emergence of successful prevention programs may help reveal causal factors in eating disorders. Given the limited efficacy of existing prevention programs, debates exist over the value of prevention research in the field. The opposition to prevention research could be applied (with rather dire consequences) to many areas of investigation within the field, including the treatment of AN and molecular genetic studies of eating disorders. However, some practitioners express concern that we may do more harm than good when prevention programs are initiated before an adequate understanding of risk factors is available. This fear has been realized in one study that found that participants in a prevention program reported greater *increases* in disordered eating compared to those in the control condition.

Chapter 11 reviewed the long-term course and outcome of eating disorders. AN is associated with a worse prognosis than BN, with a higher rate of mortality and a lower rate of recovery. Limited data are available for evaluating the long-term course and outcome of BED. Although both BN and BED are associated with relatively low rates of mortality, these results may alter as the duration of study follow-up increases. In terms of the three case studies, Jean's response to treatment and ultimate recovery represent the most likely outcome for someone with her eating disorder. Because Emily had an older age of onset and required inpatient treatment, her prognosis is less favorable. She is less likely to respond to a family-based intervention, and alternative treatments with proven efficacy are lacking. It is difficult to predict what Jamie's long-term course and outcome will be. Based on preliminary outcome data for BED, he has a good chance of recovering from BED but he may face a lifelong struggle with weight control.

Probably the greatest debate in the field of long-term outcome research is the long-term efficacy of treatment. Most studies suggest that treatment does not predict the long-term outcome in AN or BN. Some have pointed to limited evidence that treatments do impact the long-term outcome. One approach used to answer this question is to examine the impact of treatment on the long-term course, as efficacious treatments do seem to speed recovery. However, the failure of treatments to demonstrate an impact on long-term outcome represents a challenge to develop more powerful interventions. This challenge has already been raised by the significant proportion of patients who do not respond to even the most efficacious treatments available.

FUTURE DIRECTIONS

Because of the relative youth of the field of eating disorders, heated debates surround almost every topic related to these disorders. In addition, the field is expanding rapidly. In 1981, the first and only journal to focus on eating disorders, the *International Journal of Eating Disorders*, was established. Since then, four more journals have emerged: *Eating Disorders: Journal of Treatment and Prevention* (established in 1993), *European Eating Disorders Review* (established in 1993), *Eating and Weight Disorders* (established in 1996), and *Body Image* (established in 2003). A new generation of eating disorders researchers has joined the ranks of junior faculty in medical schools and colleges around the world, allowing students greater opportunities to study eating disorders and eventually specialize in the field. To promote public awareness and support for research and treatment of eating disorders, a coalition of eating disorder associations has emerged, and the National Institute of Mental Health has designated an officer to focus on the development and funding of research on these disorders. The advances made thus far and the opportunity to make significant contributions in the near future make this an exciting time in this field.

This expansion provides multiple avenues along which future research can develop. One such avenue is the expansion of controlled treatment studies to include individuals with EDNOS rather than limiting studies to individuals with full-criteria eating disorders. Another is the expansion of treatment techniques such as cognitive-behavioral therapy to incorporate features from other efficacious interventions. In addition to the examination of new psychosocial interventions, new medications are being developed and tested, and the combination of medication and therapy in stepped-treatment programs is being explored. Empirical studies examining the development of eating disorders among immigrants from non-Western nations to the United States are being initiated. Studies of neurocognitive function in eating disorders are increasing as technology in neuroimaging develops, and multinational collaborative molecular genetic studies have begun. The National Institute of Mental Health has established a focus on translational research to transcend traditional boundaries between basic science and clinical research and to encourage communication among investigators in these different lines of research. Thus, rather than curtailing certain research avenues, current debates within the field serve to keep several lines of investigation open simultaneously. In closing, what remains unknown in the field of eating disorders represents not so much a failure of past research but rather a challenge for the future.

Glossary

Affective disinhibitor: an emotional trigger for loss of restraint over eating.

Agonist: an agent that increases neurotransmitter function in the brain.

Alexythymia: inability to read different emotional states, confusion in differentiating different internal states.

Allele: one of several alternative forms of the same gene that contributes to a specific genotype.

Amenorrhea: the loss of menstrual periods for 3 consecutive months.

Analogue studies: experimental studies in which the specific hypothesis involves testing the relationship between an independent and a dependent variable in which one or both are analogous to the topic of study.

Ascetics: individuals who engage in the practice of extreme abstinence or self-control.

Association studies: molecular genetic studies that examine whether there is an association between a specific gene and the presence of a specific trait.

Candidate gene study: a study designed to examine whether individuals with a particular disorder are more likely to have a certain allele or combination of alleles for a specific gene compared to individuals who do not have the disorder.

Cholecystokinin: a neuropeptide released in the small intestine following food ingestion that is associated with eliciting a feeling of satiety.

Cognition: processes related to thinking, including attention, perception, learning, and memory.

Cognitive disinhibitor: a cognitive trigger for loss of restraint over eating.

Cognitive distortions: thoughts that do not adequately reflect reality.

Cognitive-behavioral therapy: a directive therapy that is organized around the theory that disorders are composed of reinforced behaviors to which there are healthier alternatives and irrational beliefs that need to be elicited, challenged, and replaced.

Complex inheritance: the action of multiple genes control the expression of a phenotype.

Constraint: a dimension of personality representing the tendency to inhibit impulses and show caution, restraint, and conventionalism.

Conversion disorder: a disorder characterized by expression of physical distress that appears to take the place of psychological distress that is being suppressed.

Course: path a patient follows to the outcome.

Crossover: transition from one eating disorder to another.

Deoxyribonucleic acid (DNA): a sequence of nucleic acids, generally found in and confined to the genes of higher order organisms, which store genetic information.

Dialectical behavior therapy: a form of cognitive-behavioral therapy originally designed to treat patients diagnosed with borderline personality disorder that focuses on skills in the areas of mindfulness, distress tolerance, interpersonal effectiveness, and emotional regulation.

Diathesis: a vulnerability factor for developing a mental disorder.

Dichotomous thinking: black-and-white thinking, a pattern of thinking in which things are categorized as either good or bad.

Disease-Specific Pathways Model/Disease Prevention Paradigm: theoretical approach to prevention that seeks to identify and then reduce specific risk factors for a disease.

Disengagement: condition in which boundaries between family subsystems are too strong.

Disinhibition: loss of restraint over eating.

Distress tolerance: the ability to develop safe ways of coping with painful emotions without resorting to impulsive (and often self-destructive) behaviors that will ultimately increase emotional pain.

Dizygotic (DZ) twins: twins who share, on average, 50% of their genes.

Dopamine: a neurotransmitter that appears to inhibit food intake by acting on dopamine receptors in the lateral hypothalamus and is involved in experiencing reward.

Down-regulation: a process by which neurotransmitter receptors become less sensitive due to increased neurotransmitter availability in the brain.

Dysphoria: a state of mental discomfort.

Ecological validity: a measure of how well results of an experimental study reflect events as they occur in real-world situations.

Edema: fluid retention.

Efficacy: the ability to produce change.

Emotional regulation: the ability to experience emotions without having extreme fluctuations that interfere with life function.

Empirically supported treatment: treatment that has demonstrated efficacy from research studies.

Empowerment-Relational Model: theoretical approach to prevention that seeks to empower girls to transform their social environments to eliminate sources of risk.

Enmeshment: condition in which boundaries between family subsystems are too weak.

Epidemiology: the study of the occurrence of disorders within populations.

Equal environments assumption: an assumption in twin models that there is no difference in the shared environment between monozygotic and dizygotic twin pairs reared together.

Etiology: the causes and origin of mental and physical disorders.

Experimental study: any study in which an independent variable is manipulated in order to determine its effect on a dependent variable.

Fames canina: *hist.,* a disorder characterized by large food intake followed by vomiting.

Family systems model: theory that all families are made up of subsystems (e.g., spousal, parental, and sibling) in which different roles and responsibilities occur.

Family therapy: a therapy organized around the theory that family interactions play an important role in the etiology and treatment of disorders.

First-degree relative: a biological member of one's immediate family with whom one shares 50% of one's genes (e.g., mother, father, or sibling).

Gene: a sequence of DNA that provides a code for building proteins.

Genetic markers: places in the genome where known genes reside.

Genome: the entire set of genes present in an organism.

Genome-wide linkage study: a study evaluating alleles at several genetic markers to determine whether two biological relatives who have a disorder both have specific alleles at a frequency that is higher than expected by chance.

Genotype: the specific combination of alleles for a given gene.

Harm avoidance: a dimension of temperament representing a tendency to avoid punishment through inhibiting behavior.

Health Promotion Paradigm: theoretical approach to prevention that seeks to identify and then increase protective factors at both individual and community levels to promote wellness.

Heritability estimate: a percentage representing how much genes contribute to the development of a disorder in a given group of people.

Heterozygous: a genotype in which a person has two different alleles for a gene.

Homovanillic acid (HVA): the by-product of dopamine use in the brain.

Homozygous: a genotype in which a person has two identical alleles for a gene.

Hypothalamic-pituitary-adrenal (HPA) axis: a tristructural brain system implicated in responses to stress.

Hypothalamic-pituitary-gonadal (HPG) axis: a tristructural brain system involved in the release of sex hormones and the process of maturation.

Hypothalamus: a brain structure responsible for appetite and weight control.

Incidence: the number of new cases of an illness per 100,000 people per year.

Interoceptive awareness: a personality measure of one's difficulty in recognizing different feelings and internal states.

Interpersonal effectiveness: the ability to relate to people in a way that meets personal needs, the needs of the other person, and the need for self-respect.

Interpersonal therapy: a therapy organized around the theory that disorders arise from problems patients have in negotiating their relationships with others.

Intrapsychic: occurring within the mind.

Kynorexia: hist., a disorder defined by insatiable appetite, eating that is out of control, and then compulsive vomiting as a result of excessive food intake.

Lateral: direction in the brain referring to areas that are farther away from the center.

Leptin: a neuropeptide that provides a negative feedback loop in the brain's control of weight and food intake, with receptors in the paraventricular nucleus and ventromedial hypothalamus in the brain producing decreased food intake.

Lifetime prevalence: the overall percentage of people who have had a specific disorder at some point in their lives.

Longitudinal studies: studies involving measurements of individuals or groups followed at different points over a period of time.

Melanocyte-stimulating hormone (MSH): a hormone that appears to be necessary for a response to increased leptin concentration.

Menarche: the age at which the first menstrual period occurs.

Mendelian inheritance: the action of a single gene controls the expression of a phenotype.

Meta-analysis: Analysis of data from several studies to determine overall trends and significance.

Mindfulness: the ability to be aware of internal feelings and external demands in a way that combines emotions with intellect in guiding wise choices.

Minnesota Multiphasic Personality Inventory (MMPI): a measure of personality and behavioral functioning.

Monozygotic (MZ) twins: twins who share 100% of their genes.

Muscle dysmorphia: a condition characterized by viewing one's own body as much smaller than it really is, causing significant distress and efforts to increase muscle mass.

Naturalistic investigation: a study in which natural events are observed.

Negative emotionality: a dimension of personality representing the tendency to experience negative mood states (e.g., sadness, anxiety, anger).

Negative reinforcement: something that increases the likelihood of a behavior because the behavior is associated with removal of something undesirable.

Neurasthenic disorders: a class of disorders commonly diagnosed in the late 19th and early 20th centuries in which patients complained of fatigue and various physical symptoms such as headache, muscle pain, and problems with hearing or vision.

Neuron: a brain cell.

Neuropeptide Y: a neuropeptide that increases food intake and is inhibited by leptin.

Neuropeptides: chemicals in the brain that activate specific areas of the brain but are physically larger than neurotransmitters.

Neurotransmitters: chemicals in the brain that facilitate communication between brain cells.

Nonorganic failure to thrive: a condition affecting young children in which children fail to make necessary weight gains and no biological reason can be found for low weight.

Nonspecific Vulnerability-Stressor Model: theoretical approach to prevention that seeks to identify and then reduce general risk factors for illness.

Norepinephrine: a neurotransmitter that has roles in both increasing and decreasing food intake and is involved in physiological responses to stress.

Novelty seeking: a dimension of temperament representing a tendency to pursue rewards.

Nuisance variable: anything that creates differences but that is irrelevant for understanding the problem under investigation.

Operant conditioning: a type of learning in which behaviors are associated with reinforcement (positive or negative) or punishment.

Outcome: a condition of patients assessed at some point in time after initial assessment.

Paraventricular nucleus: section of the hypothalamus that is named for its location outside of the third ventricle.

Perfectionism: a tendency to strive for perfection in all aspects of life.

Persistence: a dimension of temperament representing a tendency to continue behavior that is no longer rewarded.

Personality: a stable way in which individuals perceive, react to, and interact with their environments that is influenced by both biology and experience.

Pharmacological disinhibitor: a psychoactive substance that causes loss of restraint over eating.

Phenocopy: a condition in which a phenotype occurs in the absence of the genotype.

Phenotype: the observable manifestation of a genotype.

Positive emotionality: a dimension of personality representing the tendency to enjoy and be actively engaged in work and social interactions.

Positive reinforcement: something that increases the likelihood of a behavior because the behavior is associated with the presence of something desirable.

Proband: an individual exhibiting the trait whose inheritance is to be studied.

Prognostic: predictive of a course or an outcome.

Prolactin: a hormone produced in response to serotonin function that is involved in lactation.

Proopiomelanocortin (POMC): the precursor for melanocyte-stimulating hormone.

Psychoanalytic: referring to a theory of psychopathology as arising from unconscious intrapsychic conflicts.

Psychodynamic therapy: a nondirective therapy organized around the theory that disorders arise from internal conflicts of which the patient may not be aware. The goal is to facilitate improvement by promoting insight.

Psychoeducation: factual information that is provided in the context of therapy to educate the patient about the disorder.

Psychogenic vomiting: vomiting for which there is no physical explanation.

Punishment: something that decreases the likelihood of a behavior because the behavior is associated with the presence of something undesirable.

Pyloric sphincter: a muscle at the base of the stomach that contracts and relaxes to control the rate at which food passes from the stomach to the small intestine.

Receptor: structure in brain cells that allows them to receive neurotransmitter signals.

Reduced penetrance: a condition in which a genotype does not lead to the phenotype.

Refeeding syndrome: a life-threatening condition caused by reintroducing too much food too quickly to a person in a state of starvation.

Relapse: return of a full disorder after remission has been achieved.

Representativeness assumption: assumption in twin studies that patterns observed in twins are representative of patterns observed in non-twin population.

Reproductive fitness: one's ability to survive and have children.

Resting metabolic rate: the rate at which the body consumes energy in the form of calories when it is not exercising.

Retrospective recall bias: a bias that occurs when memory for the past is influenced by factors in the present in a way that makes memory less accurate.

Reuptake: process by which a brain cell reabsorbs neurotransmitters it has just released before they can bind to receptors on another brain cell.

Reverse anorexia: see *muscle dysmorphia.*

Reward dependence: a dimension of temperament representing a tendency to continue rewarded behavior.

Ribonucleic acid (RNA): a sequence of nucleic acids transcribed directly from DNA that are used to build chains of amino acids into proteins.

Second-degree relative: a biological relative to whom one is related through one family member and with whom one shares approximately 25% of one's genes (e.g., parents' siblings and grandparents).

Selective abstraction: a part of something comes to represent the whole and carries undue influence in the evaluation of the whole.

Selective prevention program: primary prevention designed for specific segments of the population that are at increased risk for certain problems with the goal of preventing the problems before they begin.

Serotonin (5-HT): a neurotransmitter that plays an important role in the regulation of mood, appetite, and impulse control.

Set point theory: theory that the body has evolved behavioral and biological weight defending mechanisms to maintain a certain weight.

Socioeconomic status: a combination of educational and professional attainment and income.

Somaticize: the condition in which mental conflicts are expressed as physical conditions.

Standardized mortality ratio: ratio of the observed number of deaths in a specific group to the expected number of deaths in a matched population.

Stroop Test: a method used to evaluate attentional processes in which a participant is asked to name the color of ink that words are printed in when the words are names of different colors.

Targeted prevention program: secondary prevention designed for individuals who are already experiencing some problems with the goal of preventing the problems from becoming worse.

Temperament: a biologically based predisposition to experience certain emotional and behavioral responses.

Third-degree relative: a biological relative to whom one is related through two family members and with whom one shares approximately 12.5% of one's genes (e.g., cousins).

Transmission disequilibrium test (TDT) study: a study designed to compare the frequency of allele transmission from heterozygous parents to affected offspring to that expected if there were no association between the allele and the disorder.

Tryptophan: an amino acid that is required to make serotonin.

Twin concordance: the similarity within twin pairs for specific trait.

Universal prevention program: primary prevention designed for an entire population with the goal of preventing certain problems before they begin.

Up-regulation: a process by which neurotransmitter receptors become more sensitive as a result of sustained low concentrations of a neurotransmitter in the brain.

Vagus nerve: one of 12 cranial nerves, it has both motor and sensory functions, including stimulating smooth muscle fibers in the stomach and intestine and receiving sensations from the abdomen.

Variable expressivity: a condition in which a genotype leads to variable phenotypes.

Ventromedial: a direction in the brain referring to areas that are closer to the center and down toward the belly of the brain.

References

Abou-Saleh, M. T., Younis, Y., & Karim, L. (1998). Anorexia nervosa in an Arab culture. *International Journal of Eating Disorders, 23,* 207–212.

Abrams, K. K., Allen, L. R., & Gray, J. J. (1993). Disordered eating attitudes and behaviors, psychological adjustment, and ethnic identity: A comparison of black and white female college students. *International Journal of Eating Disorders, 14,* 49–57.

Agliata, D., & Tantleff-Dunn, S. (2004). The impact of media exposure on males' body image. *Journal of Social and Clinical Psychology, 23,* 7–22.

Agras, S., Hammer, L., & McNicolas, F. (1999). A prospective study of the influence of eating-disordered mothers on their children. *International Journal of Eating Disorders, 25,* 253–262.

Agras, W. S., Telch, C. F., Arnow, B., Eldredge, K., & Marnell, M. (1994). Weight loss, cognitive-behavioral, and desipramine treatments in binge eating disorder: An additive design. *Behavior Therapy, 25,* 225–238.

Agras, W. S., Telch, C. F., Arnow, B., Eldredge, K., & Marnell, M. (1995). Does interpersonal therapy help patients with binge eating disorder who fail to respond to cognitive-behavioral therapy? *Journal of Consulting and Clinical Psychology, 63,* 356–360.

Agras, W. S., Telch, C. F., Arnow, B., Eldredge, K., & Marnell, M. (1997). One-year follow-up of cognitive-behavioral therapy for obese individuals with binge eating disorder. *Journal of Consulting and Clinical Psychology, 65,* 343–347.

Agras, W. S., Walsh, T., Fairburn, C. G., Wilson, G. T., & Kraemer, H. C. (2000). A multicenter comparison of cognitive-behavioral therapy and interpersonal psychotherapy for bulimia nervosa. *Archives of General Psychiatry, 57,* 459–466.

Allison, D. B., Heshka, S., Neale, M. C., Lykken, D. T., & Heymsfield, S. B. (1994). A genetic analysis of relative weight among 4,020 twin pairs, with an emphasis on sex effects. *Health Psychology, 13,* 362–365.

Altabe, M., & Thompson, J. K. (1992). Size estimation versus figural ratings of body image disturbance: Relation to body dissatisfaction and eating dysfunction. *International Journal of Eating Disorders, 11,* 397–402.

American Psychiatric Association. (1980). *Diagnostic and statistical manual of mental disorders* (3rd ed.). Washington, DC: Author.

American Psychiatric Association. (1994). *Diagnostic and statistical manual of mental disorders* (4th ed.). Washington, DC: Author.

American Psychiatric Association. (2000). *Diagnostic and statistical manual of mental disorders, text revision* (4th ed.). Washington, DC: Author.

Anand, B. K., & Brobeck, J. R. (1951). Hypothalamic control of food intake in rats and cats. *Yale Journal of Biology and Medicine, 24,* 123–140.

Andersen, A. E. (1984). Anorexia nervosa and bulimia in adolescent males. *Pediatric Annals, 13,* 901–904, 907.

Ando, T., Komaki, G., Karibe, M., Kawamura, N., Hara, S., Takii, M., et al. (2001). 5-HT2a promoter polymorphism is not associated with anorexia nervosa in Japanese patients. *Psychiatric Genetics, 11,* 157–160.

Apple, R. F. (1999). Interpersonal therapy for bulimia nervosa. *Journal of Clinical Psychology, 55,* 715–725.

Appolinario, J. C., Godoy-Matos, A., Fontenelle, L. F., Carraro, L., Cabral, M., Vieira, A., et al. (2002). An open-label trial of sibutramine in obese patients with binge-eating disorder. *Journal of Clinical Psychiatry, 63,* 28–30.

Arnow, B., Kenardy, J., & Agras, W. S. (1992). Binge eating among the obese: A descriptive study. *Journal of Behavioral Medicine, 15,* 155–170.

Austin, S. B. (2000). Prevention research in eating disorders: Theory and new directions. *Psychological Medicine, 30,* 1249–1262.

Bahrke, M. S., Yesalis, C. E., & Brower, K. J. (1998). Anabolic-androgenic steroid abuse and performance-enhancing drugs among adolescents. *Child and Adolescent Psychiatric Clinics of North America, 7,* 821–838.

Bailey, R., & Earle, M. (1999). *Home cooking to takeaways: Changes in food consumption in New Zealand during 1880–1990* (2nd Ed.). Palmerston North, New Zealand: Massey University.

Ball, K., Mishra, G., & Crawford, D. (2002). Which aspects of socioeconomic status are related to obesity among men and women? *International Journal of Obesity and Related Metabolic Disorders: Journal of the International Association for the Study of Obesity, 26,* 559–565.

Banks, C. G. (1992). "Culture" in culture-bound syndromes: The case of anorexia nervosa. *Social Science & Medicine, 34,* 867–884.

Banks, C. G. (1994). Anorexia nervosa: Is it the syndrome or the theorist that is culture- and gender-bound?: Response. *Transcultural Psychiatric Research Review, 31,* 321–325.

Baranowski, M. J., & Hetherington, M. M. (2001). Testing the efficacy of an eating disorder prevention program. *International Journal of Eating Disorders, 29,* 119–124.

Bardone, A. M., Vohs, K. D., Abramson, L. Y., Heatherton, T. F., & Joiner, T. E., Jr. (2000). The confluence of perfectionism, body dissatisfaction, and low self-esteem predicts bulimic symptoms: Clinical implications. *Behavior Therapy, 31,* 265–280.

Barnett, H. L., Keel, P. K., & Conoscenti, L. M. (2001). Body type preferences in Asian and Caucasian college students. *Sex Roles, 45,* 867–878.

Beck, A. T. (1970). *Depression: Causes and treatment.* Philadelphia: University of Pennsylvania Press.

Becker, A. E. (1995). *Body, self and society: The view from Fiji.* Philadelphia: University of Pennsylvania Press.

Becker, A. E., Burwell, R. A., Herzog, D. B., Hamburg, P., & Gilman, S. E. (2002). Eating behaviours and attitudes following prolonged exposure to television among ethnic Fijian adolescent girls. *British Journal of Psychiatry, 180*, 509–514.

Bell, R. M. (1985). *Holy anorexia.* Chicago: University of Chicago Press.

Bemporad, J. R. (1996). Self-starvation through the ages: Reflections on the pre-history of anorexia nervosa. *International Journal of Eating Disorders, 19*, 217–237.

Beren, S. E., Hayden, H. A., Wilfley, D. E., & Grilo, C. M. (1996). The influence of sexual orientation on body dissatisfaction in adult men and women. *International Journal of Eating Disorders, 20*, 135–141.

Bergen, A. W., Yeager, M., Welch, R., Ganjei, J. K., Deep-Soboslay, A., Haque, K., et al. (2003). The Price Foundation Collaborative Group (www.anbn.org). Candidate gene analysis of the Price Foundation anorexia nervosa affected relative pair dataset. *Current Drug Targets—CNS and Neurological Disorders, 2*, 41–51.

Berkowitz, R., Stunkard, A. J., & Stallings, V. A. (1993). Binge-eating disorder in obese adolescent girls. *Annals of the New York Academy of Sciences, 699*, 200–206.

Beumont, P. J. (1988). Bulimia: Is it an illness entity? *International Journal of Eating Disorders, 7*, 167–176.

Beumont, P. J., Garner, D. M., & Touyz, S. W. (1994). Diagnoses of eating or dieting disorders: What may we learn from past mistakes? *International Journal of Eating Disorders, 16*, 349–362.

Bliss, E. L., & Branch, C. H. H. (1960). *Anorexia nervosa.* New York: Paul Hoeber.

Boskind-Lodahl, M. (1976). Cinderella's stepsisters: A feminist perspective on anorexia nervosa and bulimia. *Signs, 2*, 342–356.

Bourke, M. P., Taylor, G. J., Parker, J. D., & Bagby, R. M. (1992). Alexithymia in women with anorexia nervosa. A preliminary investigation. *British Journal of Psychiatry, 161*, 240–243.

Brambilla, F., Bellodi, L., Arancio, C., Ronchi, P., & Limonta, D. (2001). Central dopaminergic function in anorexia and bulimia nervosa: A psychoneuroendocrine approach. *Psychoneuroendocrinology, 26*, 393–409.

Branch, C. H., & Eurman, L. J. (1980). Social attitudes toward patients with anorexia nervosa. *American Journal of Psychiatry, 137*, 631–632.

Brand, P. A., Rothblum, E. D., & Solomon, L. J. (1992). A comparison of lesbians, gay men, and heterosexuals on weight and restrained eating. *International Journal of Eating Disorders, 11*, 253–259.

Branson, R., Potoczna, N., Kral, J. G., Lentes, K. U., Hoehe, M. R., & Horber, F. F. (2003). Binge eating as a major phenotype of melanocortin 4 receptor gene mutations. *New England Journal of Medicine, 348*, 1096–1103.

Bray, G. A. (1986). Effects of obesity on health and happiness. In K. D. Brownell & J. P. Foreyt (Eds.), *Handbook of eating disorders* (pp. 3–44). New York: Basic Books.

Brewerton, T. D., Brandt, H. A., Lesem, M. D., Murphy, D. L., & Jimerson, D. C. (1990). Serotonin in eating disorders. In E. F. Coccaro & D. L. Murphy (Eds.), *Serotonin in major psychiatric disorders: Progress in psychiatry* (pp. 155–184). Washington, DC: American Psychiatric Press.

Brewerton, T. D., Lesem, M. D., Kennedy, A., & Garvey, W. T. (2000). Reduced plasma leptin concentration in bulimia nervosa. *Psychoneuroendocrinology, 25*, 649–658.

Brewerton, T. D., Mueller, E. A., Lesem, M. D., Brandt, H. A., Quearry, B., George, D. T., et al. (1992). Neuroendocrine responses to *m*-chlorophenylpiperazine and L-tryptophan in bulimia. *Archives of General Psychiatry, 49*, 852–861.

Brinch, M., Isager, T., & Tolstrup, K. (1988). Anorexia nervosa and motherhood: Reproduction pattern and mothering behavior of 50 women. *Acta Psychiatrica Scandinavica, 77*, 611–617.

Brotman, A. W., Herzog, D. B., & Hamburg, P. (1988). Long-term course in 14 bulimic patients treated with psychotherapy. *Journal of Clinical Psychiatry, 49*, 157–160.

Bruch, H. (1966). Anorexia nervosa and its differential diagnosis. *Journal of Nervous and Mental Disease, 14*, 555–566.

Bruch, H. (1978). *The golden cage: The enigma of anorexia nervosa.* Cambridge, MA: Harvard University Press.

Bruins-Slot, L., Gorwood, P., Bouvard, M., Blot, P., Ades, J., Feingold, J., et al. (1998). Lack of association between anorexia nervosa and D_3 dopamine receptor gene. *Biological Psychiatry, 43,* 76–78.

Brumberg, J. J. (1989). *Fasting girls: The history of anorexia nervosa.* New York: Plume.

Brunzell, C., & Henrickson-Nelson, M. (2001). An overview of nutrition. In J. E. Mitchell (Ed.), *The outpatient treatment of eating disorders: A guide for therapists, dietitians and physicians* (pp. 216–241). J. E. Mitchell (Ed.), Minneapolis: University of Minnesota Press.

Buchan, T., & Gregory, L. D. (1984). Anorexia nervosa in a black Zimbabwean. *British Journal of Psychiatry, 145,* 326–330.

Buddeberg-Fischer, B., & Reed, V. (2001). Prevention of disturbed eating behavior: An intervention program in Swiss high school classes. *Eating Disorders: The Journal of Treatment and Prevention, 9,* 109–124.

Buhrich, N. (1981). Frequency of presentation of anorexia nervosa in Malaysia. *Australian and New Zealand Journal of Psychiatry, 15,* 153–155.

Bulik, C. M., Devlin, B., Bacanu, S. A., Thornton, L., Klump, K. L., Fichter, M. M., et al. (2003). Significant linkage on chromosome 10p in families with bulimia nervosa. *American Journal of Human Genetics, 72,* 200–207.

Bulik, C. M., Sullivan, P. F., Carter, F. A., & Joyce, P. R. (1997). Initial manifestations of disordered eating behavior: Dieting versus binging. *International Journal of Eating Disorders, 22,* 195–201.

Bulik, C. M., Sullivan, P. F., Carter, F. A., MacIntosh, V. V., & Joyce, P. R. (1998a). The role of exposure with response prevention in the cognitive behavioral therapy for bulimia nervosa. *Psychological Medicine, 28,* 611–623.

Bulik, C. M., Sullivan, P. F., & Kendler, K. S. (1998b). Heritability of binge-eating and broadly defined bulimia nervosa. *Biological Psychiatry, 44,* 1210–1218.

Bulik, C. M., Sullivan, P. F., Weltzin, T. E., & Kaye, W. H. (1995). Temperament in eating disorders. *International Journal of Eating Disorders, 17,* 251–261.

Burckes-Miller, M. E., & Black, D. R. (1988). Eating disorders: A problem in athletics? *Health Education, 19,* 22–25.

Bushnell, J. A., Wells, J. E., Hornblow, A. R., Oakley-Browne, M. A., & Joyce, P. (1990). Prevalence of three bulimia syndromes in the general population. *Psychological Medicine, 20,* 671–680.

Byely, L., Archibald, A. B., Graber, J., & Brooks-Gunn, J. (2000). A prospective study of familial and social influences on girls' body image and dieting. *International Journal of Eating Disorders, 28,* 155–164.

Bynum, C. W. (1987). *Holy feast and holy fast. The religious significance of food to medieval women.* Berkeley: University of California Press.

Cachelin, F. M., & Maher, B. A. (1998). Is amenorrhea a critical criterion for anorexia nervosa? *Journal of Psychosomatic Research., 44,* 435–440.

Cachelin, F. M., Striegel-Moore, R. H., Elder, K. A., Pike, K. M., Wilfley, D. E., & Fairburn, C. G. (1999). Natural course of a community sample of women with binge eating disorder. *International Journal of Eating Disorders, 25,* 45–54.

Campbell, D. A., Sundaramurthy, D., Markham, A. F., & Pieri, L. F. (1998). Lack of association between 5-HT2A gene promoter polymorphism and susceptibility to anorexia nervosa. *Lancet, 351,* 499.

Carlat, D. J., & Camargo, C. A. (1991). Review of bulimia nervosa in males. *American Journal of Psychiatry, 148,* 831–843.

Carlat, D. J., Camargo, C. A., Jr., & Herzog, D. B. (1997). Eating disorders in males: A report on 135 patients. *American Journal of Psychiatry, 154,* 1127–1132.

Carlson, N. R. (1994). *Physiology of behavior* (5th ed.). Boston: Allyn and Bacon.

Carter, J. C., Stewart, D. A., Dunn, V. J., & Fairburn, C. G. (1997). Primary prevention of eating disorders: Might it do more harm than good? *International Journal of Eating Disorders, 22,* 167–172.

Cash, T. F., & Deagle, E. A., III (1997). The nature and extent of body-image disturbances in anorexia nervosa and bulimia nervosa: A meta-analysis. *International Journal of Eating Disorders, 22,* 107–125.

Casper, R. C. (1990). Personality features of women with good outcome from restricting anorexia nervosa. *Psychosomatic Medicine, 52,* 156–170.

Casper, R. C., Hedeker, D., & McClough, J. F. (1992). Personality dimensions in eating disorders and their relevance for subtyping. *Journal of the American Academy of Child and Adolescent Psychiatry, 31,* 830–840.

Casper, R. C., & Troiani, M. (2001). Family functioning in anorexia nervosa differs by subtype. *International Journal of Eating Disorders, 30,* 338–342.

Cauffman, E., & Steinberg, L. (1996). Interactive effects of menarcheal status and dating on dieting and disordered eating among adolescent girls. *Developmental Psychology, 32,* 631–635.

Celio, A. A., Winzelberg, A. J., Wilfley, D. E., Eppstein-Herald, D., Springer, E. A., Dev, P., et al. (2000). Reducing risk factors for eating disorders: Comparison of an Internet- and a classroom-delivered psychoeducational program. *Journal of Consulting and Clinical Psychology, 68,* 650–657.

Chamorro, R., & Flores-Ortiz, Y. (2000). Acculturation and disordered eating patterns among Mexican American women. *International Journal of Eating Disorders, 28,* 125–129.

Chandler, S. B., Abood, D. A., Lee, D. T., Cleveland, M. Z., & Daly, J. A. (1994). Pathogenic eating attitudes and behaviors and body dissatisfaction differences among Black and White college students. *Eating Disorders: The Journal of Treatment and Prevention, 2,* 319–328.

Chipley, W. J. (1860). On sitomania. *Journal of Psychological Medicine and Mental Pathology, 13,* 266–270.

Chun, Z. F., Mitchell, J. E., Li, K., Yu, W. M., Lan, Y. D., Jun, Z. et al. (1992). The prevalence of anorexia nervosa and bulimia nervosa among freshman medical college students in China. *International Journal of Eating Disorders, 12,* 209–214.

Ciano, R., Rocco, P. L., Angarano, A., Biasin, E., & Balestrieri, M. (2002). Group-analytic and psychoeducational therapies for binge-eating disorder: An exploratory study on efficacy and persistence of effects. *Psychotherapy Research, 12,* 231–239.

Claude-Pierre, P. (1998). *The secret language of eating disorders: How you can understand and work to cure anorexia and bulimia.* New York: Random House.

Cloninger, C. R. (1987). A systematic method for clinical description and classification of personality variants. A proposal. *Archives of General Psychiatry, 44,* 573–588.

Cloninger, C. R., Svrakic, D. M., & Przybeck, T. R. (1993). A psychobiological model of temperament and character. *Archives of General Psychiatry, 50,* 975–990.

Cohn, L. D., Adler, N. E., Irwin, C. E., Millstein, S. G., Kegeles, S. M., & Stone, G. (1987). Body-figure preferences in male and female adolescents. *Journal of Abnormal Psychology, 96,* 276–279.

Collier, D. A., Arranz, M. J., Li, T., Mupita, D., Brown, N., & Treasure, J. (1997). Association between 5-HT2A gene promoter polymorphism and anorexia nervosa. [comment]. *Lancet, 350,* 412.

Collings, S., & King, M. (1994). Ten-year follow-up of 50 patients with bulimia nervosa. *British Journal of Psychiatry, 164,* 80–87.

Cooper, M., & Todd, G. (1997). Selective processing of three types of stimuli in eating disorders. *British Journal of Clinical Psychology, 36,* 279–281.

Cooper, P. J., & Fairburn, C. G. (1993). Confusion over the core psychopathology of bulimia nervosa. *International Journal of Eating Disorders, 13,* 385–389.

Craighead, L. W., Allen, H. N., Craighead, W. E., & DeRosa, R. (1996). Effect of social feedback on learning rate and cognitive distortions among women with bulimia. *Behavior Therapy, 27,* 551–563.

Craik, K. H., Hogan, R., & Wolfe, R. N. (1993). *Fifty years of personality psychology.* New York: Plenum Press.

Crandall, C. S., & Biernat, M. (1990). The ideology of antifat attitudes. *Journal of Applied Social Psychology, 20,* 227–243.

Crandall, C. S., & Martinez, R. (1996). Culture, ideology, and antifat attitudes. *Personality and Social Psychology Bulletin, 22,* 1165–1176.

Crichton, P. (1996). Were the Roman emperors Claudius and Vitellius bulimic? *International Journal of Eating Disorders, 19,* 203–207.

Crisp, A. H., Callender, J. S., Halek, C., & Hsu, L. G. (1992). Long-term mortality in anorexia nervosa. A 20-year follow-up of the St. George's and Aberdeen cohorts. *British Journal of Psychiatry, 161,* 104–107.

Crisp, A. H., Gelder, M. G., Rix, S., Meltzer, H. I., & Rowlands, O. J. (2000). Stigmatisation of people with mental illnesses. *British Journal of Psychiatry, 177,* 4–7.

Crisp, A. H., Palmer, R. L., & Kalucy, R. S. (1976). How common is anorexia nervosa? A prevalence study. *British Journal of Psychiatry, 128,* 549–554.

Crocker, J., & Major, B. (1989). Social stigma and self-esteem: The self-protective properties of stigma. *Psychological Review, 96,* 608–630.

Cusumano, D. L., & Thompson, J. K. (1997). Body image and body shape ideals in magazines: Exposure, awareness, and internalization. *Sex Roles, 37,* 701–721.

Dare, C., Eisler, I., Russell, G. F., & Szmukler, G. I. (1990). The clinical and theoretical impact of a controlled trial of family therapy in anorexia nervosa. *Journal of Marital and Family Therapy, 16,* 39–57.

Davis, C., & Woodside, D. B. (2002). Sensitivity to the rewarding effects of food and exercise in the eating disorders. *Comprehensive Psychiatry, 43,* 189–194.

Davis, C., & Yager, J. (1992). Transcultural aspects of eating disorders: A critical literature review. *Culture, Medicine and Psychiatry, 16,* 377–394.

de Castro, J. M. (1999). Behavioral genetics of food intake regulation in free-living humans. *Nutrition, 15,* 550–554.

de Zwaan, M., Nutzinger, D. O., & Schoenbeck, G. (1992). Binge eating in overweight women. *Comprehensive Psychiatry, 33,* 256–261.

Dejong, W., & Kleck, R. (1986). The social psychological effects of overweight. In C. Herman, M. Zanna, & E. Higgins (Eds.), *Physical appearance stigma and social behavior: The Ontario Symposium* (pp. 65–87). Hillsdale, NJ: Erlbaum.

Demitrack, M. A., Putnam, F. W., Rubinow, D. R., Pigott, T. A., Altemus, M., Krahn, D. D., et al. (1993). Relation of dissociative phenomena to levels of cerebrospinal fluid monoamine metabolites and beta-endorphin in patients with eating disorders: A pilot study. *Psychiatry Research, 49,* 1–10.

Devlin, M. J., Goldfein, J. A., Carino, J. S., & Wolk, S. L. (2000). Open treatment of overweight binge eaters with phentermine and fluoxetine as an adjunct to cognitive-behavioral therapy. *International Journal of Eating Disorders, 28,* 325–332.

Devlin, M. J., Walsh, B. T., Guss, J. L., Kissileff, H. R., Liddle, R. A., & Petkova, E. (1997). Postprandial cholecystokinin release and gastric emptying in patients with bulimia nervosa. *American Journal of Clinical Nutrition, 65,* 114–120.

Diamond, R. J. (2002). *Instant psychopharmacology: A guide for the nonmedical mental health professional* (2nd ed.). New York: Norton.

Di Bella, D. D., Catalano, M., Cavallini, M. C., Riboldi, C., & Bellodi, L. (2000). Serotonin transporter linked polymorphic region in anorexia nervosa and bulimia nervosa. *Molecular Psychiatry, 5,* 233–234.

Di Carlo, C., Tommaselli, G. A., De Filippo, E., Pisano, G., Nasti, A., Bifulco, G., et al. (2002). Menstrual status and serum leptin levels in anorectic and in menstruating women with low body mass indexes. *Fertility and Sterility, 78,* 376–382.

DiNicola, V. F. (1990a). Anorexia multiforme: Self-starvation in historical and cultural context: I. Self-starvation as a historical chameleon. *Transcultural Psychiatric Research Review, 27,* 165–196.

DiNicola, V. F. (1990b). Anorexia multiforme: Self-starvation in historical and cultural context: II. Anorexia nervosa as a culture-reactive syndrome. *Transcultural Psychiatric Research Review, 27,* 245–286.

Dolan, B. (1991). Cross-cultural aspects of anorexia nervosa and bulimia: A review. *International Journal of Eating Disorders, 10,* 67–79.

Dolan, B., & Ford, K. (1991). Binge eating and dietary restraint: A cross-cultural analysis. *International Journal of Eating Disorders, 10,* 345–353.

Doerr-Zegers, O. (1994). About a particular type of oral perversion in the female: Hyperphasia followed by vomiting. *International Journal of Eating Disorders, 16,* 117–132.

Drewnowski, A., Kurth, C. L., & Krahn, D. D. (1995). Effects of body image on dieting, exercise, and anabolic steroid use in adolescent males. *International Journal of Eating Disorders, 17,* 381–386.

Eagles, J. M., Johnston, M. I., Hunter, D., Lobban, M., & Millar, H. R. (1995). Increasing incidence of anorexia nervosa in the female population of northeast Scotland. *American Journal of Psychiatry, 152,* 1266–1271.

East, R., & Joseph, T. (1994). *Cassell dictionary of modern politics.* London: Cassell.

Eastwood, H., Brown, K. M., Markovic, D., & Pieri, L. F. (2002). Variation in the *ESR1* and *ESR2* genes and genetic susceptibility to anorexia nervosa. *Molecular Psychiatry, 7,* 86–89.

Eckert, E. D., Halmi, K. A., Marchi, P., Grove, W., & Crosby, R. (1995). Ten-year follow-up of anorexia nervosa: Clinical course and outcome. *Psychological Medicine, 25,* 143–156.

Eddy, K. T., Keel, P. K., Dorer, D. J., Delinsky, S. S., Franko, D. L., & Herzog, D. B. (2002). Longitudinal comparison of anorexia nervosa subtypes. *International Journal of Eating Disorders, 31,* 191–201.

Edmunds, H., & Hill, A. J. (1999). Dieting and the family context of eating in young adolescent children. *International Journal of Eating Disorders, 25,* 435–440.

Edwards-Hewitt, T., & Gray, J. J. (1993). The prevalence of disordered eating attitudes and behaviours in Black-American and White-American college women: Ethnic, regional, class, and media differences. *European Eating Disorders Review, 1,* 41–54.

Eisler, I., Dare, C., Russell, G. F., Szmukler, G., le Grange, D., & Dodge, E. (1997). Family and individual therapy in anorexia nervosa. A 5-year follow-up. *Archives of General Psychiatry, 54,* 1025–1030.

Engel, K., Wittern, M., Hentze, M., & Meyer, A. E. (1989). Long-term stability of anorexia nervosa treatments: Follow-up study of 218 patients. *Psychiatric Developments, 7,* 395–407.

Enns, M. P., Drewnowski, A., & Grinker, J. A. (1987). Body composition, body size estimation, and attitudes toward eating in male college athletes. *Psychosomatic Medicine, 49,* 56–64.

Enoch, M. A., Kaye, W. H., Rotondo, A., Greenberg, B. D., Murphy, D. L., & Goldman, D. (1998). 5-HT2A promoter polymorphism–1438G/A, anorexia nervosa, and obsessive-compulsive disorder. *Lancet, 351,* 1785–1786.

Epel, E. S., Spanakos, A., Kasl-Godley, J., & Brownell, K. D. (1996). Body shape ideals across gender, sexual orientation, socioeconomic status, race, and age in personal advertisements. *International Journal of Eating Disorders, 19,* 265–273.

Fairburn, C. G. (1981). A cognitive behavioural approach to the treatment of bulimia. *Psychological Medicine, 11,* 707–711.

Fairburn, C. (1995) *Overcoming binge eating.* New York: Guilford Press.

Fairburn, C. G., Cooper, Z., Doll, H. A., Norman, P., & O'Connor, M. (2000). The natural course of bulimia nervosa and binge eating disorder in young women. *Archives of General Psychiatry, 57,* 659–665.

Fairburn, C. G., Cooper, Z., Doll, H. A., & Welch, S. L. (1999). Risk factors for anorexia nervosa: Three integrated case-control comparisons. *Archives of General Psychiatry, 56,* 468–476.

Fairburn, C. G., Doll, H. A., Welch, S. L., Hay, P. J., Davies, B. A., & O'Connor, M. E. (1998). Risk factors for binge eating disorder: A community-based, case-control study. *Archives of General Psychiatry, 55,* 425–432.

Fairburn, C. G., Jones, R., Peveler, R. C., Hope, R. A., & O'Connor, M. (1993). Psychotherapy and bulimia nervosa. Longer-term effects of interpersonal psychotherapy, behavior therapy, and cognitive behavior therapy. *Archives of General Psychiatry, 50,* 419–428.

Fairburn, C. G., Kirk, J., O'Connor, M., & Cooper, P. J. (1986). A comparison of two psychological treatments for bulimia nervosa. *Behavior Research & Therapy, 24,* 629–643.

Fairburn, C. G., Norman, P. A., Welch, S. L., O'Connor, M. E., Doll, H. A., & Peveler, R. C. (1995). A prospective study of outcome in bulimia nervosa and the long-term effects of three psychological treatments. *Archives of General Psychiatry, 52,* 304–312.

Fairburn, C. G., Welch, S. L, Doll, H. A, Davies, B. A., & O'Connor, M. E. (1997). Risk factors for bulimia nervosa: A community-based case-control study. *Archives of General Psychiatry, 54,* 509–517.

Fairburn, C. G., Welch, S. L., Norman, P. A., O'Connor, M. E., & Doll, H. A. (1996). Bias and bulimia nervosa: How typical are clinic cases? *American Journal of Psychiatry, 153,* 386–391.

Fallon, A. E., & Rozin, P. (1985). Sex differences in perceptions of desirable body shape. *Journal of Abnormal Psychology, 94,* 102–105.

Fallon, B. A., Walsh, B. T., Sadik, C., Saoud, J. B., & Lukasik, V. (1991). Outcome and clinical course in inpatient bulimic women: A 2- to 9-year follow-up study. *Journal of Clinical Psychiatry, 52,* 272–278.

Farmer, R. F., Nash, H. M., & Field, C. E. (2001). Disordered eating behaviors and reward sensitivity. *Journal of Behavior Therapy and Experimental Psychiatry, 32,* 211–219.

Fassino, S., Abbate-Daga, G., Amianto, F., Leombruni, P., Boggio, S., & Rovera, G. G. (2002a). Temperament and character profile of eating disorders: A controlled study with the Temperament and Character Inventory. *International Journal of Eating Disorders, 32,* 412–425.

Fassino, S., Abbate-Daga, G., Amianto, F., Leombruni, P., Fornas, B., Garzaro, L., et al. (2001). Outcome predictors in anorectic patients after 6 months of multimodal treatment. *Psychotherapy and Psychosomatics, 70,* 201–208.

Fassino, S., Piero, A., Daga, G. A., Leombruni, P., Mortara, P., & Rovera, G. G. (2002b). Attentional biases and frontal functioning in anorexia nervosa. *International Journal of Eating Disorders, 31,* 274–283.

Fernstrom, J. D. (1994). Dietary amino acids and brain function. *Journal of the American Dietetic Association, 94,* 71–77.

Ferraro, F. R., Wonderlich, S., & Zeljko, J. (1997). Performance variability as a new theoretical mechanism regarding eating disorders and cognitive processing. *Journal of Clinical Psychology, 53,* 117–121.

Fetissov, S. O., Meguid, M. M., Chen, C., & Miyata, G. (2000). Synchronized release of dopamine and serotonin in the medial and lateral hypothalamus of rats. *Neuroscience, 101,* 657–663.

Fichter, M. M., & Noegel, R. (1990). Concordance for bulimia nervosa in twins. *International Journal of Eating Disorders, 9,* 255–263.

Fichter, M. M., & Quadflieg, N. (1997). Six-year course of bulimia nervosa. *International Journal of Eating Disorders, 22,* 361–384.

Fichter, M. M., & Quadflieg, N. (1999). Six-year course and outcome of anorexia nervosa. *International Journal of Eating Disorders, 26,* 359–385.

Fichter, M. M., Quadflieg, N., & Gnutzmann, A. (1998). Binge eating disorder: Treatment outcome over a 6-year course. *Journal of Psychosomatic Research, 44,* 385–405.

Field, A. E., Herzog, D. B., Keller, M. B., West, J., Nussbaum, K., & Colditz, G. A. (1997). Distinguishing recovery from remission in a cohort of bulimic women: How should asymptomatic periods be described? *Journal of Clinical Epidemiology, 50,* 1339–1345.

Fitzgibbon, M. L., Spring, B., Avellone, M. E., Blackman, L. R., Pingitore, R., & Stolley, M. R. (1998). Correlates of binge eating in Hispanic, black, and white women. *International Journal of Eating Disorders, 24,* 43–52.

Flegal, K. M., Carrol, M. D., Ogden, C. L., & Johnson, C. L. (2002). Prevalence and trends in obesity among U.S. adults, 1999–2000. *Journal of the American Medical Association, 288,* 1723–1727.

Flegal, K. M., & Troiano, R. P. (2000). Changes in the distribution of body mass index of adults and children in the U.S. population. *International Journal of Obesity and Related Metabolic Disorders: Journal of the International Association for the Study of Obesity, 24,* 807–818.

Flynn, S. V., & McNally, R. J. (1999). Do disorder-relevant cognitive biases endure in recovered bulimics? *Behavior Therapy, 30,* 541–553.

Formea, G. M., & Burns, L. (1996). Selective processing of food, weight, and body-shape words in nonpatient women with bulimia nervosa: Interference on the Stroop task. *Journal of Psychopathology and Behavioral Assessment, 18,* 105–118.

Franko, D. L. (1998). Secondary prevention of eating disorders in college women at risk. *Eating Disorders: The Journal of Treatment and Prevention, 6,* 29–40.

Franko, D. L., & Erb, J. (1998). Managed care or mangled care?: Treating eating disorders in the current healthcare climate. *Psychotherapy: Theory, Research, Practice, Training, 35,* 43–53.

Franko, D. L., Keel, P. K., Dorer, D. J., Blais, M., Delinsky, S. S., Eddy, K. T., et al. (in press). Suicide and suicide attempts in women with eating disorders. *Psychological Medicine.*

French, S. A., Story, M., Remafedi, G., Resnick, M. D., & Blum, R. W. (1996). Sexual orientation and prevalence of body dissatisfaction and eating disordered behaviors: A population-based study of adolescents. *International Journal of Eating Disorders, 19,* 119–126.

Friedman, J. M., & Halaas, J. L. (1998). Leptin and the regulation of body weight in mammals. *Nature, 395,* 763–770.

Fulkerson, J. A., Keel, P. K., Leon, G. R., & Dorr, T. (1999). Eating-disordered behaviors and personality characteristics of high school athletes and nonathletes. *International Journal of Eating Disorders, 26,* 73–79.

Furnham, A., & Alibhai, N. (1983). Cross-cultural differences in the perception of female body shapes. *Psychological Medicine, 13,* 829–837.

Furnham, A., & Baguma, P. (1994). Cross-cultural differences in the evaluation of male and female body shapes. *International Journal of Eating Disorders, 15,* 81–89.

Garfinkel, P. E., & Garner, D. M. (1982). *Anorexia nervosa: A multidimensional perspective.* New York: Brunner/Mazel.

Garfinkel, P. E., Garner, D. M., Rose, J., Darby, P. L., Brandes, J. S., O'Hanlon, J., et al. (1983). A comparison of characteristics in the families of patients with anorexia nervosa and normal controls. *Psychological Medicine, 13,* 821–828.

Garfinkel, P. E., Lin, E., Goering, P., Spegg, C., Goldbloom, D. S., Kennedy, S., et al. (1995b). Bulimia nervosa in a Canadian community sample: Prevalence and comparison of subgroups. *American Journal of Psychiatry, 152,* 1052–1058.

Garner, D. M., Garfinkel, P. E., Schwartz, D., & Thompson, M. (1980). Cultural expectations of thinness in women. *Psychological Reports, 47,* 483–491.

Garner, D. M., Olmstead, M. P., & Polivy, J. (1983). Development and validation of a multidimensional eating disorder inventory for anorexia nervosa and bulimia. *International Journal of Eating Disorders, 2,* 15–34.

Garner, D. M., Rockert, W., Davis, R., Garner, M. V., Olmsted, M. P., & Eagle, M. (1993). Comparison of cognitive-behavioral and supportive-expressive therapy for bulimia nervosa. *American Journal of Psychiatry, 150,* 37–46.

Gendall, K. A., Kaye, W. H., Altemus, M., McConaha, C. W., & La Via, M. C. (1999). Leptin, neuropeptide Y, and peptide YY in long-term recovered eating disorder patients. *Biological Psychiatry, 46,* 292–299.

Geracioti, T. D., & Liddle, R. A. (1988). Impaired cholecystokinin secretion in bulimia nervosa. *New England Journal of Medicine, 319*, 683–688.

Gerner, R. H., Cohen, D. J., Fairbanks, L., Anderson, G. M., Young, J. G., Scheinin, M., et al. (1984). CSF neurochemistry of women with anorexia nervosa and normal women. *American Journal of Psychiatry, 141*, 1441–1444.

Gershon, E. S., Schreiber, J. L., Hamont, J. R., Dibble, E. D., Kaye, W, Nurnberger, J. L., et al. (1983). Anorexia nervosa and major affective disorders associated in families: A preliminary report. In S. B. Guze, F. J. Earls, & J. E. Barret (Eds.), *Childhood Psychopathology and Development* (pp. 279–284). New York: Raven Press.

Gibbs, J., & Smith, G. P. (1977). Cholecystokinin and satiety in rats and rhesus monkeys. *American Journal of Clinical Nutrition, 30*, 758–761.

Gibbs, J., Young, R. C., & Smith, G. P. (1972). Effect of gut hormones on feeding behavior in the rat. *Federation Proceedings, 31*, 397.

Gladis, M. M., Wadden, T. A., Vogt, R., Foster, G., Kuehnel, R. H., & Bartlett, S. J. (1998). Behavioral treatment of obese binge eaters: Do they need different care? *Journal of Psychosomatic Research, 44*, 375–384.

Goh, S. E., Ong, S. B., & Subramaniam, M. (1993). Eating disorders in Hong Kong. *British Journal of Psychiatry, 162*, 276–277.

Goldbloom, D. S., Hicks, L. K., & Garfinkel, P. E. (1990). Platelet serotonin uptake in bulimia nervosa. *Biological Psychiatry, 28*, 644–647.

Golden, N. H., & Shenker, I. R. (1994). Amenorrhea in anorexia nervosa: Neuroendocrine control of hypothalamic dysfunction. *International Journal of Eating Disorders, 16*(1), 53–60.

Goldfein, J. A., Walsh, B. T., & Midlarsky, E. (2000). Influence of shape and weight on self-evaluation in bulimia nervosa. *International Journal of Eating Disorders, 27*, 435–445.

Goldstein, D. J., Wilson, M. G., Thompson, V. L., Potvin, J. H., & Rampey, A. H., Jr. (1995). Long-term fluoxetine treatment of bulimia nervosa. Fluoxetine Bulimia Nervosa Research Group. *British Journal of Psychiatry, 166*, 660–666.

Gordon, K. H., Perez, M., & Joiner, T. E., Jr. (2002). The impact of racial stereotypes on eating disorder recognition. *International Journal of Eating Disorders, 32*, 219–224.

Gorwood, P., Ades, J., Bellodi, L., Cellini, E., Collier, D. A., Di Bella, D., et al. (2002). The 5-HT(2A)-1438G/A polymorphism in anorexia nervosa: A combined analysis of 316 trios from six European centres. *Molecular Psychiatry, 7*, 90–94.

Götestam, K. G., Eriksen, L., Heggestad, T., & Nielsen, S. (1998). Prevalence of eating disorders in Norwegian general hospitals 1990–1994: Admissions per year and seasonality. *International Journal of Eating Disorders, 23*, 57–64.

Gowen, L. K., Hayward, C., Killen, J. D., Robinson, T. N., & Taylor, C. B. (1999). Acculturation and eating disorder symptoms in adolescent girls. *Journal of Research on Adolescence, 9*, 67–83.

Grave, R. D., De Luca, L., & Campello, G. (2001). Middle school primary prevention program for eating disorders: A controlled study with a twelve-month follow-up. *Eating Disorders: The Journal of Treatment and Prevention, 9*, 327–337.

Gray, J. J., Ford, K., & Kelly, L. M. (1987). The prevalence of bulimia in a Black college population. *International Journal of Eating Disorders, 6*, 733–740.

Grice, D. E., Halmi, K. A., Fichter, M. M., Strober, M., Woodside, D. B., Treasure, J. T., et al. (2002). Evidence for a susceptibility gene for anorexia nervosa on chromosome 1. *American Journal of Human Genetics, 70*, 787–792.

Grilo, C. M., & Masheb, R. M. (2000). Onset of dieting vs. binge eating in outpatients with binge eating disorder. *International Journal of Obesity and Related Metabolic Disorders, 24*, 404–409.

Grinspoon, S., Miller, K., Coyle, C., Krempin, J., Armstrong, C., Pitts, S., et al. (1999). Severity of osteopenia in estrogen-deficient women with anorexia nervosa and hypothalamic amenorrhea. *Journal of Clinical Endocrinology and Metabolism, 84*, 2049–2055.

Groesz, L. M., Levine, M. P., & Murnen, S. K. (2002). The effect of experimental presentation of thin media images on body satisfaction: A meta-analytic review. *International Journal of Eating Disorders, 31,* 1–16.

Grover, V. P., Keel, P. K., & Mitchell, J. P. (2003). Gender differences in implicit weight identity. *International Journal of Eating Disorders, 34,* 125–135.

Gruner, D. C. (1930). A treatise on the canon of medicine of Avicenna, incorporating a translation of the first book. London: Luzac & Co.

Gull, W. W. (1868). The address in medicine delivered before the annual meeting of the British Medical Association at Oxford. *Lancet, 1,* 171–176.

Gull, W. W. (1874). Anorexia nervosa (apepsia hysterica, anorexia hysterica). *Transaction of the Clinical Society of London, 7,* 22–28.

Gull, W. W. (1888). Anorexia nervosa. *Lancet, 1,* 516–517.

Habermas, T. (1989). The psychiatric history of anorexia nervosa and bulimia nervosa: Weight concerns and bulimic symptoms in early case reports. *International Journal of Eating Disorders, 8,* 259–273.

Habermas, T. (1991). The role of psychiatric and medical traditions in the discovery and description of anorexia nervosa in France, Germany, and Italy, 1873–1918. *Journal of Nervous and Mental Disease, 179,* 360–365.

Habermas, T. (1992a). Further evidence on early case descriptions of anorexia nervosa and bulimia nervosa. *International Journal of Eating Disorders, 11,* 351–359.

Habermas, T. (1992b). Historical continuities and discontinuities between religious and medical interpretations of extreme fasting. The background to Giovanni Brugnoli's description of two cases of anorexia nervosa in 1875. *History of Psychiatry, 3,* 431–55.

Hall, A., & Hay, P. J. (1991). Eating disorder patient referrals from a population region 1977–1986. *Psychological Medicine, 21,* 697–701.

Halmi, K. A., McBride, P. A., & Sunday, S. R. (1993). Serotonin responsivity and hunger and satiety in eating disorders. In E. Tierraie & F. Brambilla (Eds.), *Advances in Bioscience* (pp. 123–131). Pergamon Press.

Hargreaves, D., & Tiggemann, M. (2002). The effect of television commercials on mood and body dissatisfaction: The role of appearance-schema activation. *Journal of Social & Clinical Psychology, 21,* 287–308.

Harris, E. C., & Barraclough, B. (1998). Excess mortality of mental disorder. *British Journal of Psychiatry, 173,* 11–53.

Harris, M. B., Walters, L. C., & Waschull, S. (1991). Gender and ethnic differences in obesity-related behaviors and attitudes in a college sample. *Journal of Applied Social Psychology, 21,* 1545–1566.

Haudek, C., Rorty, M., & Henker, B. (1999). The role of ethnicity and parental bonding in the eating and weight concerns of Asian-American and Caucasian college women. *International Journal of Eating Disorders, 25,* 425–433.

Hausenblas, H. A., & Carron, A. V. (1999). Eating disorder indices and athletes: An integration. *Journal of Sport and Exercise Psychology, 21,* 230–258.

Hay, P. J., Fairburn, C. G., & Doll, H. A. (1996). The classification of bulimic eating disorders: A community-based cluster analysis study. *Psychological Medicine, 26,* 801–812.

Heatherton, T. F., & Baumeister, R. F. (1991). Binge eating as escape from self-awareness. *Psychological Bulletin, 110,* 86–108.

Heatherton, T. F., Mahamedi, F., Striepe, M., Field, A. E., & Keel, P. (1997). A 10-year longitudinal study of body weight, dieting, and eating disorder symptoms. *Journal of Abnormal Psychology, 106,* 117–125.

Heatherton, T. F., Nichols, P., Mahamedi, F., & Keel, P. (1995). Body weight, dieting, and eating disorder symptoms among college students, 1982 to 1992. *American Journal of Psychiatry, 152,* 1623–1629.

Hebebrand, J., Blum, W. F., Barth, N., Coners, H., Englaro, P., Juul, A., et al. (1997). Leptin levels in patients with anorexia nervosa are reduced in the acute stage and elevated upon short-term weight restoration. *Molecular Psychiatry, 2,* 330–334.

Heffernan, K. (1994). Sexual orientation as a factor in risk for binge eating and bulimia nervosa: A review. *International Journal of Eating Disorders, 16,* 335–347.

Heinberg, L. J., & Thompson, J. K. (1995). Body image and televised images of thinness and attractiveness: A controlled laboratory investigation. *Journal of Social and Clinical Psychology, 14,* 325–338.

Hermes, S. F., & Keel, P. K. (2003). The influence of puberty and ethnicity on awareness and internalization of the thin ideal. *International Journal of Eating Disorders, 33,* 465–467.

Herzog, D. B., Dorer, D. J., Keel, P. K., Selwyn, S. E., Ekeblad, E. R., Flores, A. T., et al. (1999). Recovery and relapse in anorexia and bulimia nervosa: A 7.5-year follow-up study. *Journal of the American Academy of Child and Adolescent Psychiatry, 38,* 829–837.

Herzog, D. B., Keller, M. B., & Lavori, P. W. (1988). Outcome in anorexia nervosa and bulimia nervosa. A review of the literature. *Journal of Nervous and Mental Disease, 176,* 131–143.

Herzog, D. B., Norman, D. K, Gordon, C., & Pepose, M. (1984). Sexual conflict and eating disorders in 27 males. *American Journal of Psychiatry, 141,* 989–990.

Herzog, W., Deter, H. C., Fiehn, W., & Petzold, E. (1997). Medical findings and predictors of long-term physical outcome in anorexia nervosa: A prospective, 12-year follow-up study. *Psychological Medicine, 27,* 269–279.

Hetherington, A. W., & Ranson, S. W. (1942). The spontaneous activity and food intake of rats with hypothalamic lesions. *American Journal of Physiology, 136,* 609–617.

Hettema, J. M., Neale, M. C., & Kendler, K. S. (1995). Physical similarity and the equal-environment assumption in twin studies of psychiatric disorders. *Behavior Genetics, 25,* 327–335.

Heymsfield, S. B., Greenberg, A. S., Fujioka, K., Dixon, R. M., Kushner, R., Hunt, T., et al. (1999). Recombinant leptin for weight loss in obese and lean adults: A randomized, controlled, dose-escalation trial. [comment]. *Journal of the American Medical Association, 282,* 1568–1575.

Hill, A. J., Weaver, C., & Blundell, J. E. (1990). Dieting concerns of 10-year-old girls and their mothers. *British Journal of Clinical Psychology, 29*(Pt 3), 346–348.

Hinney, A., Barth, N., Ziegler, A., von Prittwitz S., Hamann, A., Hennighausen, K., et al. (1997a). Serotonin transporter gene-linked polymorphic region: Allele distributions in relationship to body weight and in anorexia nervosa. *Life Sciences, 61,* 295–303.

Hinney, A., Bornscheuer, A., Depenbusch, M., Mierke, B., Tolle, A., Middeke, K., et al. (1998). No evidence for involvement of the leptin gene in anorexia nervosa, bulimia nervosa, underweight or early onset extreme obesity: Identification of two novel mutations in the coding sequence and a novel polymorphism in the leptin gene linked upstream region. *Molecular Psychiatry, 3,* 539–543.

Hinney, A., Herrmann, H., Lohr, T., Rosenkranz, K., Ziegler, A., Lehmkuhl, G., et al. (1999a). No evidence for an involvement of alleles of polymorphisms in the serotonin1Dbeta and 7 receptor genes in obesity, underweight or anorexia nervosa. *International Journal of Obesity & Related Metabolic Disorders, 23,* 760–763.

Hinney, A., Lentes, K. U., Rosenkranz, K., Barth, N., Roth, H., Ziegler, A., et al. (1997b). Beta 3-adrenergic-receptor allele distributions in children, adolescents and young adults with obesity, underweight or anorexia nervosa. *International Journal of Obesity and Related Metabolic Disorders, 21,* 224–230.

Hinney, A., Schneider, J., Ziegler, A., Lehmkuhl, G., Poustka, F., Schmidt, M. H., et al. (1999b). No evidence for involvement of polymorphisms of the dopamine D_4 receptor gene in anorexia nervosa, underweight, and obesity. *American Journal of Medical Genetics, 88,* 594–597.

Hinney, A., Ziegler, A., Nothen, M. M., Remschmidt, H., & Hebebrand, J. (1997c). 5-HT2A receptor gene polymorphisms, anorexia nervosa, and obesity. *Lancet, 350,* 1324–1325.

Hoek, H. W., Bartelds, A. I., Bosveld, J. J., van der Graaf, Y., Limpens, V. E., Maiwald, M., et al. (1995). Impact of urbanization on detection rates of eating disorders. *American Journal of Psychiatry, 152,* 1272–1278.

Hotta, M., Shibasaki, T., Sato, K., & Demura, H. (1998). The importance of body weight history in the occurrence and recovery of osteoporosis in patients with anorexia nervosa: Evaluation by dual X-ray absorptiometry and bone metabolic markers. *European Journal of Endocrinology, 139*, 276–283.

Hsu, L. K. G. (1990). *Eating disorders.* New York: Guilford Press.

Hu, X., Giotakis, O., Li, T., Karwautz, A., Treasure, J., & Collier, D. A. (2003). Association of the 5-HT2c gene with susceptibility and minimum body mass index in anorexia nervosa. *Neuroreport, 14*, 781–783.

Humphrey, L. L. (1986). Family relations in bulimic-anorexic and nondistressed families. *International Journal of Eating Disorders, 5*, 223–232.

Humphrey, L. L. (1988). Relationships within subtypes of anorexic, bulimic, and normal families. *Journal of the American Academy of Child and Adolescent Psychiatry, 27*, 544–551.

Humphrey, L. L. (1989). Observed family interactions among subtypes of eating disorders using structural analysis of social behavior. *Journal of Consulting and Clinical Psychology, 57*, 206–214.

Humphrey, L. L., Apple, R. F., & Kirschenbaum, D. S. (1986). Differentiating bulimic-anorexic from normal families using interpersonal and behavioral observational systems. *Journal of Consulting and Clinical Psychology, 54*, 190–195.

Hurley, J. B., Palmer, R. L., & Stretch, D. (1990). The specificity of the Eating Disorders Inventory: A reappraisal. *International Journal of Eating Disorders, 9*, 419–424.

Jansen, A., van den Hout, M. A., & Griez, E. (1989). Does bingeing restore bulimics' alleged 5-HT deficiency? *Behaviour Research and Therapy, 27*, 555–560.

Jimerson, D. C., Lesem, M. D., Kaye, W. H., & Brewerton, T. D. (1992). Low serotonin and dopamine metabolite concentrations in cerebrospinal fluid from bulimic patients with frequent binge episodes. *Archives of General Psychiatry, 49*, 132–138.

Jimerson, D. C., Mantzoros, C., Wolfe, B. E., & Metzger, E. D. (2000). Decreased serum leptin in bulimia nervosa. *Journal of Clinical Endocrinology and Metabolism, 85*, 4511–4514.

Jimerson, D. C., Wolfe, B. E., Metzger, E. D., Finkelstein, D. M., Cooper, T. B., & Levine, J. M. (1997). Decreased serotonin function in bulimia nervosa. *Archives of General Psychiatry, 54*, 529–34.

Joergensen, J. (1992). The epidemiology of eating disorders in Fyn County, Denmark, 1977–1986. *Acta Psychiatrica Scandinavica, 85*, 30–34.

Johnson, C. L., Lewis, C., Love, S., Lewis, L., & Stuckey M. (1984). Incidence and correlates of bulimic behavior in a female high school population. *Journal of Youth and Adolescence, 13*, 15–26.

Joiner, T. E., Jr. (1999). Self-verification and bulimic symptoms: Do bulimic women play a role in perpetuating their own dissatisfaction and symptoms? *International Journal of Eating Disorders, 26*, 145–151.

Joiner, T. E., Jr., Heatherton, T. F., & Keel, P. K. (1997). Ten-year stability and predictive validity of five bulimia-related indicators. *American Journal of Psychiatry, 154*, 1133–1138.

Jones, D. J., Fox, M. M., Babigian, H. M., & Hutton, H. E. (1980). Epidemiology of anorexia nervosa in Monroe County, New York: 1960–1976. *Psychosomatic Medicine, 42*, 551–558.

Jones-Chesters, M. H., Monsell, S., & Cooper, P. J. (1998). The disorder-salient Stroop effect as a measure of psychopathology in eating disorders. *International Journal of Eating Disorders, 24*, 65–82.

Kandel, E. R., Schwartz, J. H., & Jessell, T. M. (1991). *Principles of Neural Science* (3rd ed.). New York: Elsevier.

Kaplan, A. S., Garfinkel, P. E., Warsh, J. J., & Brown, G. M. (1989). Clonidine challenge test in bulimia nervosa. *International Journal of Eating Disorders, 8*, 425–435.

Karwautz, A., Rabe-Hesketh, S., Hu, X., Zhao, J., Sham, P., Collier, D. A., et al. (2001). Individual-specific risk factors for anorexia nervosa: A pilot study using a discordant sister-pair design. *Psychological Medicine, 31*, 317–329.

Kater, K., Rohwer, J., & Levine, M. P (2000). An elementary school project for developing healthy body image and reducing risk factors for unhealthy and disordered eating. *Eating Disorders: The Journal of Treatment and Prevention, 8*, 3–16.

Katzman, D. K., Zipursky, R. B., Lambe, E. K., & Mikulis, D. J. (1997). A longitudinal magnetic resonance imaging study of brain changes in adolescents with anorexia nervosa. *Archives of Pediatrics and Adolescent Medicine, 151,* 793–797.

Katzman, M. A., & Lee, S. (1997). Beyond body image: The integration of feminist and transcultural theories in the understanding of self-starvation. *International Journal of Eating Disorders, 22,* 385–394.

Kaye, W. H. (1997). Anorexia nervosa, obsessional behavior, and serotonin. *Psychopharmacology Bulletin, 33,* 335–344.

Kaye, W. H., Ballenger, J. C., Lydiard, R. B., Stuart, G. W., Laraia, M. T., O'Neil, P., et al. (1990a). CSF monoamine levels in normal-weight bulimia: Evidence for abnormal noradrenergic activity. *American Journal of Psychiatry, 147,* 225–229.

Kaye, W. H., Berrettini, W. H., Gwirtsman, H. E., Chretien, M., Gold, P. W., George, D. T., et al. (1987). Reduced cerebrospinal fluid levels of immunoreactive pro-opiomelanocortin related peptides (including beta-endorphin) in anorexia nervosa. *Life Sciences, 41,* 2147–2155.

Kaye, W. H., Berrettini, W., Gwirtsman, H., & George, D. T. (1990b). Altered cerebrospinal fluid neuropeptide Y and peptide YY immunoreactivity in anorexia and bulimia nervosa. *Archives of General Psychiatry, 47,* 548–556.

Kaye, W. H., Ebert, M. H., Gwirtsman, H. E., & Weiss, S. R. (1984a). Differences in brain serotonergic metabolism between nonbulimic and bulimic patients with anorexia nervosa. *American Journal of Psychiatry, 141,* 1598–1601.

Kaye, W. H., Ebert, M. H., Raleigh, M., & Lake, R. (1984b). Abnormalities in CNS monoamine metabolism in anorexia nervosa. *Archives of General Psychiatry, 41,* 350–355.

Kaye, W. H., Frank, G. K. W., & McConaha, C. (1999). Altered dopamine activity after recovery from restricting-type anorexia nervosa. *Neuropsychopharmacology, 21,* 503–506.

Kaye, W. H., Frank, G. K., Meltzer, C. C., Price, J. C., McConaha, C. W., Crossan, P. J., et al. (2001a). Altered serotonin 2A receptor activity in women who have recovered from bulimia nervosa. *American Journal of Psychiatry, 158,* 1152–1155.

Kaye, W. H., Gwirtsman, H. E., Brewerton, T. D., George, D. T., & Wurtman, R. J. (1988a). Bingeing behavior and plasma amino acids: A possible involvement of brain serotonin in bulimia nervosa. *Psychiatry Research, 23,* 31–43.

Kaye, W. H., Gwirtsman, H. E., George, D. T., & Ebert, M. H. (1991a). Altered serotonin activity in anorexia nervosa after long-term weight restoration. Does elevated cerebrospinal fluid 5-hydroxyindoleacetic acid level correlate with rigid and obsessive behavior? *Archives of General Psychiatry, 48,* 556–562.

Kaye, W. H., Gwirtsman, H. E., George, D. T., Jimerson, D. C., & Ebert, M. H. (1988b). CSF 5-HIAA concentrations in anorexia nervosa: Reduced values in underweight subjects normalize after weight gain. *Biological Psychiatry, 23,* 102–105.

Kaye, W. H., Jimerson, D. C., Lake, C. R., & Ebert, M. H. (1985). Altered norepinephrine metabolism following long-term weight recovery in patients with anorexia nervosa. *Psychiatry Research, 14,* 333–342.

Kaye, W. H., Nagata, T., Weltzin, T. E., Hsu, L. K., Sokol, M. S., McConaha, C., et al. (2001b). Double-blind placebo-controlled administration of fluoxetine in restricting- and restricting-purging-type anorexia nervosa. *Biological Psychiatry, 49,* 644–652.

Kaye, W. H., Weltzin, T. E., Hsu, L. K., & Bulik, C. M. (1991b). An open trial of fluoxetine in patients with anorexia nervosa. *Journal of Clinical Psychiatry, 52,* 464–471.

Keel, P. K. (1998). Long-term outcome of bulimia nervosa. *Dissertation Abstracts International: Section B: The Sciences and Engineering, 58,* 6812.

Keel, P. K., Dorer, D. J., Eddy, K. T., Delinsky, S. S., Franko, D. L., Blais, M. A., et al. (2002a). Predictors of treatment utilization among women with anorexia and bulimia nervosa. *American Journal of Psychiatry, 159,* 140–142.

Keel, P. K., Dorer, D. J., Eddy, K. T., Franko, D., Charatan, D. L., & Herzog, D. B. (2003). Predictors of mortality in eating disorders. *Archives of General Psychiatry, 60,* 179–183.

Keel, P. K., Haedt, A., & Edler, C. (in press). Purging disorder: An ominous variant of bulimia nervosa? *International Journal of Eating Disorders.*

Keel, P. K., Fulkerson, J. A., & Leon, G. R. (1997a). Disordered eating precursors in pre- and early adolescent girls and boys. *Journal of Youth and Adolescence, 26,* 203–216.

Keel, P. K., & Haedt, A. (in press). Empirically supported psychosocial interventions for eating disorders and eating problems. *Journal of Clinical Child and Adolescent Psychology.*

Keel, P. K., Heatherton, T. F., Harnden, J. L., & Hornig, C. D. (1997b). Mothers, fathers, and daughters: Dieting and disordered eating. *Eating Disorders: The Journal of Treatment and Prevention, 5,* 216–228.

Keel, P. K., & Herzog, D. B. (2004). Long-term outcome, course of illness and mortality in anorexia nervosa, bulimia nervosa, and binge eating disorder. In T. D. Brewerton (Ed.), *Eating Disorders* (pp. 97–116). New York: Marcel Dekker.

Keel, P. K., & Klump, K. L. (2003). Are eating disorders culture-bound syndromes? Implications for conceptualizing their etiology. *Psychological Bulletin, 129,* 747–769.

Keel, P. K., Klump, K. L., Leon, G. R., & Fulkerson, J. A. (1998). Disordered eating in adolescent males from a school-based sample. *International Journal of Eating Disorders, 23,* 125–132.

Keel, P. K., Mayer, S. A., & Harnden-Fischer, J. H. (2001a). Importance of size in defining binge eating episodes in bulimia nervosa. *International Journal of Eating Disorders, 29,* 294–301.

Keel, P. K., & Mitchell, J. E. (1997). Outcome in bulimia nervosa. *American Journal of Psychiatry, 154,* 313–321.

Keel, P. K., Mitchell, J. E., Davis, T. L., & Crow, S. J. (2001b). Relationship between depression and body dissatisfaction in women diagnosed with bulimia nervosa. *International Journal of Eating Disorders, 30,* 48–56.

Keel, P. K., Mitchell, J. E., Davis, T. L., & Crow, S. J. (2002b). Long-term impact of treatment in women diagnosed with bulimia nervosa. *International Journal of Eating Disorders, 31,* 151–158.

Keel, P. K., Mitchell, J. E., Davis, T. L., Fieselman, S., & Crow, S. J. (2000a). Impact of definitions on the description and prediction of bulimia nervosa outcome. *International Journal of Eating Disorders, 28,* 377–386.

Keel, P. K., Mitchell, J. E., Miller, K. B., Davis, T. L., & Crow, S. J. (1999). Long-term outcome of bulimia nervosa. *Archives of General Psychiatry, 56,* 63–69.

Keel, P. K., Mitchell, J. E., Miller, K. B., Davis, T. L., & Crow, S. J. (2000b). Predictive validity of bulimia nervosa as a diagnostic category. *American Journal of Psychiatry, 157,* 136–138.

Keesey, R. E. (1986). Set point theory of obesity. In K. D. Brownell & J. P. Foreyt (Eds.), *Handbook of eating disorders* (pp. 63–87). New York: Basic Books.

Kendell, R. E. (1989). Clinical validity. *Psychological Medicine, 19,* 45–55.

Kendell, R. E., Hall, D. J., Hailey, A., & Babigian, H. M. (1973). The epidemiology of anorexia nervosa. *Psychological Medicine, 3,* 200–203.

Kendler, K. S., & Gardner, C. O., Jr. (1998). Twin studies of adult psychiatric and substance dependence disorders: Are they biased by differences in the environmental experiences of monozygotic and dizygotic twins in childhood and adolescence? *Psychological Medicine, 28,* 625–633.

Kendler, K. S., Martin, N. G., Heath, A. C., & Eaves, L. J. (1995). Self-report psychiatric symptoms in twins and their nontwin relatives: Are twins different? *American Journal of Medical Genetics, 60,* 588–591.

Keys, A., Brozek, J., Henschel, A., Mickelsen, O., & Taylor, H. L. (1950). *The biology of human starvation.* Minneapolis: University of Minnesota Press.

Kilbourne, J. (1987). *Still killing us softly.* Cambridge: Harvard University.

Killen, J. D., Taylor, C. B., Hayward, C., Haydel, K. F., Wilson, D. M., Hammer, L., et al. (1996). Weight concerns influence the development of eating disorders: A 4-year prospective study. *Journal of Consulting and Clinical Psychology, 64*, 936–940.

King, N., Touyz, S., & Charles, M. (2000). The effect of body dissatisfaction on women's perceptions of female celebrities. *International Journal of Eating Disorders, 27*, 341–347.

Kingston, K., Szmukler, G., Andrewes, D., Tress, B., & Desmond, P. (1996). Neuropsychological and structural brain changes in anorexia nervosa before and after refeeding. *Psychological Medicine, 26*, 15–28.

Kipman, A., Bruins-Slot, L., Boni, C., Hanoun, N., Ades, J., Blot, P., et al. (2002). 5-HT(2A) gene promoter polymorphism as a modifying rather than a vulnerability factor in anorexia nervosa. *European Psychiatry, 17*, 227–229.

Kirkley, B. G., Schneider, J. A., Agras, W. S., & Bachman, J. A. (1985). Comparison of two group treatments for bulimia. *Journal of Consulting and Clinical Psychology, 53*, 43–48.

Klerman, G. L., Weissman, M. M., Rounsaville, B. J., & Chevron, E. S. (1984). *Interpersonal psychotherapy of depression.* New York: Basic Boooks.

Klump, K. L., Bulik, C. M., Pollice, C., Halmi, K. A., Fichter, M. M., Berrettini, W. H., et al. (2000a). Temperament and character in women with anorexia nervosa. *Journal of Nervous and Mental Disease, 188*, 559–567.

Klump, K. L., Holly, A., Iacono, W. G., McGue, M., & Willson, L. E. (2000b). Physical similarity and twin resemblance for eating attitudes and behaviors: A test of the equal environments assumption. *Behavior Genetics, 30*, 51–58.

Klump, K. L., Kaye, W. H., & Strober, M. (2001a). The evolving genetic foundations of eating disorders. *Psychiatric Clinics of North America, 24*, 215–225.

Klump, K. L., Keel, P. K., Leon, G. R., & Fulkerson, J. A. (1999). Risk for eating disorders in a school-based twin sample: Are twins representative of the general population for eating disorders behavior? *Eating Disorders: The Journal of Treatment and Prevention, 7*, 33–41.

Klump, K. L., McGue, M., & Iacono, W. G. (2002). Genetic relationships between personality and eating attitudes and behaviors. *Journal of Abnormal Psychology, 111*, 380–389.

Klump, K. L., McGue, M., & Iacono, W. G. (2000c). Age differences in genetic and environmental influences on eating attitudes and behaviors in preadolescent and adolescent female twins. *Journal of Abnormal Psychology, 109*, 239–251.

Klump, K. L., McGue, M., & Iacono, W. G. (2003). Differential heritability of eating attitudes and behaviors in prepubertal versus pubertal twins. *International Journal of Eating Disorders, 33*, 287–292.

Klump, K. L., Miller, K. B., Keel, P. K., McGue, M., & Iacono, W. G. (2001b). Genetic and environmental influences on anorexia nervosa syndromes in a population-based twin sample. *Psychological Medicine, 31*, 737–740.

Koeppen-Schomerus, G., Wardle, J., & Plomin, R. (2001). A genetic analysis of weight and overweight in 4-year-old twin pairs. *International Journal of Obesity and Related Metabolic Disorders, 25*, 838–844.

Koo-Loeb, J. H., Costello, N., Light, K. C., & Girdler, S. S. (2000). Women with eating disorder tendencies display altered cardiovascular, neuroendocrine, and psychosocial profiles. *Psychosomatic Medicine, 62*, 539–548.

Koronyo-Hamaoui, M., Danziger, Y., Frisch, A., Stein, D., Leor, S., Laufer, N., et al. (2002). Association between anorexia nervosa and the *hsKCa3* gene: A family-based and case control study. *Molecular Psychiatry, 7*, 82–85.

Kosslyn, S. M., & Rosenberg, R. S. (2001). *Psychology: The brain, the person, the world.* Needham Heights, MA: Allyn and Bacon.

Kraig, K. A., & Keel, P. K. (2001). Weight-based stigmatization in children. *International Journal of Obesity and Related Metabolic Disorders, 25*, 1661–1666.

Krieg, J. C., Lauer, C., Leinsinger, G., Pahl, J., Schreiber, W., Pirke, K. M., et al. (1989). Brain morphology and regional cerebral blood flow in anorexia nervosa. *Biological Psychiatry, 25,* 1041–1048.

Kuba, S., & Harris, D. (2001). Eating disturbances in women of color: An exploratory study of contextual factors in the development of disordered eating in Mexican-American women. *Health Care for Women International, 22,* 281–298.

Kuczmarski, R. J., Flegal, K. M., Campbell, S. M., & Johnson, C. L. (1994). Increasing prevalence of overweight among U.S. adults. The National Health and Nutrition Examination Surveys, 1960 to 1991. *Journal of the American Medical Association, 272,* 205–211.

Lacey, J. H. (1982). Anorexia nervosa and a bearded female saint. *British Medical Journal (Clinical Research Edition), 285,* 1816–1817.

Lai, K. Y. (2000). Anorexia nervosa in Chinese adolescents—does culture make a difference? *Journal of Adolescence, 23,* 561–568.

Laliberte, M., Boland, F. J., & Leichner, P. (1999). Family climates: Family factors specific to disturbed eating and bulimia nervosa. *Journal of Clinical Psychology, 55,* 1021–1040.

Larkin, J. E., & Pines, H. A. (1979). No fat persons need apply. *Sociology of Work Occupations, 6,* 312–327.

Lasegue, C. (1873). On hysterical anorexia. *Medical Times and Gazette, 2,* 265–266.

Lauzurica, N., Hurtado, A., Escarti, A., Delgado, M., Barrios, V., Morande, G., Soriano, J., Jauregui, I., Gonzalez-Valdermoro, M. I., Garcia-Camba, E., & Fuentes, J. A. (2003). Polymorphisms within the promoter and the intron 2 of the serotonin transporter gene in a population of bulimic patients. *Neuroscience Letters, 352,* 226–230.

Lawlor, B. A., Burket, R. C., & Hodgin, J. A. (1987). Eating disorders in American Black men. *Journal of the National Medical Association, 79,* 984–986.

le Grange, D. (1999). Family therapy for adolescent anorexia nervosa. *Journal of Clinical Psychology, 55,* 727–739.

le Grange, D., Eisler, I., Dare, C., & Russell, G. F. (1992). Evaluation of family treatments in adolescent anorexia nervosa: A pilot study. *International Journal of Eating Disorders, 12,* 347–357.

le Grange, D., Stone, A. A., & Brownell, K. D. (1998). Eating disturbances in white and minority female dieters. *International Journal of Eating Disorders, 24,* 395–403.

Lear, S. A., Pauly, R. P., & Birmingham, C. L. (1999). Body fat, caloric intake, and plasma leptin levels in women with anorexia nervosa. *International Journal of Eating Disorders, 26,* 283–288.

Lee, C. K., Kwak, Y. S., Rhee, H., Kim, Y. S., Han, J. H., Choi, J. O., et al. (1987). The nationwide epidemiological study of medical disorders in Korea. *Journal of Korean Medical Science, 2,* 19–34.

Lee, S. (1995). Self-starvation in context: Towards a culturally sensitive understanding of anorexia nervosa. *Social Science and Medicine, 41,* 25–36.

Lee, S. (2000). Eating disorders are becoming more common in the East too. *British Medical Journal, 321,* 10–23.

Lee, S., Chiu, H. F., & Chen, C. N. (1989). Anorexia nervosa in Hong Kong: Why not more in Chinese? *British Journal of Psychiatry, 154,* 683–688.

Lee, S., Ho, T. P., & Hsu, L. K. (1993). Fat phobic and non-fat phobic anorexia nervosa: A comparative study of 70 Chinese patients in Hong Kong. *Psychological Medicine, 23,* 999–1017.

Lee, S., Hsu, L. K., & Wing, Y. K. (1992). Bulimia nervosa in Hong Kong Chinese patients. *British Journal of Psychiatry, 161,* 545–551.

Lee, S., & Lee, A. M. (2000). Disordered eating in three communities of China: A comparative study of female high school students in Hong Kong, Shenzhen, and rural Hunan. *International Journal of Eating Disorders, 27,* 317–327.

Leon, G. R., Fulkerson, J. A., Perry, C. L., & Cudeck, R. (1993). Personality and behavioral vulnerabilities associated with risk status for eating disorders in adolescent girls. *Journal of Abnormal Psychology, 102,* 438–444.

Leon, G. R., Fulkerson, J. A., Perry, C. L., & Early-Zald, M. B. (1995). Prospective analysis of personality and behavioral vulnerabilities and gender influences in the later development of disordered eating. *Journal of Abnormal Psychology, 104,* 140–149.

Leon, G. R., Fulkerson, J. A., Perry, C. L., Keel, P. K., & Klump, K. L. (1999). Three to four year prospective evaluation of personality and behavioral risk factors for later disordered eating in adolescent girls and boys. *Journal of Youth and Adolescence, 28,* 181–196.

Leon, G. R., Keel, P. K., Klump K. L., & Fulkerson, J. A. (1997). The future of risk factor research in understanding the etiology of eating disorders. *Psychopharmacology Bulletin, 33,* 405–411.

Leon, G. R., Perry, C. L., Mangelsdorf, C., & Tell, G. J. (1989). Adolescent nutritional and psychological patterns and risk for the development of an eating disorder. *Journal of Youth and Adolescence, 18,* 273–282.

Lerner, R. M., & Gellert, E. (1969). Body build identification, preference, and aversion in children. *Developmental Psychology, 1,* 456–462.

Lester, R., & Petrie, T. A. (1995). Personality and physical correlates of bulimic symptomatology among Mexican American female college students. *Journal of Counseling Psychology, 42,* 199–203.

Lester, R., & Petrie, T. A. (1998). Prevalence of disordered eating behaviors and bulimia nervosa in a sample of Mexican American female college students. *Journal of Multicultural Counseling and Development, 26,* 157–165.

Levine, M. P., & Smolak, L. (2001). Primary prevention of body image disturbances and disordered eating in childhood and early adolescence. In J. K. Thompson & L. Smolak (Eds.), *Body image, eating disorders, and obesity in youth: Assessment, prevention, and treatment* (pp. 237–260). Washington; American Psychological Association.

Levine, M. P., Smolak, L., & Schermer, F. (1996). Media analysis and resistance by elementary school children in the primary prevention of eating problems. *Eating Disorders: The Journal of Treatment and Prevention, 4,* 310–322.

Lilenfeld, L. R., Kaye, W. H., Greeno, C. G., Merikangas, K. R., Plotnicov, K., Pollice, C., et al. (1998). A controlled family study of anorexia nervosa and bulimia nervosa: Psychiatric disorders in first-degree relatives and effects of proband comorbidity. *Archives of General Psychiatry, 55,* 603–610.

Littleton, H. L., & Ollendick, T. (2003). Negative body image and disordered eating behavior in children and adolescents: What places youth at risk and how can these problems be prevented? *Clinical Child and Family Psychology Review, 6,* 51–66.

Lovell, D. M., Williams, J. M., & Hill, A. B. (1997). Selective processing of shape-related words in women with eating disorders, and those who have recovered. *British Journal of Clinical Psychology, 36,* 421–432.

Lowe, M. R., Gleaves, D. H., & Murphy-Eberenz, K. P. (1998). On the relation of dieting and bingeing in bulimia nervosa. *Journal of Abnormal Psychology, 107,* 263–271.

Loxton, N. J., & Dawe, S. (2001). Alcohol abuse and dysfunctional eating in adolescent girls: The influence of individual differences in sensitivity to reward and punishment. *International Journal of Eating Disorders, 29,* 455–462.

Lucas, A. R., Beard, C. M., O'Fallon, W. M., & Kurland, L. T. (1988). Anorexia nervosa in Rochester, Minnesota: A 45-year study. *Mayo Clinic Proceedings, 63,* 433–442.

Lucas, A. R., Beard, C. M., O'Fallon, W. M., & Kurland, L. T. (1991). 50-year trends in the incidence of anorexia nervosa in Rochester, Minn.: A population-based study. *American Journal of Psychiatry, 148,* 917–922.

Lucas, A. R., Crowson, C. S., O'Fallon, W. M., & Melton, L. J., 3rd (1999). The ups and downs of anorexia nervosa. *International Journal of Eating Disorders, 26,* 397–405.

Lucero, K., Hicks, R. A., Bramlette, J., Brassington, G. S., & Welter, M. G. (1992). Frequency of eating problems among Asian and Caucasian college women. *Psychological Reports, 71,* 255–258.

Lydiard, R. B., Brady, K. T., O'Neil, P. M., Schlesier-Carter, B., Hamilton, S., Rogers, Q., et al. (1988). Precursor amino acid concentrations in normal weight bulimics and normal controls. *Progress in Neuropsychopharmacology and Biological Psychiatry, 12*, 893–898.

MacBrayer, E. K., Smith, G. T., McCarthy, D. M., Demos, S., & Simmons, J. (2001). The role of family of origin food-related experiences in bulimic symptomatology. *International Journal of Eating Disorders, 30*, 149–160.

Mangweth, B., Pope, H. G., Jr., Hudson, J. I., Olivardia, R., Kinzl, J., & Biebl, W. (1997). Eating disorders in Austrian men: An intracultural and crosscultural comparison study. *Psychotherapy and Psychosomatics, 66*, 214–221.

Mann, T., Nolen-Hoeksema, S., Huang, K., Burgard, D., Wright, A., & Hanson, K. (1997). Are two interventions worse than none? Joint primary and secondary prevention of eating disorders in college females. *Health Psychology, 16*, 215–225.

Mantzoros, C., Flier, J. S., Lesem, M. D., Brewerton, T. D., & Jimerson, D. C. (1997). Cerebrospinal fluid leptin in anorexia nervosa: Correlation with nutritional status and potential role in resistance to weight gain. *Journal of Clinical Endocrinology and Metabolism, 82*, 1845–1851.

Marazziti, D., Macchi, E., Rotondo, A., Placidi, G. F., & Cassano, G. B. (1988). Involvement of serotonin system in bulimia. *Life Science, 43*, 2123–2126.

Marcus, M. D., Wing, R. R., & Fairburn, C. G. (1995). Cognitive treatment of binge eating v. behavioral weight control in the treatment of binge eating disorder. *Annals of Behavioral Medicine, 17*, S090.

Marcus, M. D., Wing, R. R., & Hopkins, J. (1988). Obese binge eaters: Affect, cognitions, and response to behavioral weight control. *Journal of Consulting and Clinical Psychology, 56*, 433–439.

Martz, D. M., & Bazzini, D. G. (1999). Eating disorders prevention programming may be failing: Evaluation of 2 one-shot programs. *Journal of College Student Development, 40*, 32–42.

Martz, D. M., Graves, K. D., & Sturgis, E. T. (1997). A pilot peer-leader eating disorders prevention program for sororities. *Eating Disorders: The Journal of Treatment and Prevention, 5*, 294–308.

McCabe, M. P., & Ricciardelli, L. A. (2001). Parent, peer, and media influences on body image and strategies to both increase and decrease body size among adolescent boys and girls. *Adolescence, 36*, 225–240.

McDermott, B. M., Batik, M., Roberts, L., & Gibbon, P. (2002). Parent and child report of family functioning in a clinical child and adolescent eating disorders sample. *Australian and New Zealand Journal of Psychiatry, 36*, 509–514.

McEvey, G. L., & Davis, R. (2002). A program to promote positive body image: A 1-year follow-up evaluation. *Journal of Early Adolescence, 22*, 96–108.

McEvey, G. L., Pepler, D., Davis, R., Flett, G. L., & Abdolell, M. (2002). Risk and protective factors associated with disordered eating during early adolescence. *Journal of Early Adolescence, 22*, 75–95.

Miller, K. B., Keel, P. K., Mitchell, J. E., Thuras, P., & Crow, S. J. (2004). *Cognitive-behavioral therapy speeds recovery over the long-term course of bulimia nervosa.* Manuscript submitted for publication.

Miller, M. N., & Pumariega, A. J. (2001). Culture and eating disorders: A historical and cross-cultural review. *Psychiatry, 64*, 93–110.

Mills, J. S., Polivy, J., Herman, C. P., & Tiggemann, M. (2002). Effects of exposure to thin media images: Evidence of self-enhancement among restrained eaters. *Personality and Social Psychology Bulletin, 28*, 1687–1699.

Milos, G., Spindler, A., Schnyder, U., Martz, J., Hoek, H. W., & Willi, J. (2004). Incidence of severe anorexia nervosa in Switzerland: 40 years of development. *International Journal of Eating Disorders, 35*, 250–258.

Milosevic, A. (1999). Eating disorders and the dentist. *British Dental Journal, 186*, 109–113.

Mintz, L., & Kashubeck, S. (1999). Body image and disordered eating among Asian American and Caucasian college students: An examination of race and gender differences. *Psychology of Women Quarterly, 23*, 781–796.

Minuchin, S., Rosman, B. L., & Baker, L. (1978). *Psychosomatic families: Anorexia nervosa in context.* Cambridge: Harvard University Press.

Mitchell, J. E. (1990). The treatment of eating disorders. *Psychosomatics, 31,* 1–3.

Mitchell, J. E., Halmi, K., Wilson, G. T., Agras, W. S., Kraemer, H., & Crow, S. (2002). A randomized secondary treatment study of women with bulimia nervosa who fail to respond to CBT. *International Journal of Eating Disorders, 32,* 271–281.

Mitchell, J. E., Pomeroy, C., Seppala, M., & Huber, M. (1988). Diuretic use as a marker for eating problems and affective disorders among women. *Journal of Clinical Psychiatry, 49,* 267–270.

Mitchell, J. E., Pyle, R. L., Eckert, E. D., Hatsukami, D., & Lentz, R. (1983). Electrolyte and other physiological abnormalities in patients with bulimia. *Psychological Medicine, 13,* 273–278.

Mitchell, J. E., Pyle, R. L., Eckert, E. D., Hatsukami, D., Pomeroy, C., & Zimmerman, R. (1990). A comparison study of antidepressants and structured intensive group psychotherapy in the treatment of bulimia nervosa. *Archives of General Psychiatry, 47,* 149–157.

Mitchell, J. E., Raymond, N., & Specker, S. (1993). A review of the controlled trials of pharmacotherapy and psychotherapy in the treatment of bulimia nervosa. *International Journal of Eating Disorders, 14,* 229–247.

Mitchell, J. E., Seim, H. C., Colon, E., & Pomeroy, C. (1987). Medical complications and medical management of bulimia. *Annals of Internal Medicine, 107,* 71–77.

Møller-Madsen, S., & Nystrup, J. (1992). Incidence of anorexia nervosa in Denmark. *Acta Psychiatrica Scandinavica, 86,* 197–200.

Møller-Madsen, S., Nystrup, J., & Nielsen, S. (1996). Mortality in anorexia nervosa in Denmark during the period 1970–1987. *Acta Psychiatrica Scandinavica, 94,* 454–459.

Monteleone, P., Bortolotti, F., Fabrazzo, M., La Rocca, A., Fuschino, A., & Maj, M. (2000a). Plasma leptin response to acute fasting and refeeding in untreated women with bulimia nervosa. *Journal of Clinical Endocrinology and Metabolism, 85,* 2499–2503.

Monteleone, P., Brambilla, F., Bortolotti, F., & Maj, M. (2000b). Serotonergic dysfunction across the eating disorders: Relationship to eating behaviour, purging behaviour, and nutritional status and general psychopathology. *Psychological Medicine, 30,* 1099–1110.

Monteleone, P., Di Lieto, A., Tortorella, A., Longobardi, N., & Maj, M. (2000c). Circulating leptin in patients with anorexia nervosa, bulimia nervosa or binge-eating disorder: Relationship to body weight, eating patterns, psychopathology and endocrine changes. *Psychiatry Research, 94,* 121–129.

Moore, F., & Keel, P. K. (2003). Influence of sexual orientation and age on disordered eating attitudes and behaviors in women. *International Journal of Eating Disorders, 34,* 370–374.

Moran, T. H., Robinson, P. H., & McHugh, P. R. (1985). The pyloric cholecystokinin receptor: A site of mediation for satiety? *Annals of the New York Academy of Sciences, 448,* 621–623.

Moreno, A. B., & Thelen, M. H. (1993). A preliminary prevention program for eating disorders in a junior high school population. *Journal of Youth and Adolescence, 22,* 109–124.

Morgan, H. G., & Russell, G. F. (1975). Value of family background and clinical features as predictors of long-term outcome in anorexia nervosa: Four-year follow-up study of 41 patients. *Psychological Medicine, 5,* 355–371.

Morton, R. (1694). *Phthisiologia: Or, a treatise of consumptions.* London: Smith & Walford.

Mukai, T., Crago, M., & Shisslak, C. M. (1994). Eating attitudes and weight preoccupation among female high school students in Japan. *Journal of Child Psychology and Psychiatry and Allied Disciplines, 35,* 677–688.

Mukai, T., Kambara, A., & Sasaki, Y. (1998). Body dissatisfaction, need for social approval, and eating disturbances among Japanese and American college women. *Sex Roles, 39,* 751–763.

Mukai, T., & McCloskey, L. A. (1996). Eating attitudes among Japanese and American elementary school girls. *Journal of Cross-Cultural Psychology, 27,* 424–435.

Mullholland, A., & Mintz, L. (2001). Prevalence of eating disorders among African American women. *Journal of Counseling Psychology, 48*, 111–116.

Munk-Jorgensen, P., Møller-Madsen, S., Nielsen, S., & Nystrup, J. (1995). Incidence of eating disorders in psychiatric hospitals and wards in Denmark, 1970–1993. *Acta Psychiatrica Scandinavica, 92*, 91–96.

Murnen, S. K., & Smolak, L. (1997). Femininity, masculinity, and disordered eating: A meta-analytic review. *International Journal of Eating Disorders, 22*, 231–242.

Mussell, M. P., Crosby, R. D., Crow, S. J., Knopke, A. J., Peterson, C. B., Wonderlich, S. A. et al. (2000). Utilization of empirically supported psychotherapy treatments for individuals with eating disorders: A survey of psychologists. *International Journal of Eating Disorders, 27*, 230–237.

Mussell, M. P., Mitchell, J. E., Fenna, C. J, Crosby, R. D, Miller, J. P., & Hoberman, H. M. (1997). A comparison of onset of binge eating versus dieting in the development of bulimia nervosa. *International Journal of Eating Disorders, 21*, 353–360.

Nacmias, B., Ricca, V., Tedde, A., Mezzani, B., Rotella, C. M., & Sorbi, S. (1999). 5-HT2A receptor gene polymorphisms in anorexia nervosa and bulimia nervosa. *Neuroscience Letters, 277*, 134–136.

Nadaoka, T., Oiji, A., Takahashi, S., Morioka, Y., Kashiwakura, M., & Totsuka, S. (1996). An epidemiological study of eating disorders in a northern area of Japan. *Acta Psychiatrica Scandinavica, 93*, 305–310.

Nakamura, K., Yamamoto, M., Yamazaki, O., Kawashima, Y., Muto, K., Someya, T., et al. (2000). Prevalence of anorexia and bulimia nervosa in a geographically defined area in Japan. *International Journal of Eating Disorders, 28*, 173–180.

Nasser, M. (1988). Culture and weight consciousness. *Journal of Psychosomatic Research, 32*, 573–577.

Nasser, M. (1993). A prescription of vomiting: Historical footnotes. *International Journal of Eating Disorders, 13*, 129–131.

Neumark-Sztainer, D., & Hannan, P. J. (2000). Weight-related behaviors among adolescent girls and boys: Results from a national survey. *Archives of Pediatrics and Adolescent Medicine, 154*, 569–577.

Neumark-Sztainer, D., Story, M., & Coller, T. (1999a). Perceptions of secondary school staff toward the implementation of school-based activities to prevent weight-related disorders: A needs assessment. *American Journal of Health Promotion, 13*, 153–156.

Neumark-Sztainer, D., Story, M., Falkner, N. H., Beuhring, T., & Resnick, M. D. (1999b). Sociodemographic and personal characteristics of adolescents engaged in weight loss and weight/muscle gain behaviors: Who is doing what? *Preventive Medicine, 28*, 40–50.

Neumark-Sztainer, D., Story, M., Hannan, P. J., Beuhring T., & Resnick, M. D. (2000). Disordered eating among adolescents: Associations with sexual/physical abuse and other familial/psychosocial factors. *International Journal of Eating Disorders, 28*, 249–258.

Newman, M. M., & Halmi, K. A. (1989). Relationship of bone density to estradiol and cortisol in anorexia nervosa and bulimia. *Psychiatry Research, 29*, 105–112.

Nielsen, S. (1990). The epidemiology of anorexia nervosa in Denmark from 1973 to 1987: A nationwide register study of psychiatric admission. *Acta Psychiatrica Scandinavica, 81*, 507–514.

Nielsen, S. (2001). Epidemiology and mortality of eating disorders. *Psychiatric Clinics of North America, 24*, 201–214.

Nielsen, S., Møller-Madsen, S., Isager, T., Jorgensen, J., Pagsberg, K., & Theander, S. (1998). Standardized mortality in eating disorders—a quantitative summary of previously published and new evidence. *Journal of Psychosomatic Research, 44*, 413–434.

Nishiguchi, N., Matsushita, S., Suzuki, K., Murayama, M., Shirakawa, O., & Higuchi, S. (2001). Association between 5HT2A receptor gene promoter region polymorphism and eating disorders in Japanese patients. *Biological Psychiatry, 50*, 123–128.

Nobakht, M., & Dezhkam, M. (2000). An epidemiological study of eating disorders in Iran. *International Journal of Eating Disorders, 28*, 265–271.

Norring, C. E., & Sohlberg, S. (1991). Ego functioning in eating disorders: Prediction of outcome after one and two years. *International Journal of Eating Disorders, 10,* 1–13.

O'Dea, J. A., & Abraham, S. (2000). Improving the body image, eating attitudes, and behaviors of young male and female adolescents: A new educational approach that focuses on self-esteem. *International Journal of Eating Disorders, 28,* 43–57.

Ogden, J., & Steward, J. (2000). The role of the mother–daughter relationship in explaining weight concern. *International Journal of Eating Disorders, 28,* 78–83.

Okasha, A. (1977). Psychiatric symptomatology in Egypt. *Mental Health and Society, 4,* 121–125.

Olivardia, R., Pope, H. G., Jr., Mangweth, B., & Hudson, J. I. (1995). Eating disorders in college men. *American Journal of Psychiatry, 152,* 1279–1285.

Olmsted, M. P., Kaplan, A. S., & Rockert, W. (1994). Rate and prediction of relapse in bulimia nervosa. *American Journal of Psychiatry, 151,* 738–743.

Oltmanns, T. F., & Emery, R. E. (2001). *Abnormal psychology* (3rd ed.). Upper Saddle River, NJ: Prentice Hall.

Owen, P. R., & Laurel-Seller, E. (2000). Weight and shape ideals: Thin is dangerously in. *Journal of Applied Social Psychology, 30,* 979–990.

Pagsberg, A. K., & Wang, A. R. (1994). Epidemiology of anorexia nervosa and bulimia nervosa in Bornholm County, Denmark, 1970–1989. *Acta Psychiatrica Scandinavica, 90,* 259–265.

Palmer, R. L., Birchall, H., Damani, S., Gatward, N., McGrain, L., & Parker, L. (2003). A dialectical behavior therapy program for people with an eating disorder and borderline personality disorder—description and outcome. *International Journal of Eating Disorders, 33,* 281–286.

Parry-Jones, B. (1991). Historical terminology of eating disorders. *Psychological Medicine, 21,* 21–28.

Parry-Jones, B. (1992). A bulimic ruminator? The case of Dr. Samuel Johnson. *Psychological Medicine, 22,* 851–862.

Parry-Jones, B., & Parry-Jones, W. L., (1991). Bulimia: An archival review of its history in psychosomatic medicine. *International Journal of Eating Disorders, 10,* 129–143.

Pate, J. E., Pumariega, A. J., Hester, C., & Garner, D. M. (1992). Cross-cultural patterns in eating disorders: A review. *Journal of the American Academy of Child and Adolescent Psychiatry, 31,* 802–809.

Patton, G. C. (1988). Mortality in eating disorders. *Psychological Medicine, 18,* 947–951.

Patton, G. C., Johnson-Sabine, E., Wood, K., Mann, A. H., & Wakeling, A. (1990). Abnormal eating attitudes in London schoolgirls-a prospective epidemiological study: Outcome at twelve month follow-up. *Psychological Medicine, 20,* 383–394.

Pauly, R. P., Lear, S. A., Hastings, F. C., & Birmingham, C. L. (2000). Resting energy expenditure and plasma leptin levels in anorexia nervosa during acute refeeding. *International Journal of Eating Disorders, 28,* 231–234.

Paxton, S. J. (1993). A prevention program for disturbed eating and body dissatisfaction in adolescent girls: A 1 year follow-up. *Health Education Research, 8,* 43–51.

Paxton, S. J. (1996). Prevention implications of peer influences on body image dissatisfaction and disturbed eating in adolescent girls. *Eating Disorders: The Journal of Treatment and Prevention, 4,* 334–347.

Paxton, S. J., & Sculthorpe, A. (1999). Weight and health locus of control beliefs in an Australian community sample. *Psychology and Health, 14,* 417–431.

Pearson, J., Goldklang, D., & Striegel-Moore, R. H. (2002). Prevention of eating disorders: Challenges and opportunities. *International Journal of Eating Disorders, 31,* 233–239.

Pemberton, A. R., Vernon, S. W., & Lee, E. S. (1996). Prevalence and correlates of bulimia nervosa and bulimic behaviors in a racially diverse sample of undergraduate students in two universities in southeast Texas. *American Journal of Epidemiology, 144,* 450–455.

Pendleton, V. R., Willems, E., Swank, P., Poston, W. S. C., Goodrick, G. K,. Reeves, R. S., et al. (2001). Negative stress and the outcome of treatment for binge eating. *Eating Disorders: The Journal of Treatment and Prevention, 9,* 351–360.

Peterson, C. B., & Mitchell, J. E. (1999). Psychosocial and pharmacological treatment of eating disorders: A review of research findings. *Journal of Clinical Psychology, 55*, 685–697.

Peterson, C. B., & Mitchell, J. E. (2001). Cognitive-behavioral therapy for eating disorders. In J. E. Mitchell (Ed.), *The outpatient treatment of eating disorders: A guide for therapists, dietitians and physicians* (pp. 144–167). Minneapolis: University of Minnesota Press.

Peterson, C. B., Mitchell, J. E., Engbloom, S., Nugent, S., Pederson Mussell, M., Crow, S. J., & et al. (2001). Self-help versus therapist-led group cognitive-behavioral treatment of binge eating disorder at follow-up. *International Journal of Eating Disorders, 30*, 363–374.

Phares, E. J. (1988). *Introduction to personality* (2nd ed.). Manhattan: Kansas State University of Agriculture and Applied Science.

Phelps, L., Sapia, J., Nathanson, D., & Nelson, L. (2000). An empirically supported eating disorder prevention program. *Psychology in the Schools, 37*, 443–452.

Phillipp, E., Pirke, K. M., Kellner, M. B., & Krieg, J. C. (1991). Disturbed cholecystokinin secretion in patients with eating disorders. *Life Science, 48*, 2443–2450.

Phillips, K. A., O'Sullivan, R. L., & Pope, H. G., Jr. (1997). Muscle dysmorphia. *Journal of Clinical Psychiatry, 58*, 361.

Pike, K. M., & Rodin, J. (1991). Mothers, daughters, and disordered eating. *Journal of Abnormal Psychology, 100*, 198–204.

Piran, N. (1999). Eating disorders: A trial of prevention in a high risk school setting. *Journal of Primary Prevention, 20*, 75–90.

Pirke, K. M. (1996). Central and peripheral noradrenalin regulation in eating disorders. *Psychiatry Research, 62*, 43–49.

Pirke, K. M., Kellner, M. B., Friess, E., Krieg, J. C., & Fichter, M. M. (1994). Satiety and cholecystokinin. *International Journal of Eating Disorders, 15*, 63–69.

Plomin, R., DèFries, J. C., McClearn, G. E., & McGuffin, P. (2001). *Behavioral Genetics* (4th ed.). New York: Worth.

Polivy, J., & Herman, C. P. (1985). Dieting and binging. A causal analysis. *American Psychologist, 40*, 193–201.

Polivy, J., Zeitlin, S. B., Herman, C. P., & Beal, A. L. (1994). Food restriction and binge eating: A study of former prisoners of war. *Journal of Abnormal Psychology, 103*, 409–411.

Pomeroy, C. (2001). Medical evaluation and medical managment. In J. E. Mitchell (Ed.), *The outpatient treatment of eating disorders: A guide for therapists, dietitians and physicians* (pp. 306–318). Minneapolis: University of Minnesota Press.

Pope, H. G., Hudson, J. I., & Mialet, J. P. (1985). Bulimia in the late nineteenth century: The observations of Pierre Janet. *Psychological Medicine, 15*, 739–743.

Pope, H. G., Jr., Katz, D. L., & Hudson, J. I. (1993). Anorexia nervosa and "reverse anorexia" among 108 male bodybuilders. *Comprehensive Psychiatry, 34*, 406–409.

Pope, H. G., Jr., Gruber, A. J., Choi, P., Olivardia, R., & Phillips, K. A. (1997). Muscle dysmorphia: An underrecognized form of body dysmorphic disorder. *Psychosomatics, 38*, 548–557.

Pope, H. G., Jr., Olivardia, R., Gruber, A., & Borowiecki, J. (1999). Evolving ideals of male body image as seen through action toys. *International Journal of Eating Disorders, 26*, 65–72.

Pope, H. G., Phillips, K. A., & Olivardia, R. (2000). *The adonis complex: The secret crisis of male body obsession.* New York: Free Press.

Porzelius, L. K., Houston, C., Smith, M., Arfken, C., et. al. (1995). Comparison of a standard behavioral weight loss treatment and a binge eating weight loss treatment. *Behavior Therapy, 26*, 119–134.

Presnell, K., & Stice, E. (2003). An experimental test of the effect of weight-loss dieting on bulimic pathology: Tipping the scales in a different direction. *Journal of Abnormal Psychology, 112*, 166–170.

Prince, R. (1985). The concept of culture-bound syndromes: Anorexia nervosa and brain-fag. *Social Science and Medicine, 21*, 197–203.

Pryor, T., & Wiederman, M. W. (1996). Measurement of nonclinical personality characteristics of women with anorexia nervosa or bulimia nervosa. *Journal of Personality Assessment, 67,* 414–421.

Pumariega, A. J. (1986). Acculturation and eating attitudes in adolescent girls: A comparative and correlational study. *Journal of the American Academy of Child Psychiatry, 25,* 276–279.

Pumariega, A. J., Gustavson, C. R., Gustavson, J. C., & Motes, P. S. (1994). Eating attitudes in African-American women: The Essence Eating Disorders Survey. *Eating Disorders: The Journal of Treatment and Prevention, 2,* 5–16.

Rahkonen, O., Lundberg, O., Lahelma, E., & Huuhka, M. (1998). Body mass and social class: A comparison of Finland and Sweden in the 1990s. *Journal of Public Health Policy, 19,* 88–105.

Rampling, D. (1985). Ascetic ideals and anorexia nervosa. *Journal of Psychiatric Research, 19,* 89–94.

Raulin, M. L. (2003). *Abnormal psychology.* Boston: Allyn and Bacon.

Raymond, N. C., de Zwaan, M., Mitchell, J. E., Ackard, D., & Thuras, P. (2002). Effect of a very low calorie diet on the diagnostic category of individuals with binge eating disorder. *International Journal of Eating Disorders, 31,* 49–56.

Reidpath, D. D., Burns, C., Garrard, J., Mahoney, M., & Townsend, M. (2002). An ecological study of the relationship between social and environmental determinants of obesity. *Health and Place, 8,* 141–145.

Reiss, D. (1996). Abnormal eating attitudes and behaviours in two ethnic groups from a female British urban population. *Psychological Medicine, 26,* 289–299.

Rhea, D. J. (1999). Eating disorder behaviors of ethnically diverse urban female adolescent athletes and non-athletes. *Journal of Adolescence, 22,* 379–388.

Ricca, V., Mannucci, E., Mezzani, B., Moretti, S., Di Bernardo, M., Bertelli, M., et al. (2001). Fluoxetine and fluvoxamine combined with individual cognitive-behaviour therapy in binge eating disorder: A one-year follow-up study. *Psychotherapy and Psychosomatics, 70,* 298–306.

Ricca, V., Nacmias, B., Cellini, E., Di Bernardo, M., Rotella, C. M., & Sorbi, S. (2002). 5-HT2A receptor gene polymorphism and eating disorders. *Neuroscience Letters, 323,* 105–108.

Rieger, E., Touyz, S. W., Swain, T., & Beumont, P. J. (2001). Cross-cultural research on anorexia nervosa: Assumptions regarding the role of body weight. *International Journal of Eating Disorders, 29,* 205–215.

Risch, N., & Merikangas, K. R. (1993). Linkage studies of psychiatric disorders. *European Archives of Psychiatry and Clinical Neuroscience, 243,* 143–149.

Robin, A. L., Siegel, P. T., Moye, A. W., Gilroy, M., Dennis, A. B., & Sikand, A. (1999). A controlled comparison of family versus individual therapy for adolescents with anorexia nervosa. *Journal of the American Academy of Child and Adolescent Psychiatry, 38,* 1482–1489.

Robinson, P. H., McHugh, P. R., Moran, T. H., & Stephenson, J. D. (1988). Gastric control of food intake. *Journal of Psychosomatic Research, 32,* 593–606.

Robinson, T. N., Killen, J. D., Litt, I. F., Hammer, L. D., Wilson, D. M., Haydel, K. F., et al. (1996). Ethnicity and body dissatisfaction: Are Hispanic and Asian girls at increased risk for eating disorders? *Journal of Adolescent Health, 19,* 384–393.

Rocco, P. L., Ciano, R. P., & Balestrieri, M. (2001). Psychoeducation in the prevention of eating disorders: An experimental approach in adolescent schoolgirls. *British Journal of Medical Psychology, 74,* 351–358.

Roe, D. A., & Eickwort, K. R. (1976). Relationships between obesity and associated health factors with unemployment among low income women. *Journal of the American Medical Women's Association, 31,* 193–194, 198–199, 203–204.

Roediger, H. L., Capaldi, E. D., Paris, S. G., & Polivy, J. (1991). *Psychology* (3rd ed.). New York: HarperCollins.

Roehling, M. V. (1999). Weight-based discrimination in employment: Psychological and legal aspects. *Personnel Psychology, 52,* 969–1016.

Rorty, M., Yager, J., Rossotto, E., & Buckwalter, G. (2000). Parental intrusiveness in adolescence re-called by women with a history of bulimia nervosa and comparison women. *International Journal of Eating Disorders, 28,* 202–208.

Rosen, E. F., Anthony, L., Booker, K. M., Brown, T. L., Christian, E., Crews, R. C. et al. (1991). A comparison of eating disorder scores among African-American and White college females. *Bulletin of the Psychonomic Society, 29,* 65–66.

Rosen, J. C., Gross, J., & Vara, L. (1987). Psychological adjustment of adolescents attempting to lose or gain weight. *Journal of Consulting and Clinical Psychology, 55,* 742–747.

Rosen, L. W., Shafer, C. L., Dummer, G. M., Cross, L. K., Deuman, G. W., & Malmberg, S. R. (1988). Prevalence of pathogenic weight-control behaviors among Native American women and girls. *International Journal of Eating Disorders, 7,* 807–811.

Rosenkranz, K., Hinney, A., Ziegler, A., Hermann, H., & Fichter, M., Mayer, H., et al. (1998). Systematic mutation screening of the estrogen receptor beta gene in probands of different weight extremes: Identification of several genetic variants. *Journal of Clinical Endocrinology & Metabolism, 83,* 4524–4527.

Rosenkranz, K., Hinney, A., Ziegler, A., von Prittwitz, S., Barth, N., Roth, H., Mayer, H., Siegfried, W., Lehmkuhl, G., Poustka, F., Schmidt, M., Schafer, H., Remschmidt, H., & Hebebrand, J. (1998b). Screening for mutations in the neuropeptide Y Y5 receptor gene in cohorts belonging to different weight extremes. *International Journal of Obesity & Related Metabolic Disorders, 22,* 157–163.

Rosenvinge, J. H., & Borresen, R. (1999). Preventing eating disorders—time to change programmes or paradigms? Current update and further recommendations. *European Eating Disorders Review, 7,* 5–16.

Rosenvinge, J. H., & Vandereycken, W. (1994). Early descriptions of eating disorders in the Norwegian medical literature. *International Journal of Child and Adolescent Psychiatry, 56,* 279–281.

Rothblum, E. D., Brand, P. A., Miller, C. T., & Oetjen, H. A. (1990). The relationship between obesity, employment discrimination, and employment-related victimization. *Journal of Vocational Behavior, 37,* 251–266.

Rubinstein, S., & Caballero, B. (2000). Is Miss America an undernourished role model? *Journal of the American Medical Association, 283,* 1569.

Ruderman, A. J. (1986). Dietary restraint: A theoretical and empirical review. *Psychological Bulletin, 99,* 247–262.

Ruggiero, G. M., Prandin, M., & Mantero, M. (2001). Eating disorders in Italy: A historical review. *European Eating Disorders Review, 9,* 292–300.

Russell, C. J., & Keel, P. K. (2002). Homosexuality as a specific risk factor for eating disorders in men. *International Journal of Eating Disorders, 31,* 300–306.

Russell, G. (1979). Bulimia nervosa: An ominous variant of anorexia nervosa. *Psychological Medicine, 9,* 429–448.

Russell, G. F. M. (1997). The history of bulimia nervosa. In D. M. Garner & P. E. Garfinkel (Eds.), *Handbook of treatment for eating disorders* (2nd ed., pp. 11–24). New York: Guilford.

Russell, G. F., Szmukler, G. I., Dare, C., & Eisler, I. (1987). An evaluation of family therapy in anorexia nervosa and bulimia nervosa. *Archives of General Psychiatry, 44,* 1047–1056.

Russell, G. F., Treasure, J., & Eisler, I. (1998). Mothers with anorexia nervosa who underfeed their children: Their recognition and management. *Psychological Medicine, 28,* 93–108.

Rutherford, J., McGuffin, P., Katz, R. J., & Murray, R. M. (1993). Genetic influences on eating attitudes in a normal female twin population. *Psychological Medicine, 23,* 425–436.

Safer, D. L., Telch, C. F., & Agras, W. S. (2001). Dialectical behavior therapy for bulimia nervosa. *American Journal of Psychiatry, 158,* 632–634.

Sanftner, J. L., Crowther, J. H., Crawford, P. A., & Watts, D. D. (1996). Maternal influences (or lack thereof) on daughters' eating attitudes and behaviors. *Eating Disorders: The Journal of Treatment and Prevention, 4,* 147–159.

Santonastaso, P., Zanetti, T., Ferrara, S., Olivotto, M. C., Magnavita, N., & Favaro, A. (1999). A preventive intervention program in adolescent schoolgirls: A longitudinal study. *Psychotherapy and Psychosomatics, 68*, 46–50.

Schmidt, U., Jiwany, A., & Treasure, J. (1993). A controlled study of alexithymia in eating disorders. *Comprehensive Psychiatry, 34*, 54–58.

Schwartz, M. W., Baskin, D. G., Kaiyala, K. J., & Woods, S. C. (1999). Model for the regulation of energy balance and adiposity by the central nervous system. *American Journal of Clinical Nutrition, 69*, 584–596.

Seligman, M. E. P., Walker, E. F., & Rosenhan, D. L. (2001). *Abrnormal psychology* (4th ed.). New York: W. W. Norton.

Shafran, R., Keel, P. K., Haedt, A., & Fairburn, C. G. (in press). Psychological treatments for eating disorders. In *Cambridge Handbook of Effective Treatments in Psychiatry, Eating Disorders*. K. Halmi and U. Schmidt (eds).

Shinkwin, R., & Standen, P. J. (2001). Trends in anorexia nervosa in Ireland: A register study. *European Eating Disorders Review, 9*, 263–276.

Shoebridge, P., & Gowers, S. G. (2000). Parental high concern and adolescent-onset anorexia nervosa. A case-control study to investigate direction of causality. *British Journal of Psychiatry, 176*, 132–137.

Siegel, J. H., Hardoff, D., Golden, N. H., & Shenker, I. R. (1995). Medical complications in male adolescents with anorexia nervosa. *Journal of Adolescent Health, 16*, 448–453.

Sifneos, P. E. (1972). *Short-term psychotherapy and emotional crises*. Cambridge, MA: Harvard University Press.

Silber, T. J., & Robb, A. S. (2002). Eating disorders and health insurance: Understanding and overcoming obstacles to treatment. *Child and Adolescent Psychiatric Clinics of North America, 11*, 419–428.

Silverman, J. A. (1987). Robert Whytt, 1714–1766: Eighteenth century limner of anorexia nervosa and bulimia: An essay. *International Journal of Eating Disorders, 6*, 143–146.

Simmons, M. S., Grayden, S. K., & Mitchell, J. E. (1986). The need for psychiatric–dental liaison in the treatment of bulimia. *American Journal of Psychiatry, 143*, 783–784.

Smeets, M. A. M. (1999). Body size categorization in anorexia nervosa using a morphing instrument. *International Journal of Eating Disorders, 25*, 451–455.

Smith, D. E., Marcus, M. D., Lewis, C., Fitzgibbon, M., & Schreiner, P. (1998). Prevalence of binge eating disorder, obesity, and depression in a biracial cohort of young adults. *Annals of Behavioral Medicine, 20*, 227–232.

Smith, J. E., & Krejci, J. (1991). Minorities join the majority: Eating disturbances among Hispanic and Native American youth. *International Journal of Eating Disorders, 10*, 179–186.

Smith, K. A., Fairburn, C. G., & Cowen, P. J. (1999). Symptomatic relapse in bulimia nervosa following acute tryptophan depletion. *Archives of General Psychiatry, 56*, 171–176.

Smolak, L., Harris, B., Levine, M. P., & Shisslak, C. M. (2001). Teachers: The forgotten influence on the success of prevention programs. *Eating Disorders: The Journal of Treatment & Prevention, 9*, 261–265.

Smolak, L., Levine, M. P., & Schermer, F. (1998). A controlled evaluation of an elementary school primary prevention program for eating problems. *Journal of Psychosomatic Research, 44*, 339–353.

Smolak, L., Levine, M. P., & Schermer, F. (1999). Parental input and weight concerns among elementary school children. *International Journal of Eating Disorders, 25*, 263–271.

Snow, J. T., & Harris, M. B. (1989). Disordered eating in South-western Pueblo Indians and Hispanics. *Journal of Adolescence, 12*, 329–336.

Sorbi, S., Nacmias, B., Tedde, A., Ricca, V., Mezzani, B., & Rotella, C. M. (1998). 5-HT2A promoter polymorphism in anorexia nervosa. *Lancet, 351*, 1785.

Soundy, T. J., Lucas, A. R., Suman, V. J., & Melton, L. J., 3rd (1995). Bulimia nervosa in Rochester, Minnesota from 1980 to 1990. *Psychological Medicine, 25*, 1065–1071.

Spencer, J. A., & Fremouw, W. J. (1979). Binge eating as a function of restraint and weight classification. *Journal of Abnormal Psychology, 88*, 262–267.

Spitzer, R. L., Devlin, M. J., Walsh, B. T., & Hasin, D, Wing, R., Marcus, M., et al. (1992). Binge eating disorder: A multisite field trial of the diagnostic criteria. *International Journal of Eating Disorders, 11*, 191–203.

Spitzer, R. L., Yanovski, S. Z., Wadden, T., Wing, R., Marcus, M. D., Stunkard, A., et al. (1993). Binge eating disorder: Its further validation in a multisite study. *International Journal of Eating Disorders, 13*, 137–153.

Spurrell, E. B., Wilfley, D. E., Tanofsky, M. B., & Brownell, K. D. (1997). Age of onset for binge eating: Are there different pathways to binge eating? *International Journal of Eating Disorders, 21*, 55–65.

Srinivasagam, N. M., Kaye, W. H., Plotnicov, K. H., Greeno, C., Weltzin, T. E., & Rao, R. (1995). Persistent perfectionism, symmetry, and exactness after long-term recovery from anorexia nervosa. *American Journal of Psychiatry, 152*, 1630–1634.

Steiger, H., Puentes-Neuman, G., & Leung, F. Y. (1991). Personality and family features of adolescent girls with eating symptoms: Evidence for restricter/binger differences in a nonclinical population. *Addictive Behaviors, 16*, 303–314.

Steiger, H., Stotland, S., Ghadirian, A. M., & Whitehead, V. (1995). Controlled study of eating concerns and psychopathological traits in relatives of eating-disordered probands: Do familial traits exist? *International Journal of Eating Disorders, 18*, 107–118.

Stein, A., Murray, L., Copper, P., & Fairburn, C. G. (1996). Infant growth in the context of maternal eating disorders and maternal depression: A comparative study. *Psychological Medicine, 26*, 569–574.

Stein, A., Woolley, H., Cooper, S. D., & Fairburn, C. G. (1994). An observational study of mothers with eating disorders and their infants. *Journal of Child Psychology and Psychiatry and Allied Disciplines, 35*, 733–748.

Stein, A., Woolley, H., & McPherson, K. (1999). Conflict between mothers with eating disorders and their infants during mealtimes. *British Journal of Psychiatry, 175*, 455–461.

Stein, D., Lilenfeld, L. R., Plotnicov, K., Pollice, C., Rao, R., Strober, M., & Kaye, W. H. (1999). Familial aggregation of eating disorders: Results from a controlled family study of bulimia nervosa. *International Journal of Eating Disorders, 26*, 211–215.

Stein, D. M., & Laakso, W. (1988). Bulimia: A historical perspective. *International Journal of Eating Disorders, 7*, 201–210.

Steiner-Adair, C., Sjostrom, L., Franko, D. L., Pai, S., Siny Tucker, R., Becker, A. E., et al. (2002). Primary prevention of risk factors for eating disorders in adolescent girls: Learning from practice. *International Journal of Eating Disorders, 32*, 401–411.

Steinhausen, H. C. (2002). The outcome of anorexia nervosa in the 20th century. *American Journal of Psychiatry, 159*, 1284–1293.

Stewart, D. A., Carter, J. C., Drinkwater, J., Hainsworth, J., & Fairburn, C. G. (2001). Modification of eating attitudes and behavior in adolescent girls: A controlled study. *International Journal of Eating Disorders, 29*, 107–118.

Stice, E. (2002). Risk and maintenance factors for eating pathology: A meta-analytic review. *Psychological Bulletin, 128*, 825–848.

Stice, E., W. S., Agras, (1999). Subtyping bulimic women along dietary restraint and negative affect dimensions. *Journal of Consulting and Clinical Psychology, 67*, 460–469.

Stice, E., Agras, W. S., & Hammer, L. D. (1999). Risk factors for the emergence of childhood eating disturbances: A five-year prospective study. *International Journal of Eating Disorders, 25*, 375–387.

Stice, E., & Shaw, H. (2004). Eating disorder prevention programs: A meta-analytic review. *Psychological Bulletin, 130*, 206–227.

Stice, E., Chase, A., Stormer, S., & Appel, A. (2001). A randomized trial of a dissonance-based eating disorder prevention program. *International Journal of Eating Disorders, 29*, 247–262.

Stice, E., & Shaw, H. E. (1994). Adverse effects of the media portrayed thin-ideal on women and linkages to bulimic symptomatology. *Journal of Social and Clinical Psychology, 13*, 288–308.

Stice, E., Trost, A., & Chase, A. (2003). Healthy weight control and dissonance-based eating disorder prevention programs: Results from a controlled trial. *International Journal of Eating Disorders, 33*, 10–21.

Story, M., Hauck, F. R., Broussard, B. A., White, L. L., Resnick, M. D., & Blum, R. W. (1994). Weight perceptions and weight control practices in American Indian and Alaska Native adolescents. A national survey. *Archives of Pediatrics and Adolescent Medicine, 148*, 567–571.

Strauss, C. C., Smith, K., Frame, C., & Forehand, R. (1985). Personal and interpersonal characteristics associated with childhood obesity. *Journal of Pediatric Psychology, 10*, 337–343.

Striegel-Moore, R. H., Dohm, F. A., Kraemer, H. C., Taylor, C. B., Daniels, S., Crawford, P. B., & Schreiber, G. B. (2003). Eating disorders in white and black women. *American Journal of Psychiatry, 160*, 1326–1331.

Striegel-Moore, R. H., & Kearney-Cooke, A. (1994). Exploring parents' attitudes and behaviors about their children's physical appearance. *International Journal of Eating Disorders, 15*, 377–385.

Striegel-Moore, R. H., Leslie, D., Petrill, S. A., Garvin, V., & Rosenheck, R. A. (2000a). One-year use and cost of inpatient and outpatient services among female and male patients with an eating disorder: Evidence from a national database of health insurance claims. *International Journal of Eating Disorders, 27*, 381–389.

Striegel-Moore, R. H., Schreiber, G. B., Lo, A., Crawford, P., Obarzanek, E., & Rodin, J. (2000b). Eating disorder symptoms in a cohort of 11 to 16-year-old Black and White girls: The NHLBI Growth and Health Study. *International Journal of Eating Disorders., 27*, 49–66.

Striegel-Moore, R. H., Schreiber, G. B., Pike, K. M., Wilfley, D. E., & Rodin, J. E. (1995). Drive for thinness in black and white preadolescent girls. *International Journal of Eating Disorders, 18*, 59–69.

Strober, M., Freeman, R., Lampert, C., Diamond, J., & Kaye, W. (2000). Controlled family study of anorexia nervosa and bulimia nervosa: Evidence of shared liability and transmission of partial syndromes. *American Journal of Psychiatry, 157*, 393–401.

Strober, M., Freeman, R., Lampert, C., Diamond, J., & Kaye, W. (2001). Males with anorexia nervosa: A controlled study of eating disorders in first-degree relatives. *International Journal of Eating Disorders, 29*, 263–269.

Strober, M., Freeman, R., Morrell, W. (1997). The long-term course of severe anorexia nervosa in adolescents: Survival analysis of recovery, relapse, and outcome predictors over 10–15 years in a prospective study. *International Journal of Eating Disorders, 22*, 339–360.

Strober, M., Lampert, C., Morrell, W., Burroughs, J., & Jacobs, C. (1990). A controlled family study of anorexia nervosa: Evidence of familial aggregation and lack of shared transmission with affective disorders. *International Journal of Eating Disorders, 9*, 239–253.

Strober, M., Morrell, W., Burroughs, J., Salkin, B., & Jacobs, C. (1985). A controlled family study of anorexia nervosa. *Journal of Psychiatric Research, 19*, 239–246.

Strong, K. G., & Huon, G. F. (1998). An evaluation of a structural model for studies of the initiation of dieting among adolescent girls. *Journal of Psychosomatic Research, 44*, 315–326.

Stunkard, A. (1990). A description of eating disorders in 1932. *American Journal of Psychiatry, 147*, 263–268.

Stunkard, A. (1996b). Socioeconomic status and obesity. *Ciba Foundation Symposium, 201*, 174–193.

Sullivan, P. F. (1995). Mortality in anorexia nervosa. *American Journal of Psychiatry, 152*, 1073–1074.

Sullivan, P. F., Bulik, C. M., Fear, J. L., & Pickering, A. (1998a). Outcome of anorexia nervosa: A case-control study. *American Journal of Psychiatry, 155,* 939–946.

Sullivan, P. F., Bulik, C. M., & Kendler, K. S. (1998a). Genetic epidemiology of binging and vomiting. *British Journal of Psychiatry, 173,* 75–79.

Sundaramurthy, D., Pieri, L. F., Gape, H., Markham, A. F., & Campbell, D. A. (2000). Analysis of the serotonin transporter gene linked polymorphism (5-HTTLPR) in anorexia nervosa. *American Journal of Medical Genetics, 96,* 53–55.

Swayze, V. W., 2nd, Andersen, A., Arndt, S., Rajarethinam, R., Fleming, F., Sato, Y., et al. (1996). Reversibility of brain tissue loss in anorexia nervosa assessed with a computerized Talairach 3-D proportional grid. *Psychological Medicine, 26,* 381–390.

Szmukler, G., McCance, C., McCrone, L., & Hunter, D. (1986). Anorexia nervosa: A psychiatric case register study from Aberdeen. *Psychological Medicine, 16,* 49–58.

Szyrynski, V. (1973). Anorexia nervosa and psychotherapy. *American Journal of Psychotherapy, 27,* 492–505.

Teachman, B. A., & Brownell, K. D. (2001). Implicit anti-fat bias among health professionals: Is anyone immune? *International Journal of Obesity and Related Metabolic Disorders, 25,* 1525–1531.

Teachman, B. A., Gapinski, K. D., Brownell, K. D., Rawlins, M., & Jeyaram, S. (2003). Demonstrations of implicit anti-fat bias: The impact of providing causal information and evoking empathy. *Health Psychology, 22,* 68–78.

Teitelbaum, P., & Stellar, E. (1954). Recovery from the failure to eat produced by hypothalamic lesions. *Science, 120,* 894–895.

Telch, C. F., Agras, W. S., & Linehan, M. M. (2000). Group dialectical behavior therapy for binge-eating disorder: A preliminary, uncontrolled trial. *Behavior Therapy, 31,* 569–582.

Tellegen, A. (1982). *Brief manual for the multi-dimensional personality questionnaire.* Unpublished manuscript. Minneapolis: University of Minnesota.

Theander, S. (1970). Anorexia nervosa. A psychiatric investigation of 94 female patients. *Acta Psychiatrica Scandinavica Supplementum, 214,* 1–194.

Thiel, A., Gottfried, H., & Hesse, F. W. (1993). Subclinical eating disorders in male athletes: A study of the low weight category in rowers and wrestlers. *Acta Psychiatrica Scandinavica, 88,* 259–265.

Tiggemann, M., & Pickering, A. S. (1996). Role of television in adolescent women's body dissatisfaction and drive for thinness. *International Journal of Eating Disorders, 20,* 199–203.

Tiggemann, M., & Rothblum, E. D. (1988). Gender differences in social consequences of perceived overweight in the United States and Australia. *Sex Roles, 18,* 75–86.

Tiggemann, M., & Rothblum, E. D. (1997). Gender differences in internal beliefs about weight and negative attitudes towards self and others. *Psychology of Women Quarterly, 21,* 581–593.

Tobin, D. L., Griffing, A., & Griffing, S. (1997). An examination of subtype criteria for bulimia nervosa. *International Journal of Eating Disorders, 22,* 179–186.

Tolle, V., Kadem, M., Bluet-Pajot, M. T., Frere, D., Foulon, C., Bossu, C., et al. (2003). Balance in ghrelin and leptin plasma levels in anorexia nervosa patients and constitutionally thin women. *Journal of Clinical Endocrinology and Metabolism, 88,* 109–116.

Toman, E. (2002). Body mass index and its impact on the therapeutic alliance in the work with eating disorder patients. *European Eating Disorders Review, 10,* 168–178.

Tsai, G. (2000). Eating disorders in the Far East. *Eating and Weight Disorders, 5,* 183–197.

Tsai, G., & Gray, J. (2000). The Eating Disorders Inventory among Asian American college women. *Journal of Social Psychology, 140,* 527–529.

Turnbull, S., Ward, A., Treasure, J., Jick, H., & Derby, L. (1996). The demand for eating disorder care. An epidemiological study using the general practice research database. *British Journal of Psychiatry, 169,* 705–712.

Tyrka, A. R., Waldron, I., Graber, J. A., & Brooks-Gunn, J. (2002). Prospective predictors of the onset of anorexic and bulimic syndromes. *International Journal of Eating Disorders, 32,* 282–290.

Urwin, R. E., Bennetts, B. H., Wilcken, B., Beumont, P. J., Russell, J. D., & Nunn, K. P. (2003). Investigation of epistasis between the serotonin transporter and norepinephrine transporter genes in anorexia nervosa. *Neuropsychopharmacology, 28,* 1351–1355.

Urbszat, D., Herman, C. P., & Polivy, J. (2002). Eat, drink, and be merry, for tomorrow we diet: Effects of anticipated deprivation on food intake in restrained and unrestrained eaters. *Journal of Abnormal Psychology, 111,* 396–401.

Valanne, E. H., Taipale, V., Larkio-Miettinen, A. K., Moren, R., & Aukee, M. (1972). Anorexia nervosa: A follow-up study. *Psychiatria Fennica,* 265–269.

van der Ham, T., van Strien, D. C., & van Engeland, H. (1998). Personality characteristics predict outcome of eating disorders in adolescents: A 4-year prospective study. *European Child and Adolescent Psychiatry, 7,* 79–84.

van Deth, R., & Vandereycken, W. (1995). Was late-nineteenth-century nervous vomiting an early variation of bulimia nervosa? *History of Psychiatry, 6,* 333–347.

van Wezel-Meijler, G., & Wit, J. M. (1989). The offspring of mothers with anorexia nervosa: A high-risk group for undernutrition and stunting? *European Journal of Pediatrics, 149,* 130–135.

Vandereycken, W., & Beaumont, P. J. (1990). The first Australian case description of anorexia nervosa. *Australian and New Zealand Journal of Psychiatry, 24,* 109–112.

Vandereycken, W., Habermas, T., van Deth, R., & Meermann, R. (1991). German publications on anorexia nervosa in the nineteenth century. *International Journal of Eating Disorders, 10,* 473–490.

Vandereycken, W., & Lowenkopf, E. L. (1990). Anorexia nervosa in 19th century America. *Journal of Nervous and Mental Disease, 178,* 531–535.

Vandereycken, W., & van Deth, R. (1994). *From fasting saints to anorexic girls: The history of self-starvation.* New York: New York University Press.

Varnado-Sullivan, P. J., Zucker, N., Williamson, D. A., Reas, D., Thaw, J., & Netemeyer, S. B. (2001). Development and implementation of the Body Logic Program for adolescents: A two-stage prevention program for eating disorders. *Cognitive and Behavioral Practice, 8,* 248–259.

Vedhara, K., Hyde, J., Gilchrist, I. D., Tytherleigh, M., & Plummer, S. (2000). Acute stress, memory, attention and cortisol. *Psychoneuroendocrinology, 25,* 535–549.

Viken, R. J., Treat, T. A., Nosofsky, R. M., McFall, R. M., & Palmeri, T. J. (2002). Modeling individual differences in perceptual and attentional processes related to bulimic symptoms. *Journal of Abnormal Psychology, 111,* 598–609.

Vink, T., Hinney, A., van Elburg, A. A., van Goozen, S. H., Sandkuijl, L. A., Sinke, R. J., et al. (2001). Association between an agouti-related protein gene polymorphism and anorexia nervosa. *Molecular Psychiatry, 6,* 325–328.

Vitousek, K., & Manke, F. (1994). Personality variables and disorders in anorexia nervosa and bulimia nervosa. *Journal of Abnormal Psychology, 103,* 137–147.

Vohs, K. D., Bardone, A. M., Joiner, T. E., Jr., Abramson, L. Y., & Heatherton, T. F. (1999). Perfectionism, perceived weight status, and self-esteem interact to predict bulimic symptoms: A model of bulimic symptom development. *Journal of Abnormal Psychology, 108,* 695–700.

von Ranson, K. M., Kaye, W. H., Weltzin, T. E., Rao, R., & Matsunaga, H. (1999). Obsessive-compulsive disorder symptoms before and after recovery from bulimia nervosa. *American Journal of Psychiatry, 156,* 1703–1708.

Wade, T., Martin, N. G, Neale, M. C, Tiggemann, M, Treloar, S. A, Bucholz, K. K, et al. (1999). The structure of genetic and environmental risk factors for three measures of disordered eating. *Psychological Medicine., 29,* 925–934.

Wade, T. D., Bulik, C. M., & Kendler, K. S. (2001). Investigation of quality of the parental relationship as a risk factor for subclinical bulimia nervosa. *International Journal of Eating Disorders, 30,* 389–400.

Wade, T. D., Davidson, S., & O'Dea, J. A. (2003). A preliminary controlled evaluation of a school-based media literacy program and self-esteem program for reducing eating disorder risk factors. *International Journal of Eating Disorders, 33,* 371–383.

Walsh, B. T., Wilson, G., T., Loeb, K. L., Devlin, M. J., Pike, K. M., Roose, S. P. et al., (1997). Medication and psychotherapy in the treatment of bulimia nervosa. *American Journal of Psychiatry, 154,* 523–531.

Walsh, J. M., Wheat, M. E., & Freund, K. (2000). Detection, evaluation, and treatment of eating disorders the role of the primary care physician. *Journal of General Internal Medicine, 15,* 577–590.

Ward, A., Ramsay, R., Turnbull, S., Benedettini, M., & Treasure, J. (2000). Attachment patterns in eating disorders: Past in the present. *International Journal of Eating Disorders, 28,* 370–376.

Waters, B. G., Beumont, P. J., Touyz, S., & Kennedy, M. (1990). Behavioural differences between twin and non-twin female sibling pairs discordant for anorexia nervosa. *International Journal of Eating Disorders, 9,* 265–273.

Watson, T. L., & Andersen, A. E. (2003). A critical examination of the amenorrhea and weight criteria for diagnosing anorexia nervosa. *Acta Psychiatrica Scandinavica, 108,* 175–182.

Waugh, E., & Bulik, C. M. (1999). Offspring of women with eating disorders. *International Journal of Eating Disorders, 25,* 123–133.

Weizman, R., Carmi, M., Tyano, S., Apter, A., & Rehavi, M. (1986). High affinity [3H] imipramine binding and serotonin uptake to platelets of adolescent females suffering from anorexia nervosa. *Life Sciences, 38,* 1235–1242.

Weltzin, T. E., Fernstrom, M. H., Fernstrom, J. D., Neuberger, S. K., & Kaye, W. H. (1995). Acute tryptophan depletion and increased food intake and irritability in bulimia nervosa. *American Journal of Psychiatry, 152,* 1668–1671.

Westberg, L., Bah, J., Rastam, M., Gillberg, C., Wentz, E., Melke, J., et al. (2002). Association between a polymorphism of the 5-HT2C receptor and weight loss in teenage girls. *Neuropsychopharmacology, 26,* 789–793.

Westen, D., & Harnden-Fischer, J. (2001). Personality profiles in eating disorders: Rethinking the distinction between axis I and axis II. *American Journal of Psychiatry, 158,* 547–562.

White, W. C., & Boskind-White, M. (1981). An experiential-behavioral approach to the treatment of bulimarexia. *Psychotherapy: Theory, Research and Practice, 18,* 501–507.

Whitehouse, A. M., Cooper, P. J., Vize, C. V., Hill, C., & L. Vogel (1992). Prevalence of eating disorders in three Cambridge general practices: Hidden and conspicuous morbidity. *British Journal of General Practice, 42,* 57–60.

Wilfley, D. E., Agras, W. S., Telch, C. F., & Rossiter, E. M. (1993). Group cognitive-behavioral therapy and group interpersonal psychotherapy for the nonpurging bulimic individual: A controlled comparison. *Journal of Consulting and Clinical Psychology, 61,* 296–305.

Wilfley, D. E., Schreiber, G. B., Pike, K. M., & Striegel-Moore, R. H. (1996). Eating disturbance and body image: A comparison of a community sample of adult black and white women. *International Journal of Eating Disorders, 20,* 377–387.

Wilfley, D. E., Welch, R. R., Stein, R. I., Spurrell, E. B., Cohen, L. R., Saelens, B. E., et al. (2002). A randomized comparison of group cognitive-behavioral therapy and group interpersonal psychotherapy for the treatment of overweight individuals with binge-eating disorder. *Archives of General Psychiatry, 59,* 713–721.

Willi, J., Giacometti, G., & Limacher, B. (1990). Update on the epidemiology of anorexia nervosa in a defined region of Switzerland. *American Journal of Psychiatry, 147,* 1514–1517.

Willi, J., & Grossmann, S. (1983). Epidemiology of anorexia nervosa in a defined region of Switzerland. *American Journal of Psychiatry, 140,* 564–567.

Williams, P., & King, M. (1987). The "epidemic" of anorexia nervosa: Another medical myth? *Lancet, 1,* 205–207.

Williamson, D. A., Womble, L. G., Smeets, M. A., Netemeyer, R. G., Thaw, J. M., Kutlesic, V., et al. (2002). Latent structure of eating disorder symptoms: A factor analytic and taxometric investigation. *American Journal of Psychiatry, 159,* 412–418.

Williamson, I. (1999). Why are gay men a high risk group for eating disturbance? *European Eating Disorders Review, 7,* 1–4.

Williamson, L. (1998). Eating disorders and the cultural forces behind the drive for thinness: Are African American women really protected? *Social Work in Health Care, 28,* 61–73.

Wilson, G. T., Loeb, K. L., Walsh, B. T., Labouvie, E., Petkova, E., Liu, X., et al. (1999). Psychological versus pharmacological treatments of bulimia nervosa: Predictors and processes of change. *Journal of Consulting and Clinical Psychology, 67,* 451–459.

Winzelberg, A. J., Taylor, C. B., Sharpe, T., Eldredge, K. L., Dev, P., and Constantinou, P. S. (1998). Evaluation of a computer-mediated eating disorder intervention program. *International Journal of Eating Disorders, 24,* 339–349.

Wiseman, C. V., Gray, J. J., Mosimann, J. E., & Ahrens, A. H. (1992). Cultural expectations of thinness in women: An update. *International Journal of Eating Disorders, 11,* 85–89.

Wisniewski, L., & Kelly, E. (2003). The application of dialectical behavior therapy to the treatment of eating disorders. *Cognitive and Behavioral Practice, 10,* 131–138.

Withers, G. F., Twigg, K., Wertheim, E. H., & Paxton, S. J. (2002). A controlled evaluation of an eating disorders primary prevention videotape using the Elaboration Likelihood Model of Persuasion. *Journal of Psychosomatic Research, 53,* 1021–1027.

Wolfe, B. E., Metzger, E. D., Levine, J. M., Finkelstein, D. M., Cooper, T. B., & Jimerson, D. C. (2000). Serotonin function following remission from bulimia nervosa. *Neuropsychopharmacology, 22,* 257–263.

Woodside, D. B., Bulik, C. M., Halmi, K. A., Fichter, M. M., Kaplan, A., Berrettini, W. H., et al. (2002). Personality, perfectionism, and attitudes toward eating in parents of individuals with eating disorders. *International Journal of Eating Disorders, 31,* 290–299.

Woodside, D. B., Field, L. L., Garfinkel, P. E., & Heinmaa, M. (1998). Specificity of eating disorders diagnoses in families of probands with anorexia nervosa and bulimia nervosa. *Comprehensive Psychiatry, 39,* 261–264.

World Health Organization. (1998). *International statistical classification of diseases and related health problems* (10th revision. ed.). Geneva: World Health Organization.

Wurtman, R. J., & Wurtman, J. J. (1986). Carbohydrate craving, obesity, and brain serotonin. *Appetite, 7 (Supplement),* 99–103.

Yager, J., Kurtzman, F., Landsverk, J., & Wiesmeier, E. (1988). Behaviors and attitudes related to eating disorders in homosexual male college students. *American Journal of Psychiatry, 145,* 495–497.

Yates, A., Shisslak, C. M., Allender, J., Crago, M., & Leehey, K. (1992). Comparing obligatory to nonobligatory runners. *Psychosomatics, 33,* 180–189.

Yoshimura, K. (1995). Acculturative and sociocultural influences on the development of eating disorders in Asian-American females. *Eating Disorders: The Journal of Treatment and Prevention, 3,* 216–228.

Zabinski, M. F., Pung, M. A., Wilfley, D. E., Eppstein, D. L., Winzelberg, A. J., Celio, A., et al. (2001). Reducing risk factors for eating disorders: Targeting at-risk women with a computerized psychoeducational program. *International Journal of Eating Disorders, 29,* 401–408.

Ziegler, A., Hebebrand, J., Gorg, T. Rosenkranz, K., Fichter, M., Herpertz-Dahlmann, B., et al. (1999). Further lack of association between the 5-HT2A gene promoter polymorphism and susceptibility to eating disorders and a meta-analysis pertaining to anorexia nervosa. *Molecular Psychiatry, 4,* 410–412.

Ziolko, H. U. (1994). Hyperorexia nervosa. *International Journal of Eating Disorders, 16,* 133–135.

Ziolko, H. U. (1996). Bulimia: A historical outline. *International Journal of Eating Disorders, 20,* 345–358.

Zipfel, S., Lowe B., Reas, D. L., Deter, H. C., & Herzog, W. (2000). Long-term prognosis in anorexia nervosa: Lessons from a 21-year follow-up study. *Lancet, 355,* 721–722.

Name Index

Subject Index